DESTROYERS AT WAR

DESTROYERS AT WAR

A PERSONAL RETROSPECTIVE OF THE PACIFIC THEATER

Adm. James L. Holloway III, USN

EDITED BY DAVID F. WINKLER

NAVAL INSTITUTE PRESS
Annapolis, Maryland

Naval Institute Press
291 Wood Road
Annapolis, MD 21402

© 2025 by the U.S. Naval Institute
All rights reserved. No part of this book may be reproduced or utilized in any form or by any means, electronic or mechanical, including photocopying and recording, or by any information storage and retrieval system, without permission in writing from the publisher.

Library of Congress Cataloging-in-Publication Data

Names: Holloway, James L., III, 1922-2019, author. | Winkler, David F. (David Frank), 1958- editor.
Title: Destroyers at war : a personal retrospective of the Pacific Theater / by Admiral James L. Holloway III, United States Navy (Ret.) ; edited by David F. Winkler.
Description: Annapolis, MD : Naval Institute Press, 2025. | Includes bibliographical references and index.
Identifiers: LCCN 2024037323 (print) | LCCN 2024037324 (ebook) | ISBN 9781682473344 (hardcover) | ISBN 9781682473665 (ebook)
Subjects: LCSH: Holloway, James L., III, 1922-2019. | Bennion (Destroyer) | World War, 1939-1945—Campaigns—Pacific Area. | United States. Navy—Officers—Biography. | Admirals—United States—Biography. | Leyte Gulf, Battle of, Philippines, 1944. | Ringgold (Destroyer) | World War, 1939-1945—Naval operations, American. | World War, 1939-1945—Personal narratives, American.
Classification: LCC D774.B366 H65 2025 (print) | LCC D774.B366 (ebook) | DDC 940.54/5973092 [B]—dc23/eng/20250123
LC record available at https://lccn.loc.gov/2024037323
LC ebook record available at https://lccn.loc.gov/2024037324

♾ Print editions meet the requirements of ANSI/NISO z39.48-1992 (Permanence of Paper).
Printed in the United States of America.

10 9 8 7 6 5 4 3 2 1

CONTENTS

List of Photos and Maps   v
Preface   ix
Prologue   vx

PART I.	**THE USNA YEARS AND HARVARD**	1
CHAPTER 1:	My Midshipman Experience	3
CHAPTER 2:	Harvard and Boston	21

PART II.	**USS *RINGGOLD* (DD 500)**	29
CHAPTER 3:	Joining the Fleet	31
CHAPTER 4:	To Sea	42
CHAPTER 5:	Sidetracked	54

PART III.	**USS *BENNION* (DD 662)**	67
CHAPTER 6:	Back to Square One	69
CHAPTER 7:	Pacific Bound	82
CHAPTER 8:	The Marianas Campaign	96
CHAPTER 9:	Eniwetok and Crossing the Line	144
CHAPTER 10:	The Palau Campaign	160
CHAPTER 11:	On Manus and at the Invasion of the Philippines	180
CHAPTER 12:	Leyte Gulf: The Battle of Surigao Strait	192
CHAPTER 13:	My Time in Destroyers Comes to a Close	211

Epilogue: Later Years, Final Honors   223
Notes   253
Selected Bibliography   269
Index   271

PHOTOS AND MAPS

PHOTOS

1.	Young Jimmy dressed as a sailor	xix
2.	Young Jimmy posing with his mother Jean	xix
3.	Big and Little Jimmies on board the USS *Truxtun* en route to Olongapo, January 4, 1923	xx
4.	USS *Truxtun*	xx
5.	USS *West Virginia*	xxiii
6.	Maj. Gen. Johnson Hagood	xxvii
7.	Jimmy Holloway at St. James	xxxviii
8.	Holloway as a member of the U.S. Naval Academy's varsity wrestling team, August 1941	7
9.	Holloway's portrait photograph, August 1941	7
10.	Dabney Rawlins with Jimmy Holloway on graduation day	19
11.	Ensign Holloway	22
12.	USS *Ringgold* at anchor off New York Navy Yard, May 1943	35
13.	USS *Bennion* under way during World War II	72
14 & 15.	Destroyers conducting shore bombardment at Saipan in the Marianas	105
16.	Underwater demolition team members working just off Saipan Beach	106

17. Six-inch naval gun mounted in hillside — 140
18. First bombardment wave hitting the beach at Tinian, July 24, 1944 — 141
19. Peleliu shore during the final stages of the preinvasion bombardment, September 15, 1944 — 165
20. Gun flashes of U.S. cruisers during the battle of Surigao Strait, October 24–25, 1944 — 200
21. Lieutenant Holloway's Bronze Star citation — 202
22. Vice Adm. James L. Holloway Jr., Chief of Naval Personnel and Deputy Chief of Naval Operations, October 11, 1956 — 239
23. Holloway family holiday photograph, circa 1954 — 242
24. Chief of Naval Operations with his father, 1974 — 247

MAPS

1. Marianas Islands: Saipan and Tinian — 98
2. Peleliu — 163
3. Battle of Surigao Strait — 204

PREFACE

I WAS BORN in Charleston, South Carolina, on February 23, 1922.

So stated James Lemuel Holloway III, speaking into a cassette recorder, shortly after the turn of the third millennium as he was approaching his eightieth birthday—the first of thousands of sentences that he would record in the ensuing weeks and months. Holloway was familiar with recording devices and the process of recording oneself. In the wake of a family gathering in 1974 where he witnessed his father regaling those present with tales of the old Navy, his son, the then Chief of Naval Operations, sent the senior Holloway a large gift-wrapped box with a card that said: "Open Christmas Morning. Plug into a wall socket, press the 'on' button, followed by the 'play' switch and then speak into the microphone and say 'I was born in Fort Smith Arkansas in 1898.' Then you are on your own." On Christmas morning Holloway's father opened the box to find a reel-to-reel tape recorder.

Ten days later, the son received the first reel in the mail. It opened with, "I was born in Fort Smith, Arkansas, on the Arkansas River, a little after midnight on the 20th of June, 1898." The son sequentially received numerous completed tapes over the next two years. His bride of over three decades, Dabney, transcribed her father-in-law's recollections using an ancient Underwood typewriter. With the advent of word processing, the raw transcript was digitized by Cdr. Lawrence "Skid" Heyworth III, who was the senior Holloway's grandson (and nephew to the junior Holloway). Such initiative to capture his father's recollections should not be surprising in a man who, after retiring from active duty, would serve as the president and then chairman of the nonprofit Naval Historical Foundation for twenty-eight years.

He took great pride in the fact that he was the junior partner of the first and to date only father-and-son combination to serve on active duty in the U.S. Navy at the rank of full admiral. Yet as shall be seen, the relationship between father and son was not emotionally close. Of note, in 1974 when the junior Holloway took office as the Chief of Naval Operations, Harry Chapin premiered the ballad "Cat's in the Cradle," a sad tale about a father whose career prevented his participation in his young son's activities and a son whose own career and family kept him from visiting with Dad. Each stanza closed with a promise from one to the other to get together... "and you know we'll have a good time then." It was a ballad that likely spoke to the junior Holloway as he reviewed the transcripts. He had opportunities to discuss them with his father, a unique chance for late-in-life bonding, before the senior Holloway died in 1984.

Capturing his father's recollections helped Holloway when it came time to put his own words on tape. Before a recording session, Holloway outlined the subjects that he intended to cover and gathered source materials for reference. His father's transcript helped inform him about his early years. Now an octogenarian himself, Holloway followed in his father's footsteps, producing tape after tape. He sent them for transcription to Chief Yeoman Frank Arre, who in retirement served as the office manager of the Naval Historical Foundation. For Arre, who was compensated directly by Holloway, this was a challenging experience. Besides incorporating Holloway's edits and reedits of his original transcript, Arre often found himself retranscribing previously recorded recollections that Holloway had edited and reedit. With the assistance of the Naval Historical Foundation's executive director, retired Capt. Todd Creekman, Arre managed to place Holloway's stream of thoughts in chronological order.

As with his father's transcript, which Holloway would self-publish for limited distribution in 2009 under the title *Lord Jim*, he now envisioned the creation of a primary source document that could be deposited with his papers at the Naval History and Heritage Command for use by future researchers. However, with the end of the Cold War many analysts challenged the Navy's force structure and in particular the viability of big-deck aircraft carriers, with which the Holloway was firmly identified, as the third commanding officer of *Enterprise* (CVAN 65) and then in 1968 head of the Navy's nuclear-powered carrier program, which brought about the introduction of *Nimitz*-class supercarriers. Holloway took strong issue with those who called for more modestly sized flight decks, a return to fossil-fueled carriers, or the elimination of carriers period.

He responded to them with a book drawn from the latter draft chapters of his memoir, in which Holloway had recorded extensively about his experiences as a naval aviator and how carriers, both those he served on and others, fought in Korea and Vietnam and responded to crises in Lebanon and the Mediterranean, Middle East, western Pacific, Caribbean, Indian Ocean, and elsewhere. Signing a contract with the Naval Institute Press, Holloway refined the material within the framework of the ongoing Cold War. For fact-checking assistance Holloway turned to the late John C. Reilly, who in retirement from federal service held the J. William Middendorf II history chair at the foundation. Reilly had once managed the Navy's ship history program and had overseen the publication of the indispensable *Dictionary of American Naval Fighting Ships*. Reilly's diligent work and editorial recommendations, along with additional proofreading and editing by other members of the foundation staff, helped ready Holloway's manuscript for prime time.

When it was published in 2007, *Aircraft Carriers at War: A Personal Retrospective of Korea, Vietnam, and the Soviet Confrontation* received favorable reviews, earned accolades, placement on the Chief of Naval Operations' reading list, and sold well for the Naval Institute Press. Among those who praised the book was Henry Kissinger, who wrote, "No one is more qualified than Admiral Holloway to write about the role that has been played by aircraft carriers in shaping America's military strength."

However, to focus his manifesto on behalf of big-deck carriers, Holloway set aside his recollections about his youth, his time at the U.S. Naval Academy, and his service in destroyers during World War II. Holloway died in 2019 without publishing that material, but it is a story that ought to be shared. Not only is Holloway a good storyteller but his insights on training and combat in the western Pacific could contribute to our understanding of the war and our appreciation for the role destroyers played. In preparing Holloway's earlier recollections, I arranged for fact-checking much like Reilly's and incorporated corrections as Holloway had done for *Aircraft Carriers at War*. Passages were compared to wartime diaries and deck logs. In several cases I found Holloway's recollections spot on—but simply out of chronological order.

The most problematic chapters concerned his early years. Looking back seven decades later, Holloway simply lacked many details that now, thanks to his father's recordings combined with secondary sources, I could add, with mistakes corrected. All that produced a text that could not properly be presented as the admiral's. Thus, the years leading to his entrance into the U.S. Naval Academy have been adapted as a biographical portrait in the prologue.

Thereafter the bulk of this book's narrative—his time at the Naval Academy, his short stint at Harvard, and his surface "tours" in *Ringgold* and *Bennion*—are Admiral Holloway's own. The endnotes and insertions within square brackets are mine. Because the material on his subsequent years in naval aviation and leadership has already appeared in *Aircraft Carriers at War*, I have added an epilogue to discuss the fate of Holloway's two destroyers and the postwar career of the father whose elevation to the rank of four-star admiral had an impact on that of the son in several, if tangential, ways. The epilogue ends with an observation and an implied recommendation: given the service of these two men for their navy and their nation, a USS *James L. Holloway* is long overdue.

Many thanks go to Captain Creekman and Capt. Skid Heyworth, now retired, for "sanity checks" on my revisions. I am grateful also to Paul Cogan at the National Archives and Records Administration, who provided the digital access and copies needed to ensure accuracy, and to Jane Holloway, who lent some family photographs. At the Naval Institute Press a huzzah goes to Emily Hegranes, who assisted with finding illustrations, to Padraic "Pat" Carlin for shepherding this manuscript through the production process, and to Pelham Boyer, who also copyedited *America's First Aircraft Carrier: USS* Langley *and the Dawn of U.S. Naval Aviation* just a year ago. Finally, hugs go to my wife Mary and my daughters Xepher and Carolyn for their continued support as I pursue numerous other naval history–related projects.

DAVID F. WINKLER
Alexandria, Virginia
June 2024

PROLOGUE

FAMILY BACKGROUND AND EARLY YEARS

THE SEPARATION BETWEEN father and son started at birth. Charleston, South Carolina, was Jean Gordon Hagood's (Mrs. Holloway) hometown, and during the pregnancy, with father at sea, mother stayed with her parents. Of note, Holloway's pedigree pointed to a career in the Army. Holloway's father, who graduated the U.S. Naval Academy with the accelerated war class of 1919, had hoped to earn an appointment to West Point. He was first-generation Navy, in contrast to his maternal grandfather, Maj. Gen. Johnson Hagood (pronounced *Haguewood*) (1873–1948), who had earned an appointment to the U.S. Military Academy and graduated with the class of 1896.[1] Also a South Carolinian, Hagood had a strong military legacy, including relatives who had fought for the Confederacy. Hagood's uncle, also Johnson Hagood (1829–98), graduated at the top of his class at the South Carolina Military Academy (The Citadel) and fought for South Carolina, rising in rank to brigadier general.[2]

On his paternal side, the Holloway lineage went back to the arrival in Virginia's Culpepper County of George Holloway from the north of London in the 1750s. The expatriate would marry Francis Tiller and then migrate west with Daniel Boone into Kentucky. Two subsequent generations would farm in Kentucky and then Indiana. It would be James Lemuel Holloway (1860–1961) in the late nineteenth century who chose to leave the plow, for an appointment as superintendent of schools in Fort Smith, Arkansas. There he married a schoolteacher by the name of Mary Leaming, who gave birth to Keith Leaming Holloway on November 3, 1890. Eight years later Keith would welcome a baby brother, James Lemuel Holloway Jr., who came into this world on June 20, 1898.

The senior Holloway, a medical degree in osteopathy at Washington University School of Medicine in St. Louis in hand, moved his family to Oak Cliff, Texas, on the outskirts of Dallas. There Admiral Holloway's grandfather established a practice that would serve the community over the next four decades. The younger son excelled in school, eventually playing football and competing on the Oak Cliff High School debate team. As already noted, the younger Holloway expressed interest in West Point, but his congressman suggested he take the entrance exam for the Naval Academy. He passed, and an appointment was secured. James Lemuel Holloway Jr. subsequently entered the Naval Academy in 1915, with the Class of 1919 and graduated in June 1918, his class accelerated by World War I. The Navy detailed the newly commissioned ensign as navigator on the *Paulding*-class destroyer *Monaghan* (DD 32). Commissioned in 1911, *Monaghan* escorted convoys and hunted for German U-boats during several transatlantic crossings. Following the war, the destroyer returned to Charleston to be overhauled and then went on to Philadelphia to be decommissioned in late 1919.

During his time in Charleston, the young officer met Jean Gordon Hagood during a dance at the Carolina Yacht Club. The courtship continued from a distance; in 1920 Holloway received orders to the battleship *Florida* (BB 30), where he served as flag lieutenant to Rear Adm. Frederick Bassett Jr. during a diplomatic cruise to South America. On May 11, 1921, after *Florida* returned to Hampton Roads, the couple married at St. Michael's church in Charleston. They briefly settled in Newport, Rhode Island, where he had been assigned as the commanding officer (CO) of *Wainwright* (DD 62). Commissioned in 1916, *Wainwright* was part of Cdr. Joseph Taussig's destroyer squadron, which when the United States entered World War I immediately deployed to Ireland, where Taussig's widely reported "We are ready now!" made him famous.

Late in 1921, the Newport-based flotilla to which *Wainwright* was assigned transferred to Charleston, and *Wainwright* was scheduled for decommissioning; the Bureau of Navigation at the Main Navy Building in Washington, which handled personnel in those years, detailed Lieutenant (junior grade) Holloway to serve a short stint as CO of the destroyer *McCormick* (DD 223). Granted leave, Holloway traveled with his bride and new son, christened James L. Holloway III, to Dallas where mother and infant son would stay with Holloway's paternal grandparents for a few months. Holloway then headed to Newport with orders in hand as executive officer (XO) of *Truxtun* (DD 229), a new flush-deck, four-stack, *Clemson*-class destroyer that had been commissioned in Philadelphia in February 1921.

Promoted to lieutenant, Holloway had specifically asked for *Truxtun*, because it was to leave that summer for the Asiatic station, an assignment coveted by some and assiduously avoided by others. *Truxtun* departed Newport in June 1922 for the Far East via the Mediterranean Sea and the Indian Ocean. That meant for Jean Gordon Holloway, who had returned to Charleston where her parents helped care for little Jimmy, a journey of her own. "So my mother and I traveled by Pullman in an upper berth from Charleston to San Francisco. From there we embarked in the Army transport *Thomas* at the Army marine terminal at Oakland."[3]

Following a transpacific crossing that included riding out a typhoon, mother and son arrived at Manila, in the Philippines, to find that the Asiatic Fleet destroyers, including *Truxtun*, had gone to Chefoo (today Yantai), a Chinese port on the Yellow Sea where for some two decades the fleet had spent the months when Manila's heat was insupportable. As for accommodations, they were sent to the Army and Navy Club Annex. The senior Holloway described the quarters as "such as you would find in a World War II Camp. The walls were cut away at the top for ventilation and it really was rather grim." *Truxtun*'s XO made this assessment following the return of the

Asiatic Squadron to Manila Bay. By fortunate coincidence, Jean's father had received orders to the Philippines to be posted north of Manila at Fort Stotsenburg, later Clark Air Force Base. Fort Stotsenburg featured large bungalows built in the British colonial style, with enormous verandahs surrounded by bamboo groves. With inexpensive subsidized local labor at his disposal, then-colonel Hagood oversaw grooms for the horses, chauffeurs for the cars, gardeners, butlers, cooks, and general helpers; the Holloway family soon occupied one of the bungalows. An amah, or Chinese nurse, was detailed to look after the baby around the clock, sleeping on a cot in the nursery.

Hagood commanded a regiment of infantry, a regiment of cavalry, and a battalion of mountain artillery, as well as large numbers of Filipinos and Igarots attached for training. The Filipinos were organized into conventional infantry and cavalry units for instruction by American soldiers. The Igarots, dark-skinned aborigines of the Philippine jungle, trained as scouts for jungle warfare.

When in Manila, the destroyers underwent upkeep and maintenance at the Cavite Naval Base nearby. Lieutenant Holloway often broke away during the week to drive to Fort Stotsenburg, about sixty miles north. On Saturday nights when Manila's Army-Navy Club hosted gala events, Jean left the baby with the amah and dined there with her husband and socialized with senior military officers, local businessmen, and foreign diplomats.

The baby's first birthday had been celebrated when the destroyers returned to Chefoo and the routine changed. While many of the brides and children followed their sailors on board a destroyer tender, Jean could not take advantage of this opportunity, as the commander in chief of the U.S. Asiatic Fleet selected passengers based on reverse order of husband's rank. Effectively, those who had the least money had the first chance to ride free. Holloway would recall, "Consequently, mother [i.e., Jean] and I went from Manila up to Shanghai on a steamer of the Butterfield and Squire Line, a British shipping company. From Shanghai we took the train to Chefoo.

1 & 2. Young Jimmy dressed as a sailor and posing with his mother Jean
Courtesy of Jane Holloway

Mother recalled the trip because she was terrified. Chinese bandits had been stopping the trains, looting them, and assaulting the passengers. The roofs of our train were covered with soldiers from the Chinese Army."

Holloway arranged for his wife and son to stay for the entire summer of 1923 at a small hotel next to a stream with a name that would translate as "Smell Creek," a conduit for the city's wastewater. To look after Jean and little Jimmy, the senior Holloway brought on a household staff of five Chinese headed by a "number one boy," an amah, a maid, a laundress, and a cook. Low labor costs allowed a married lieutenant to lead an elegant existence. The presence of British, French, and Japanese contingents provided weekend opportunities for receptions and balls and excuses for the officers to deck themselves in their fancy, decorated dress uniforms and dress their wives in lavish gowns. In contrast, life for little Jimmy was hardly elegant. He became seriously ill with dysentery, recovering thanks to the destroyer squadron's physician, who prescribed a seven-day diet consisting exclusively of barley water. Still, concerns about gangs of bandits did not deter Jean from taking her baby and amah on sightseeing trips. Family albums later featured photographs of mother and son posing in front of the Forbidden City in Peking (Beijing) and Baby Holloway sitting between the humps of a Bactrian camel with the Great Wall in the background.

With the return of milder temperatures to Manila that autumn the Asiatic Fleet destroyers returned for winter maintenance. Photographs from the family album suggest that mother, son, and amah were allowed to travel with the father in *Truxtun*. Once back in Manila the couple renewed their social acquaintances. As their young lad approached his second birthday his vocabulary—in

3 & 4. Big and little Jimmies on board USS *Truxtun* en route to Olongapo, January 4, 1923
Courtesy of Jane Holloway

Chinese—rapidly increased to the point where only the amah could tell him what to do. Little Jimmy would have to learn English as a second language when Lieutenant Holloway received orders back to the states. Back in Chefoo in the spring of 1924, Holloway received new orders but remained on board long enough for an historic occasion, when *Truxtun* joined five other destroyers to form a line of picket ships across the Yellow Sea under the flight path of the three remaining Army Air Service aircraft during what would be the first aerial circumnavigation of the world.

Soon after, Lieutenant Holloway detached from *Truxtun* to rejoin his wife and son at Manila and board the Navy transport *Argonne*.[4] The month-long return voyage had its moments for the couple, who had depended on an amah for raising their child. Frustrated that little Jimmy was not consuming the *Argonne*'s culinary offerings, the father lost his temper and placed the lad into the stateroom clothes closet, slammed the door, and "nipped the end of his finger off, which absolutely petrified us." The couple spent the rest of the cruise improving their parenting skills. From the Army terminal in Oakland, California, the family traveled by rail to Baltimore, Maryland. The timing enabled Lieutenant Holloway to report at the Naval Academy for duty as an instructor in ordnance, gunnery, and mathematics for the coming scholastic year.

ANNAPOLIS 1924–1926

Little Jimmy's first American home would be a small rental property on Charles Street in the historic district of Annapolis, a location that allowed his father a short walking commute to the Academy's campus, known as the Yard. There he earned a reputation as an instructor; the son later recalled, "My father was apparently a tough instructor but a good teacher because the members of the classes of '28 and '29 have told me his nickname was 'Bucket of Blood.'"

In the month after Jimmy turned four the small house on Charles Street became a bit more crowded as Jean Gordon Holloway came into the world.⁵ Charles Street itself also gained a new resident vehicle, Holloway's secondhand Model T. Apparently not as skilled a driver as a ship handler, the lieutenant ran into a telephone pole while turning a corner, throwing his four-year-old boy into the dashboard, leaving a small scar on his cheek that would stay with him for the rest of his life.

BATTLESHIPS IN THE PACIFIC FLEET, CALIFORNIA

Upon completion of his two-year instructor tour in June 1926, Lieutenant Holloway detached with orders to *West Virginia* (BB 48), where he would serve as turret officer of 16-inch gun turret 2. With a 16-inch main battery and an admiral and flag staff embarked, "Wee Vee" represented an opportunity and also peril for its officers. In 1925, under Capt. Arthur J. Hepburn, the battleship scored first in competitive short-range target practices and earned the coveted battle efficiency pennant. Traversing the continent once again by rail to join his ship, but this time alone, Lieutenant Holloway must have foreseen pressure to defend a pennant that other battleships would be literally gunning for. Meanwhile, Jean was taking Jimmy and his baby sister to Fort Totten in Queens, a borough of New York City, where her father commanded the 2nd Coast Artillery. Following a summer along the southern shores of the Long Island Sound near the approaches to Throggs Neck, the mother and two children rejoined the father, who had found in Long Beach, California, a small rented house on Second Street within walking distance of the fleet landing.⁶

Now entering elementary school, Jimmy found it difficult to make lasting friendships. The young lads he did bond with hailed from Navy families and would inevitably move on as soon as he got to know them well. As a result, Jimmy spent a lot of time at home with books and playing with lead soldiers, favoring those from the English toymaker W. Britain. Over time, the young Holloway amassed a sizable collection that his father used to recreate the opposing formations at

5. USS *West Virginia* Naval History and Heritage Command

famous battles such as Cannae and Waterloo, teaching his son such tactical principles as "enfilading fire" and "defilade."

Though most childhood memories fade with time, one remained strong for Jimmy in his later years—dinner on board the battleship when his father had the duty. Walking down to the fleet landing from Second Street Jimmy would look on as a dozen or so motorboats from the ships "anchored out"—launches, commanding officers' gigs, and admirals' barges—jockeyed for berths at the fleet landing to disembark and embark passengers. Overall, the boats went alongside in order of arrival but yielded to gigs and barges. Holloway later recalled, "The boats themselves were showpieces, varnished, painted and polished to perfection. The boat crews were especially smart with their tailor-made [better fitting than Navy issue] bell-bottom uniforms. The cabins were immaculate in white duck [canvas] seat cushions with lace trim."

Since the battleships' anchorages were in open water not protected by a breakwater, even light winds and seas did not assure a smooth transfer to or from gangways (ladders with pivoted landings lowered temporarily to water level). Heavy swells challenged not only the coxswain's skill in bringing the boat alongside but the ability of personnel to time their leaps across the gap as the craft bounced up and down.

Doubtless, boat crews made sure Jean and her two kids made it safely. Climbing up the gangway, the impressionable Jimmy would have been awed by yet another spectacle. *West Virginia*'s teak decks, scrubbed daily by sailors with holystones, were free of blemishes. Brass fittings were brightly polished, the woodwork varnished, and the steel freshly painted. "The quarterdeck was formidably formal," Holloway would recalled, "with the Officer of the Deck (OOD) in a cocked hat, white gloves and a long glass (telescope) under his arm."

Met by Lieutenant Holloway, the family was led below for a visit in his stateroom, which contained a bunk on top of a built-in chest of drawers, one chair, and a desk that pulled down out of the bulkhead (wall), and a sink. The bunk linen was stretched taut, and like the rest of the battleship, the staterooms were scrubbed, painted, and polished.

The Holloway family then made their way to the wardroom for the 6:30 p.m. seating, to be joined by about a dozen other officers in the duty section, several of whom had invited their own families to dine. Jimmy recalled the food as rather simple but the silverware (owned collectively by the officers) extensive and impressively engraved and the service elaborate: the entrée was always preceded by soup and followed by dessert. After dinner, when it had gotten dark, all went topside and aft to the fantail to watch a movie. During the first change of reels, as the temperatures dropped, officers would go below to bring up blankets for their guests. Once the movie concluded, boats would come alongside to take the families back to fleet landing.

The future Chief of Naval Operations (CNO) and staunch proponent of large carriers was to credit Charles Lindbergh with planting the seed that would eventually lead to his own decision to shift career paths and become a naval aviator. Though he was only five at the time, the news of "Lucky Lindy's" successful transatlantic crossing and the images in the local paper of the young pilot left a lasting impression. Also appearing in the local paper were images of the young lad's own father and his gun crew. His father's Turret 2 had earned the best score for all 16-inch turrets during short-range battle practice. Thanks in part to performance of Holloway's turret, *West Virginia* again earned the "Battle E" in 1927.

NORFOLK

At the completion of his two-year tour in *West Virginia,* Lieutenant Holloway and his family endured a seven-day train journey back across the country to the town of Hampton, Virginia. "Upon arrival, my father arranged for us to live at the Sherwood Inn, an old white clapboard building held up by external cables, which served as the bachelor officers quarters (BOQ) and mess [dining] for junior Army officers at Fort Monroe." His father, ordered as aide and flag lieutenant to Rear Adm. Harris Laning, crossed Hampton Roads to report for duty in Norfolk. Laning, a graduate of the Class of 1895, had risen to command Battleship Division 2 of the East Coast–based Scouting Fleet. Shortly after settling in, the left-behind Holloways may have stood on the ramparts of the giant Fort Monroe, not quite three miles away, to witness units of Scouting Fleet steam by into the Thimble Shoal Channel and the turn southward for Guantanamo Bay, in Cuba, to conduct exercises to be followed by a series of port visits along the east coast of South America.

Holloway recalled the subsequent months "as being one of the lowest points in my young life. Even at the age of eight it was clear to me that my mother was depressed and distraught." Being stuck in the large boarding house pushed Jean to the breaking point. After six months she rented a very small house in the Hampton suburb of Phoebus. In retrospect the residence proved hardly an upgrade. "The roof leaked, and the place smelled of mildew"; the neighborhood was such that Jimmy feared being beaten up on his way home from school. Following the long South American deployment, the Scouting Fleet returned to Norfolk to prepare to leave again, for a trip to Europe. The family reunion did not go well. Arriving right after a room had been painted, the senior Holloway got what he called a "painters colic" and could not keep anything in his stomach for forty-eight hours. Furthermore, he also contracted chicken pox from his two children and needed to be hospitalized as soon he returned to his battleship, now berthed in New York City. Left behind with no friends and nothing to do except take care of the two children, Jean corresponded morosely with her husband, who was now making port visits in Europe. The replies must have done little to boost her morale; they recounted how as the admiral's aide he had accompanied him on calls to presidents and princes and visited such splendid ports as Barcelona, Naples, Gibraltar, and Portsmouth, England.

THE ARMY, FORT OMAHA

Returning from overseas in 1929, Lieutenant Holloway recognized the toll his time away had taken on the family. With little prospect of any letup in sea duty, the senior Holloway prevailed upon his wife to stay with her father, who had just completed his second tour of duty in the Philippines and now had orders to command the VII Corps area, with headquarters at Fort Omaha, Nebraska. Jimmy, who had limited experience living on Army posts during his early years, found life "on post" a contrast from Annapolis, Long Beach, and Hampton, where he had lived out in town. Jimmy was moving to a post in what is now North Omaha founded in the mid-nineteenth century as Camp Sherman, a supply depot for a growing network of Army posts being built on the western frontier.[7]

Within Fort Omaha, Jean and her two kids lived in old but roomy and well-maintained quarters within a self-contained community that had its own hospital, military police station, commissary, and post exchange. For small boys, the parade grounds and drill fields offered ample space for sports. However, for Jimmy the true dividend of coming to this post in the middle of the country was the bond he was able to forge there with his grandfather: "He had a wonderful

PROLOGUE xxvii

6. Maj. Gen. Johnson Hagood proved to be a superb tutor for young Jimmy. Library of Congress

library that I was free to read, and he had an interest in young people and a lively wit." Frequently on Saturday afternoons the major general took his grandson downtown. Hagood enjoyed movies, but his real passion was vaudeville. Holloway would remember, "He seemed to get a great kick out of the comedy skits and I enjoyed them with him."

Holloway had the good fortune to spend time with his grandfather during the twilight years of an interesting career. After graduating from West Point in 1896 Hagood served in a number of coast artillery assignments until World War I, when he went to France with the first contingent of the American Expeditionary Force (AEF) as the commander of a detachment of coastal artillery that would be trained on French-made railway guns. Shortly after his arrival in France, however, Gen. John Pershing picked him to head the SOS (Services of Supply) for the AEF. Logistics support for the American troops, right from the beginning, had become hopelessly snarled. Although neither a supply officer nor a logistician by training, Hagood did such a good job that Pershing refused to let him return to his battery. He served as Pershing's head of SOS for the duration of the war.

As noted earlier, Hagood had had opportunities to see his grandson after his birth in Charleston, in the Far East, and for a few months at Fort Totten. However, Jimmy found the interlude with Hagood at Fort Omaha exceptional: "Although I loved and admired my father, he was very seldom around, and when he was, he was usually preoccupied with naval or more pressing family matters. On the other hand, my grandfather was a born teacher. He showed me how to use his library and was always willing to talk to me about military history, which with my toy soldiers was my primary interest at that time."

Holloway was doing poorly in math in the local Omaha public school. Hagood took it upon himself to tutor the lad, writing up the multiplication tables on two-by-three-inch cards in crayon and posting them around the walls in Jimmy's bedroom "so that I was exposed all day long to these tables. He drilled me constantly in multiplication, reading and spelling, but in such a way that I found it interesting rather than a chore. I believe it was the clarity of his explanations, the soundness and logic in his descriptions, and his emphasis on drilling and reiteration that became an important part of my study habits in later years."

Holloway would later attribute his ability to get through Adm. Hyman G. Rickover's course in nuclear reactor physics to study habits instilled by his grandfather in Omaha.

NAVAL WAR COLLEGE, NEWPORT, RHODE ISLAND

After about a year in the Midwest, Jean and her two children returned to the East Coast, this time to Newport, Rhode Island, where the senior Holloway had followed Rear Admiral Laning as aide and flag lieutenant when his boss assumed duties as the Naval War College's president on June 16, 1930. Once again, the family lived out "on the local economy," renting a small two-bedroom row house on Marin Street near the center of Newport. For the fall semester Jimmy would attend an excellent public school about ten blocks away. He connected with other Navy dependents through membership in the local Sea Scout organization. He recalled, "We met at nine o'clock every Saturday and wore uniforms, we drilled with wooden guns and we were taught close order drill and other nautical skills such as knot tying and rowing by Navy chiefs. It was here that I first met Ike Kidd, Jack Kane, Victor Delano, and Joe Taussig, all of whom I would later serve with in the Navy."[8]

As the junior Holloway continued his elementary school education over the next two years, the senior Holloway enrolled in several Naval War College's courses. If Laning had had his wish granted, he would have retained Holloway as his aide for his third and final year as president. However, the officer detailers in the Bureau of Navigation recognized that remaining at Laning's side for a fourth year could prove detrimental to young Holloway's career in the long term. Holloway needed to get back to sea and was issued orders to report as assistant gunnery officer on the battleship *Nevada* (BB 36), in what was now called the Battle Force, based in Long Beach.

LONG BEACH, CALIFORNIA

The orders meant another cross-country train adventure to California. Upon arrival the family rented a small but pleasant apartment on Livingston Street, just blocks from the ocean. The reopening of schools coincided with *Nevada*'s departure north to operate off the coast of the Pacific Northwest. The ship returned to the San Pedro naval base, within Los Angeles just west of Long Beach, for much of October and into early December, excepting a short trip north to San Francisco to commemorate the fifteenth anniversary of the World War I armistice in November. In December it was off to Bremerton, Washington, for maintenance and the installation of antiaircraft guns. There Lieutenant Holloway cracked the books to study for the lieutenant commander examination then required and found time to take holiday leave to travel to Dallas to visit his parents. After dry-docking, the battleship took on 1,354 containers of powder for the 14-inchers and over a thousand rounds for the secondary guns. She cleared the Puget Sound Navy Yard on March 11 to rejoin the fleet for exercises off California but had no sooner entered Puget

Sound before news came of a disaster that had occurred at *Nevada*'s homeport.⁹

Perhaps a mere few hours had spared the two Holloway children their lives on Friday, March 10, 1933, when at 5:54 p.m. a magnitude 6.4 earthquake devastated the region, flattening nearly all the schools in Long Beach just hours after they had dismissed their classes for the weekend. Riding out the tremors in their apartment, the Holloways (minus the father, safely at sea) suffered only cracked china.

When *Nevada* returned on the 15th, Holloway likely was aware of pending orders to head back east. Harris Laning, promoted to the rank of vice admiral, had prevailed upon the bureau to reassign Holloway as his aide and flag lieutenant to support him in his new role as Commander, Cruisers Scouting Force (as the Scouting Fleet was now known), embarked in his flagship, the recently commissioned heavy cruiser *Chicago* (CA 29). The Scouting Force was at the moment deployed to the West Coast, so Holloway would be spared the cross-country train trip. Rejoining Laning, Holloway, having successfully passed his exams, was promoted to lieutenant commander. With the prospect of her husband spending more time at sea that summer, Jean and the two children caught a train back to Omaha to stay six weeks with her father before Major General Hagood moved westward to the Presidio in San Francisco to take command of the Fourth Army.

Perhaps one of Lieutenant Commander Holloway's more memorable days in *Chicago* occurred in the fog off Point Sur on the California coast on October 24, 1933. On that day the British merchantman *Silverpalm* suddenly appeared as the mist cleared away and rammed the cruiser on the port side just ahead of the forward gun turret. The impact of the collision instantly killed the chief pay clerk and a scout plane pilot; a Marine officer later succumbed to his injuries. As a result of the collision *Chicago* would spend months at the Mare Island Navy Yard. Emerging from the yard in early

1934, *Chicago* made her way back to the East Coast to rejoin the Scouting Force. By this time, Lieutenant Commander Holloway had been notified that he would be the next commanding officer of the Scouting Force *Clemson*-class destroyer *Hopkins* (DD 249). He was not pleased, having requested orders to a West Coast Battle Force destroyer. The feedback from the bureau was that Holloway's counterparts in the Battle Force had priority in the assignment of those billets (perhaps to save travel funds in that era of Depression-constrained budgets).

DESTROYERS AND CARRIER AIRPLANES, SAN DIEGO

Hopkins was based in New York City, and Holloway arranged for his wife and two children to travel there on a banana boat through the Panama Canal, to be deposited just before *Chicago*'s arrival. *Hopkins* had a reputation for lax discipline. The new skipper sent a stern message at his first Captain's Mast (where commanding officers assigned "nonjudicial punishment" to enlisted crew members brought before them) with the punishment he meted out to a drunken sailor who had punched a quarterdeck petty officer of the watch: "Ten days bread and water with a full ration every third day. Master-at-Arms, take charge." Another challenge was senior enlisted leadership—he had none! Years later he recalled, "I went over to see Frank Beatty in the Class of '16 who was the scouting force flag secretary and personnel officer and showed him my personnel roster and he said, 'Jimmy, we'll take care of it immediately.' Well, the next day about six of the finest chief petty officers I've ever seen and about a dozen splendid first class [petty officers] came aboard."

During June *Hopkins* joined the Scouting Force for exercises off Provincetown, at the tip of Cape Cod. For the Fourth of July holiday, Holloway oversaw a long Sea and Anchor Detail up the James River taking the destroyer to Richmond, Virginia, for that city's observances. Meanwhile, his wife and two children were staying with family friends in New York. Then to Holloway's surprise he received news that Main Navy had decided to make *Hopkins* a Battle Force destroyer with a new homeport in San Diego. Soon the four-stacker was steaming south, stopping at Guantanamo Bay before heading through the Panama Canal.

There was yet another family reunion in San Diego upon the destroyer's arrival and another new abode, this time across the bay in Coronado, connected to the mainland only by a narrow isthmus, the Silver Strand. The junior Holloway would record, "My family rented a small but very comfortable bungalow in Coronado and I attended Coronado Junior High School." This was decades before a bridge was built, and Coronado could only be reached by ferry or by a long (forty-mile) trip up the strand from where it connected with the mainland just north of the Mexican border. Essentially a residential island city, it was a wonderful place for youngsters.

Jimmy's two best friends were Dick Whitney and Joe Bolger, sons of pilots assigned to carrier air squadrons based at Naval Air Station San Diego on North Island (so named because, except for a beachfront strip of land connecting the government acreage with residential Coronado, the station was surrounded by water). "It was at this point in my life that I made up my mind that I wanted to be a Navy pilot," Holloway would recall. "The three of us would ride our bicycles down to the causeway between Coronado and North Island and watch the Navy planes landing and taking off."[10]

Not surprisingly, the three lads became aviation enthusiasts, subscribing to aviation magazines and building model airplanes. Holloway remembered how each aircraft's markings enabled identification from a distance; for example, the color of the tail identified the carrier to which its squadron was assigned. It was a complex scheme:

> On the side of the fuselage under the cockpit, in large letters, were marked the type of squadron, the number of the squadron and the number of the plane in the squadron. For example,

3-F-12 would be the twelfth plane in Fighter Squadron 3 (or "Fighting 3" as it was known). The commanding officer's plane had a red cowling and a red stripe around the fuselage in the area of the cockpit. The tactical organization was made up of three-plane sections, and the commanding officer's right wingman would have the top half of his engine cowling painted red but no stripe around the fuselage. His left wingman would have the bottom half of the engine cowling painted red and again, no stripe. The second section leader had a white cowling and a white stripe around the cockpit and his wingmen similarly identified. So each section leader was distinguished by both a full colored cowling and a stripe around the cockpit of a different color.

Because each pilot flew an assigned aircraft, Holloway could spot his friends' fathers when they zipped by. Joe Bolger's father was XO of an F4B-4 fighter squadron off the *Saratoga*, so Holloway could identify him in the open cockpit of his Boeing-built biplane with a green tail, a blue cowling, and a blue stripe around the cockpit. During Holloway's time in Coronado the Navy began to phase out the stubby little F4B-4s, with their fixed landing gear, at first replacing it with the Grumman FF-1, a biplane with retractable landing gear and a rear-seat gunner, and then with the Grumman F2F, a single-seat biplane, also with retractable landing gear. The FF-1 would be relegated to scouting squadrons.

The young lads may have seen San Pedro–based aircraft carriers *Lexington* (CV 2) and *Saratoga* (CV 3) out beyond Point Loma (the harbor had yet to be dredged deep enough to allow them to enter). *Langley* (CV 1), a fixture at North Island since her arrival in late 1924, had spent much of 1934 on the East Coast, returning in November with two Marine Corps squadrons embarked. Surely April 15, 1935, was a memorable day, with the arrival at North Island of the recently commissioned aircraft carrier *Ranger* (CV 4).

NAVY DEPARTMENT, WASHINGTON, DC

However, the now thirteen-year-old Holloway would have little opportunity to see the new flattop in operation, as his father received orders to the Office of the Chief of Naval Operations in the gunnery section of the Navy Department's Fleet Training Division. Once again, the Holloways traveled east by rail, with stopovers in Texas. Major General Hagood now commanded the VIII Corps, headquartered at Fort Sam Houston, so Jimmy and sister Jean would have an opportunity to see both sets of grandparents. From Texas the family continued to the nation's capital, where the children's grandaunt Daisey had found a rowhouse on Allen Place, a short street in the Northwest quadrant of the city, near Rock Creek Park between 18th Street and Connecticut Avenue. Lieutenant Commander Holloway commuted to the Main Navy Building, which bracketed the National Mall and Constitution Avenue; there he sat at a big double desk opposite of Cdr. Willis "Ching" Lee. The younger Holloway entered Western High School as a freshman and joined the school's cadet corps.[11]

Segregation was in full force. Holloway recalled that Eastern, Central, Tech, Western, and Wilson high schools excluded Blacks. Of these, all except Tech had cadet corps, in which membership was mandatory for male students unless excused for physical reasons or the family could not afford a uniform. Holloway remembered the uniform he procured secondhand from a graduating senior: "a white shirt, black necktie, light blue trousers with dark blue stripe, a blue military jacket with brass buttons and a visor cap." He wore this outfit to school on Tuesday and Thursday drill days, remaining after school to march with Springfield rifles until 5 p.m. An aim of the after-school drills was to prepare for the competition held each spring at the old Griffith Stadium (the home of the Washington Senators baseball team) to determine which company marched with the greatest precision and presented the best appearance.

Besides drill, Holloway played football on the lightweight team, which competed against similar squads from the other white public high schools. In class, young Holloway benefited from ancient history and chemistry courses. Perhaps knowledge that those subjects appeared in the Naval Academy written entrance exams led him to enroll in those classes. Father and son shared a goal: that Jimmy earn an appointment to Annapolis.

That academic and career objective faced the Holloways with a difficult decision. Young Jimmy had started his junior year at Western High School when his father learned he could expect orders to go back to sea that winter on a West Coast ship. His mother and sister expected to accompany him. Accordingly, the family began to consider enrolling Jimmy in a local boarding school. Jimmy and his father had different explanations regarding the decision to pull Jimmy from Western. Both were likely true. Years later, the son would recall his father being concerned that a transfer from Western to some unknown school system on the West Coast, with the potential for yet another change during his senior year, would disrupt his preparations for the Academy entrance examinations. However, the father himself later claimed that Holloway's mother simply was not satisfied with their son's education at Western.

Having received a positive recommendation about Saint James School, in the Shenandoah Valley in Maryland, the family drove their new Buick up to Hagerstown for tea with the headmaster, Mr. Adrian Onderdonk. The parents decided then and there to enroll their son. Though tuition had dropped due to the Depression at the school, which listed Alfred Thayer Mahan amongst its graduates, the salary of a lieutenant commander needed to be augmented with a loan from Major General Hagood in Dallas.

SAINT JAMES SCHOOL

So in January of that year, as the younger Holloway, then a junior, would recall, "My father drove me up to Saint James and dropped me off with my trunk and his best wishes." Saint James proved to be an excellent match, and he took advantage of the academic opportunities, especially since there was not much else to do. "The boarding students (we were all boarders) were able to go into Hagerstown for a movie and a soda on Saturday afternoon, but that was about it." Classes were small, ranging from a minimum of six to a maximum of twelve, and were taught generally by older men. "Saint James seemed to be blessed with people who could really teach in the finest sense of the word," Holloway remembered, adding that almost all the teachers were widowers or bachelors and they lived at the school, mostly in little apartments in the dormitories. This made them accessible to assist students during the evening study period. When not studying Holloway played football, soccer, and tennis. He was able to compete, but short in stature at an age when many of his peers were in growth "spurts," he never became a star athlete. As for studies, Holloway had never been a particularly good student in other schools, but that all would change at Saint James.

Back in Washington, knowing that he was due to rotate back to sea, Lieutenant Commander Holloway corresponded with Capt. Alexander Sharp, who had orders to be the next commanding officer of the battleship *Idaho* (BB 42), about the availability of his navigator billet. Sharp expressed delight at Holloway's interest, and following additional correspondence the Bureau of Navigation "cut" the orders sending Holloway west at midyear. First, in April, he visited his parents in Dallas, where he expressed his appreciation for their willingness to help with their grandson's boarding school costs. However, he left shaken by how much they had aged since his last visit—especially his mother.

After his return to Washington and with the Saint James academic year wrapped up, the Holloway family packed their Buick for a cross-country trip to the Puget Sound Navy Yard in Bremerton.

Both father and son were to keep fond memories of the long drive, which included a visit to Yellowstone National Park. The father recalled, "We went out just to the east of Cheyenne [Wyoming], turned sharply northwest and went up to the Shoshone Canyon and as we drove through it there was a herd of horses galloping wildly on the other side of the stream and at one place Jim, who had on a baseball cap, caused much amusement because I think he made eyes at the waitress so that when she got around to him she said, "What do you want to drink, Sonny, milk?" The teenager was deeply embarrassed, much to his younger sister's amusement.

Arriving at Bremerton, where *Idaho* was undergoing routine maintenance, the Holloways settled into a nice boarding house, and the father reported for duty. After a few weeks in the yard, Holloway faced his first navigational challenge, clearing the shipyard, squeezing through Rich Passage into Puget Sound, and heading north and west through the Strait of Juan de Fuca. Once out in the Pacific, Holloway plotted a track down to San Pedro. The rest of the family followed by car. Resettled at Long Beach, a bit of Holloway's off-duty time was devoted to lining up an appointment for his son to attend the Academy.

PURSUING THE APPOINTMENT

Holloway's dilemma arose from his having been faithful to the unwritten law at the time that career military officers did not vote; having as they did an obligation to serve the commander in chief, it was thought, taking a political position by voting for or against the incumbent president (the commander in chief) could somehow jeopardize or strain that allegiance. Consequently, Holloway—along with most of his contemporaries—had no political attachments and thus no opportunity to appeal to a like-minded member of Congress.

One option was to seek one of the presidential appointments set aside for the sons of veterans. The junior Holloway recalled "that there were about 50 for each academy, with 200–300 service juniors usually applying for them each year—it was viciously competitive." It is pure conjecture, but it may have been the now-precarious standing of the younger Holloway's maternal grandfather with the Franklin D. Roosevelt administration that dissuaded the family

7. Jimmy Holloway at Saint James
Courtesy Jane Holloway

from pursuing this route. In early 1936, Major General Hagood had testified before the Senate Armed Services and offered frank assessments of the Army's readiness and commentary on the Works Progress Administration, both bleak enough that when made public they led to his relief from command. At the behest of Senator James F. Byrnes of Hagood's home state of South Carolina, Hagood was granted an opportunity to articulate his concerns in person to the commander in chief, who asked him to stay on active duty. He accepted command of the VI Corps region headquartered in Chicago and assumed the post on May 1, 1936—but the next day, he requested and was promptly granted retirement from active duty. After thirty days of leave, Hagood left the service at the end of May.[12]

So it was that the Holloways opted for a congressional appointment. Family connections came into play. Lieutenant Commander Holloway's first cousin, Paul D. Carrington, a prominent attorney in Dallas who would eventually preside over the Texas Bar Association, thought he could exploit his own connections with Congressman Hatton W. Sumners, a Democrat representing the Dallas congressional district, to secure an appointment. The problem was that Jimmy had been to Dallas only to visit his grandparents. However, since Lieutenant Commander Holloway had been appointed from Dallas and the corpus of the family still lived there, Carrington thought it was worth a shot. He had initial success, getting Sumners to authorize Holloway to take the September 1938 test as a resident of his district. Now it was incumbent on young Jimmy, having just returned to Saint James for his senior year, to do well. Holloway later recalled being driven to the Hagerstown post office to take the test. The subjects covered included "math (algebra and geometry), physics, English, American history and ancient history." With the solid grounding the Saint James curriculum had provided him, Holloway felt sure he would be competitive.

In October he learned that he stood first in a field of eighteen. Awaiting news that his exam results had secured him an appointment, Holloway was stunned when Carrington called to tell him that Sumners had reneged; apparently, a runner-up complained that Holloway was not a resident of the district and had the unfair advantage of attendance at a boarding school. Carrington assured Holloway he would do what he could do down in Dallas but suggested the young man pay a call on Sumners to allow the congressman to place a face on a name. Arriving in Washington on a Greyhound bus, Holloway took a taxi over to the House Office Building and found his way to Sumners's office. Holloway recalled: "I had never met a person as old as him. He was tall, thin, and erect, with a white mane and a gaunt face above a very high starched collar." Holloway seems to have made a favorable impression. On the way out Sumners congratulated him: he was now a candidate for the Naval Academy.

As Jimmy began preparations for a naval career, his father's career nearly came to a premature conclusion. In mid-January, much of the Battle Force including *Idaho* passed through the Panama Canal to meet the Scouting Force in the Caribbean for a series of exercises, including Fleet Problem XX, that would last into March. The opening of the New York World's Fair was set for the end of April, and the intent was to retain the whole fleet on the East Coast for a presidential review and New York City port call—perhaps an opportunity for a father/son reunion. However, tensions were flaring in the Far East as China began mounting counteroffensives against the Japanese, and in mid-April President Roosevelt ordered the bulk of the Battle Force to return to the West Coast. During her return passage through the Panama Canal's Gaillard Cut (now Culebra Cut), in the Cucaracha Reach, *Idaho* experienced a loss of electrical power to her steering engines. When the helmsman reported seeing no response on the rudder-position indicator, Holloway called down from the bridge to "after steering," at the stern, an order to bring the backup steam engine on line. However, within the narrow channel the action proved too late. The battleship bumped the steep shore of the passage, and jagged rocks pierced a recently installed exterior belt of steel designed to "predetonate" incoming torpedoes in "explosion chambers" before they smacked directly against the ship's armor belt. The chambers slowly filled with water—hardly a threat to the ship's stability.

Having engaged the steam backup engine, *Idaho* passed through the Miraflores Locks and stopped at Balboa to put divers in the water to assess the damage further and assemble a court of inquiry. The head of the inquiry, Vice Adm. Ernest J. King (then Commander, Aircraft, Battle Force and future Chief of Naval Operations, with a fearsome reputation—his nickname "Ernie," below, was not used in his presence), was joined on the board by the captains of two other battleships. Ironically, Holloway had just been selected for full commander. Now he worried that his third full stripe (lieutenant commanders wear on their coat sleeves two half-inch gold stripes and a quarter-inch stripe between) might be in jeopardy.

> We were in the cabin of the *Idaho*, the flag [admiral's] cabin, I think we had a spare cabin with Ernie King at the head of the table and this board and they called witnesses and went through the whole thing and I told my troops [enlisted men who had been present] and I said, "Now listen, don't try to

rationalize this thing and dream up something. You just tell what you saw, nothing else, and tell the absolute truth because, in the long run, there's nothing as strong as the truth." This they proceeded to do and I sat there and sort of halfway turned my back on the court saying to myself, "I'm not going to let that SOB Ernie King see me show any trepidation or show the white feather or appear worried at all. If I sink, I'm going to sink with my colors flying."

Holloway became concerned less about King than about the two battleship captains:

I could see the two captains on the board sort of looking at us and rubbing their hands and saying, "Well, maybe we'd better hang the sons of bitches just to be on the safe side!" But you know, Ernie wasn't that way, and he went down to the steering engine room and duplicated the casualty and by the great horn spoon [originally a Scots saying], he held the Bureau of Ships responsible. Well, for one thing, you know, with all of Ernie's supposed to be so harsh and brutal he had the strongest friendships and he was very beholden to Sharp's father, in the Navy, and Alexander Sharp and I were, of course, defendants together and I don't think Ernie would have found Alex Sharp guilty for a million dollars.[13]

Having surmounted a career-jeopardizing situation, Holloway put on his third full stripe and "brass hat" (the visors of uniform peaked caps of commanders and above bear gold embroidered oak leaves, often dubbed "scrambled eggs") and accepted orders to command the cargo ship *Sirius* (AK 15), then undergoing maintenance at the Norfolk Navy Yard. Having once been a passenger on sister ship *Vega* (AK 17), the new commander was less than enthusiastic about the Hog Island–built steamship but rationalized that when given an opportunity for command, you need to take it. The Holloways once again packed their Buick and drove back across the continent, arriving in time to witness a graduation ceremony in Hagerstown.

The family must have been greatly impressed when Jimmy graduated at the top of his class at Saint James. Years later he remembered, "I was almost always in the top 10 in the entire school, and quite often ranked number two or three." When the final grades came in Holloway found himself in line to receive the John Downes Prize for all-around student performance. Having received his diploma on June 16, 1939, the soon-to-be midshipman joined some of his classmates for a trip to New York to see the World's Fair.

Upon his return the family drove to Annapolis to drop him off. There a problem arose: Jimmy flunked his physical due to albumin deficiency detected by a blood test. Commander Holloway was having none of it: "Jim had been unable to pass his physical examination because of albumin and I was throwing a cartwheel with Johnny Roper [John W. Roper, later a vice admiral and then on the Academy staff] on the phone, who was on duty down there [in Annapolis], but apparently Ray Swartz, the wrestling coach came through and decided Jim could wrestle in a good weight and gave Jim a bottle of barley water, which he drank and the next day he passed the physical exam with flying colors."

Having been sworn in and now safely ensconced in Bancroft Hall, Jimmy bid farewell to his family, which then drove south to find a boarding school for sister Jean, now entering her high school years. After placing her at Ashley Hall in Charleston, South Carolina, Commander Holloway headed back north to Norfolk to take command of *Sirius*. He would remain in command for all of two months before being recruited to be the operations officer and chief of staff for Rear Adm. Hayne Ellis of the Atlantic Squadron, who flew his flag on *Texas* (BB 35). By this time the academic year had begun at the Naval Academy. But news now came of the German invasion of Poland.

PART I
THE USNA YEARS AND HARVARD

CHAPTER 1

MY MIDSHIPMAN EXPERIENCE

ADMISSION TO THE U.S. NAVAL ACADEMY

THAT SUMMER, the "youngsters" (third classmen—that is, sophomores) and first classmen (seniors) were on cruise, and the second classmen (juniors) remained at the Academy to be responsible for inducting the incoming "plebes." In order to avoid overburdening the command and administrative structure, the incoming plebe class arrived at the Academy in small groups almost daily over the period of the summer. (Later this system was changed, and now all members of the new plebe class arrive at the Academy on one specific day, known as "Induction Day.") My father drove me to Annapolis and dropped me off at a boarding house like the one in which he had stayed twenty-four years before. These boarding houses were very important to the Naval Academy's social and support structure. They were usually old houses run by elderly widows or spinsters with four or five bedrooms and usually just one bath. In the summer they put up the incoming plebes during the four-day admissions process, and during the rest of the year they catered to the families and "drags" (dates) of midshipmen who came to Annapolis for a "hop" (school dance) or some other Academy social event.

The reason for the four-day admissions procedure was the physical examination. Although all of us had passed a preliminary physical, the Naval Academy insisted on doing its own examination as the candidate was being admitted. Two afflictions worried us most: myopia, a dysfunction of the eye that none of us (including our family eye doctors) understood, and albumin in the urine (for which our family physicians had no rational explanation, though today it is understood as a potential sign of kidney disease). We were told the latter often occurred due to anxiety, something that all of us entering the Naval Academy certainly experienced. To address the albumin issue I was given a bottle of barley water. I was able to pass the eye exam and it was with great relief that when the results of the new urine tests came back on the third day, I was OK'ed for admission.

One of my classmates-to-be was Roger McNeil. McNeil's problem was his height: he just barely could make the height requirement. His doctor had told him that brisk walking from his boarding house could shorten his height by a quarter to three-eighths of an inch. So on the day of his physical examination he took a taxi from his boarding house to the Academy and rode the freight elevator to the fourth-floor sickbay where the examinations were conducted. McNeil passed the physical, but just barely. McNeil later became a carrier pilot and was killed as an A-4 Skyhawk squadron commander during a night carrier landing in 1959.[1]

During our four-day stay at the boarding houses, most of us made friendships with our classmates-to-be, and mine were long-lasting. One was Bill Maxson, a tall Texan from Wichita Falls. Bill had been the senior captain at Culver Military Academy in Indiana and was one of its most outstanding graduates. The year before he had been pictured on the cover of *Boys' Life* magazine, which was doing a story on military prep schools. He had been recruited by the athletic department at the Naval Academy for football and track. This judgment was well justified, because by his junior year he was an All Eastern end in football and held the record in the conference for the 440-yard dash. I roomed with Bill for my three years at the Academy and during that time he established a brilliant record. He was the "five-striper," or regimental commander (the highest position a midshipman could hold), and I believe he was the first midshipman to graduate from the Academy without ever having received a demerit for misconduct.

Upon graduation Bill Maxson went to submarine school and then immediately to the fleet. He was lost in 1943 when the submarine to which he was assigned was on plane-guard duty in the Pacific campaign. This required the submarine to take station in the vicinity of the island being attacked by our carrier aircraft and to pick up any aircraft crews that were shot down by the Japanese. While picking up a downed aviator near Truk, his submarine was strafed by a Japanese dive-bomber. Bill was part of the rescue detail on the submarine's weather deck; he had taken cover behind the conning tower, but a ricocheting bullet pierced his upper body. His submarine did not carry a doctor; the ship's corpsman said that Maxson could have been saved if he had been gotten to a medical facility. The submarine CO requested permission for the submarine to leave station to deliver Maxson to the nearest cruiser or carrier equipped with a better sickbay, but this request was denied and Bill Maxson died of his wound three days later.[2]

Another friendship established during these four preadmission days was with Tazewell T. Shepard Jr. from Alabama. Bill and I tried to get into a three-man room in Bancroft Hall with Tazewell but none were available. During World War II Shepard was an ensign in USS *San Francisco* (CA 38). During the Naval Battle of Guadalcanal on the night of November 12–13, 1942, *San Francisco* was badly shot up and took a direct hit to the bridge. Shepard administered first aid to the ship's captain, who died in his arms, and then Shepard took command of the ship until a more senior officer could relieve him a half hour later. He received the Navy Cross for this action. Taz was married to the daughter of Alabama's Senator John Sparkman and in 1961 was appointed naval aide to President John F. Kennedy, a job that he carried out with great distinction and considerable credit to the Navy.[3]

PLEBE YEAR

Plebe year was not much different then from the way it is now. During plebe summer we wore a uniform called "white works," a very blousy sailor suit of white cotton, the trousers of which tied at the waist like a pajama bottom. We were required to stencil our names boldly across the chest of the "middie blouse," so any upper-classman could identify us for purposes of "instruction" or hazing (which were quite often indistinguishable). White works were only a summer working uniform. Within two weeks after our admission, each of us went to the tailor shop (operated under a contract by Jacob Reed's Sons, a prominent Philadelphia clothier) in the basement of Bancroft Hall, where we were meticulously measured for tailor-made uniforms. These were delivered in September and consisted of two suits of blue service dress (identical to what officers were wearing) and a suit of full dress with high-waisted trousers and a short jacket with twin rows of brass buttons and a choke collar. (These uniform styles have changed little since their introductions—the service-dress blues in 1919 and the full-dress blues sometime in the 1800s—and are still worn at the Naval Academy.)

During plebe year, academics did not give me a problem but I had to study hard, using all of the time available in our schedule for that purpose. Like most of my classmates, I was enthusiastic about organized team sports and wanted very much to participate on one of the Academy teams. During "plebe summer" each of us was required to undergo instruction in all of the Academy sports. At 150 pounds I was too light for football, so I had to find another sport. Boxing and wrestling caught my attention because of the different weight classes, which permitted people of similar size and capability to compete. After a classmate pounded me pretty hard in an exhibition boxing match during plebe summer, I decided to go out for wrestling. (It should be noted that boxing was an important intercollegiate sport in those days, and the Naval Academy was among its leaders on the East Coast. The matches went for three two-minute rounds, and the contestants wore large gloves but no protective headgear.)

That fall I joined the wrestling squad and found myself among about twenty other aspirants in the 145-pound class of the plebe team. The Naval Academy had a fine wrestling tradition and was seeking to boost its prominence in the sport by bringing in a coaching staff from Oklahoma A&M University, now Oklahoma State University, a national powerhouse. One member of the plebe team with me, John P. Harrell, came to the Academy after two years at Oklahoma A&M, where he had won the NCAA heavyweight championship and world amateur championship in 1939. The plebe coach was Stan Henson, who was personable, patient, and a very good teacher. By that winter

8 & 9. Holloway as a member of the U.S. Naval Academy's varsity wrestling team and in a portrait photograph taken in August 1941.
Adm. James L. Holloway III (Ret.) donation to Naval History and Heritage Command, 2006

when the wrestling season began I had worked my way up to the number-one position in the 145-pound class out of a group of eight to ten contenders. Stan Henson was very fair about this. On every Monday, in each weight class, we began a three-day tournament, and the wrestler who won the tournament (that is, was undefeated) wrestled in the match on Saturday. I consider it a credit to the Navy coaching staff's teaching ability that I wrestled every match plebe year and "won my numeral," never having seen a wrestling mat before plebe summer.[4]

Plebe year was confining. As plebes we were not allowed out "on liberty"—that is, out of the Yard—during all of plebe summer. In the fall after the academic year began we could go into Annapolis only after the varsity home football game was over. We had to be back in Bancroft Hall for evening meal. We plebes also were allowed liberty after mandatory Chapel on Sundays but were required to return to Bancroft Hall for evening meal. Plebes' parents often came on Sunday afternoons to take their midshipmen to Sunday dinner, but I discouraged my family from visiting. My father was a commander at the time and I was very anxious that I not be identified as a "Navy junior." Navy juniors at the Academy had the reputation of being very cliquish and know-it-alls. They tended to room together, and in the afternoons they rendezvoused at the "Gedunk" (soda fountain) where they enjoyed each other's company over banana splits. Midshipmen like Ike Kidd and Joe Taussig were sons of prominent naval officers (admirals) who were well known in the Navy and to other members of the regiment of midshipmen and to the Academy staff. I considered it fortunate that my father was relatively junior and not well known, and I didn't particularly want him to visit me at Annapolis.

Hazing was not a problem as far as I was concerned. It was generally just good-natured buffoonery, and most plebes were immature enough to enjoy the attention that the hazing brought. Each plebe was assigned to a first classman, supposedly to polish his shoes and close his windows at 4 a.m. during the winter so the room would be comfortably warm when he arose at 6:15 reveille. My first classman, Monty Whitehead (Class of 1940), was a football player and the first-team running back. As a plebe I was proud to serve as his "lackey": like many of the first classmen, he saw his role as not to be waited on but to provide refuge and guidance to his plebes.

That fall, after a satisfying 14–12 football victory over the University of Virginia, Monty came back to his room with more than a few beers under his belt (strictly against regulations but unless a midshipman was obviously tight he was seldom spotted and put on report). I came by Monty's room and he "spooned" me, by shaking my hand, which meant that the plebe/upperclassman relationship no longer existed between us and we could be just friends. Of course, the difference in our ages—I was seventeen and he was probably twenty-three—precluded our becoming buddies, but I could use his room to escape the hazing of other upper-classmen and to relax and listen to his record collection.[5] Plebes were not allowed to have radios or record players. I have to say that I was never subjected to any brutal hazing and further never saw any improper hazing or treatment of plebes by upper-classmen. I am convinced that those occasions of overzealous hazing that did occur were brought on by stupidity on the part of the upper-classmen or an intolerable attitude on the part of the plebe.

During the fall of 1939 an important event occurred. At a noon meal, the superintendent made a rare appearance in the mess hall to read a message from President Franklin D. Roosevelt that went something like this: "In view of the possibility of a major world war in which the United States will probably play a major role, the demands on our military professionals will be unprecedented. In view of this, the president is eliminating the existing ban that prevents graduates from the Naval Academy on active duty in the Navy or Marine Corps from getting married during their first two years of commissioned service."[6] I remember a moment of stunned silence, and then the reaction was surprising: most first classmen, who could now get married after graduation, cheered. But a significant number gripped their heads in their hands and shook their heads miserably. Even though I was young and naïve, I think I understood their problem.

ARMY-NAVY GAME

In November 1939, the week before the Army-Navy game, Bancroft Hall was in pandemonium. I had never seen anything like the hysteria that gripped the regiment during this time. The football players were lionized, carried to their meals on the shoulders of their comrades, and implored to win the "big one." Plebe-year restrictions were largely ignored during this time and fourth classmen could run wild. In 1939 neither Army nor Navy had a particularly good team, but *Time* magazine had built up the game by noting that each team had an All-American tackle—Harry Stella from West Point and Al Bergner from the Naval Academy—who had played on the same high school football team in Kankakee, Illinois.[7] In those days, the quality of college football was fairly level among the major universities. For example, in 1941 Navy beat eighth-ranked Penn and was tied by Harvard.

Saturday morning on the day of the game, the regiment rose at 4 a.m., dressed in blue service uniforms and overcoats, fell in and marched four miles to the railroad station on the outskirts of Annapolis. There we boarded trains and headed for Philadelphia. We were fed cold box lunches en route and upon arrival at the stadium, the companies of midshipmen disembarked from the train, fell in on the adjacent tracks and marched onto the playing field right on schedule for the pregame parade.

Navy won the game that year as we did the next two years during my undergraduate days, and the midshipmen were granted liberty until the train departed at 11 p.m.[8] For the plebes it was a glorious occasion, our first time out of Bancroft Hall after dark since we entered the Academy the previous summer. Some midshipmen had dates, but most of us met college girls at one of the many parties organized for that purpose at the various hotels around town. Almost all of us had a few drinks and some of us even had a good meal. It was a wonderful break from plebe year.

BATTLESHIP CRUISE

In June 1940 graduation came at the end of a very glamorous period called "June Week," and the fourth classmen shed the opprobrium of being plebes. As our former first classmen headed out to the fleet, we newly elevated third classmen, or youngsters, embarked in three old battleships, *Texas* (BB 35), *New York* (BB 34), and *Arkansas* (BB 33), for our youngster cruise. During this time we would function in the role of seamen first class on board these ships, while the new first classmen (the Class of 1941) would take up the duties of junior officers, "JOs." This was the first brush my class had with the real Navy, and it was a fascinating and important experience. Boarding the *Texas* with my seabag, I was assigned to one of the deck divisions.[9] My seabag, with everything I was taking with me on the cruise, was then put in a "hammock netting," which was a space between the hull of the ship and the living spaces. In the days of sailing ships, such as USS *Constitution*, the hammocks and seabags were put into actual hammock nettings when not in use, to provide additional side protection from cannon balls. At the bugle call "Tattoo" each evening after the movie, we retired to the hammock nettings and were issued our hammocks, which we then swung from two hooks fastened in the overhead of the passageways and compartments. This took a little getting used to, but after a week we were able to be in our hammocks when Taps was sounded and all lights were turned off.

Each night we all stood one four-hour watch, either the 8 p.m.-to-midnight "evening watch," the midnight-to-4 a.m. "midwatch," or the 4 a.m.-to 8 a.m. "morning watch." This meant that a messenger had to find your hammock to wake you. Then you got up, dressed and reported to your watch station. With the inexperience of the messengers and of us in our hammocks, during the first week "calling the watch" was pretty confusing. Reveille was sounded at 5:30 a.m. and everybody hit the deck, rolled up their hammocks and stowed them in the hammock netting. Then, clad in rolled-up trousers and an undershirt (today's T-shirt), with bare feet, we holystoned and swabbed the teak decks. At about 6 o'clock the coffee cans came up from the galley and we took a short break for a cup of "joe."

By this time the decks were drying out, and the mess cooks—enlisted members of the crew plus assigned midshipmen—took down the mess tables that were stowed in the overhead of the compartments and passageways by hooks and racks. After these folding tables were set up, the mess cooks went to the galley and they returned with a china plate and cup, a knife, fork, and spoon for each member of the mess. Each mess consisted of those of us who ate at a particular table. On the mess cook's next trip he brought breakfast, which was contained in large nested metal pots. Breakfast generally consisted of dried toast and something to go over it, such as scrambled eggs, creamed chip beef or an unusual dish that was browned hamburger meat in a dark gravy. Each of these food items had affectionately scatological names that were standard throughout the fleet. After breakfast the boatswain's mate piped down "mess gear," and the tables were returned to the overhead and the plates, flatware, and containers taken back to the galley. By 8 a.m. the ship's routine began.

The ship's daily routine was published in a "plan of the day" and was carried out by the boatswain's mates. They were stationed on the bridge and received their orders from the officer of the deck (OOD). Then five or six boatswain's mates deployed about the ship in strategic locations blew their boatswain's pipes to announce each evolution. For example, the boatswain's mates would use their boatswain's pipe to call for "all hands to mess" and then in a seagoing rasp announce "All hands, pipe down chow." We midshipmen found it was almost impossible to understand what the boatswain's mates were saying, and none of us knew the pipe calls yet. It was necessary for us to rush to the nearest bulletin board, find a Plan of the Day, and check the time so we could identify the evolution.

The three battleships making up the midshipmen cruise embarked the new first- and third-class midshipmen by motor launches in Annapolis Roads, and then steamed south through Chesapeake Bay. The first port of call was Guantanamo Bay, Cuba. There we rendezvoused with some four-stacker destroyers and conducted fleet operations. One of these exercises was a simulated night torpedo attack on the two battleships by destroyers. At that time there was no radar and no voice radio for talk between the ships. The destroyers conducted a successful attack, making their presence known by turning on their searchlights when they were only five hundred yards from the battleships in torpedo-launch position.

The antiaircraft defenses of that day are worthy of note. This was in the summer of 1940, only a year and a half before Pearl Harbor. For antiaircraft practice, land-based aircraft towing cloth sleeves at the end of a five-thousand-foot towline flew over the battleships at right angles to their course at an altitude of five to ten thousand feet. The ship's antiaircraft officer was stationed on a platform just above the bridge with a wooden drawing board covered with a sheet of drafting paper annotated with various curves. As the planes approached, the elevation of the target and its distance (based on an optical range-finder measurement) were passed to the AA officer through sound-powered telephones. He plotted the data with a pencil on his sheet thumbtacked to the drawing board. When he "obtained a solution" he gave an order to a talker who passed the sight setting to the 5-inch antiaircraft gun (5-inch/51-caliber) crews that then manually set their sights and commenced firing on order. I didn't observe anything close to a hit on the sleeve. Later that day the planes flew in at about a thousand feet and the automatic antiair weapons fired at the target. These machine guns constantly seemed to jam. I decided that my earlier intention to become an aviator was probably a sound one!

Following fleet operations and some "all hands" picnics ashore in Guantanamo Bay, the battleships visited several ports in Puerto Rico, Haiti and the Dominican Republic. After the ships returned to Guantanamo, selected groups of midshipmen were transferred to destroyers. These four-stackers took six midshipmen per DD up to Santiago where we threaded the river and had an afternoon's liberty there. This was a very interesting visit, and the experience of riding a destroyer after being on the battleship was actually exhilarating.

The training squadron returned to Annapolis at the end of August 1940, and we disembarked from the battleships. After a couple of days in Bancroft Hall to get all of our gear stowed away, we departed on thirty days of leave for the month of September. "September leave" was a tradition at the Naval Academy dating from before my father's time, and it was wonderful to be able to go home and show off our new uniforms. Because we had served on board the battleships *Texas, Arkansas,* and *New York* in the Caribbean while they were conducting neutrality patrol against the German U-boats, we were entitled to wear the American Defense Service Medal's colorful ribbon. This ribbon stood out boldly on our brand-new blues.

WAR CLOUDS

We returned to the Naval Academy in October 1940 to commence our academic year as sophomores and as we marched to our classes, we followed the progress of the war, shocked with the fall of France and the aerial onslaught by the Luftwaffe on the British Isles.

The second shocker came just a month later, when again at noon meal, the superintendent showed up to announce that the Class of 1942 would graduate in December 1941—six months early—and that the Class of 1943 (my class) would be accelerated one full year to graduate in June 1942. This was not the bad part of the news. What bothered us was that, to make this accelerated schedule, there would be no leave either at Christmas or in September for midshipmen until our graduation.

The atmosphere at the Naval Academy during the fall of 1941 was one of somber drudgery, as we saw our academic load increase and our privileges and time off reduced. In October we assembled for a talk given during our noon meal in Bancroft Hall to the entire regiment by Lord Louis Mountbatten, then a captain in the Royal Navy. He had just returned from the Mediterranean where he had commanded a squadron of five British destroyers at the evacuation of the British Expeditionary Force from Souda Bay in Crete. Every one of his destroyers had been sunk by German Stuka dive-bombers, and he had been fortunate to be able to get ashore and air evacuated. Much of the British Expeditionary Force in Crete was captured when, shortly after Mountbatten's evacuation, the Germans air-assaulted several divisions of troops into Crete. Captain Mountbatten told his story in a very matter of fact, almost humorous fashion, but it was the first time that we future naval officers had been exposed to what was going on in World War II. We were appalled at the losses of what were to be our allies.[10]

On Sunday, December 7, 1941, I had gone into Annapolis with some friends for lunch with some young ladies of our acquaintance. When we returned to Bancroft Hall at about 5 p.m., I noticed that the "Jimmy Legs" (civilian security guards) at the main gate of the Academy were wearing web belts and .45-caliber pistols and were checking the IDs of everyone not in uniform entering the Academy. As our group approached the gate we asked "Why?" The Jimmy Legs responded "the country is at war; the Japanese have attacked Pearl Harbor." That's all we knew, and as we walked to our rooms in Bancroft some midshipman said, "Where the hell is Pearl Harbor?" People have subsequently been surprised that those of us at the Academy did not know about Pearl Harbor prior to the attack or its importance to the fleet. We were actually surprisingly naïve about the fleet itself, the mode of operations and its operating bases. We studied Greek and Roman naval warfare, the battle of Trafalgar and American naval history, but we really couldn't tell you much about what the fleet was doing in 1941 or even how it was organized by flotillas, squadrons, or divisions. The "task force" was a term that was never used in our instruction at the Academy. Perhaps it had not yet come into prominence as an operating system in the fleet.

NAVAL ACADEMY AT WAR

The true facts of the disaster at Pearl Harbor were not immediately made known to us as midshipmen and really not to the American public. It was only after several months of bits and pieces of news and pictures filtering through, that the American people became aware that many of the Pacific Fleet ships had been sent to the bottom of Pearl Harbor on December 7.

We midshipmen had never been given any information that could be considered intelligence, and we knew very little about Japanese military capabilities. Our general impression of their technology and production ability was based on the cheap Japanese wooden toys that we had seen in Woolworth's five-and-dime store. For a week after Pearl Harbor we laughed and joked about the disaster that had probably befallen the fabric-covered Japanese biplanes that had dared to strike the U.S. fleet in Pearl Harbor. It was inconceivable to us that the Japanese could have had aircraft and weapons that were even close to being as good as ours. We believed that the war would be short-lived once the U.S. fleet steamed west and defeated the Japanese battle forces at sea.

Christmas 1941 came and went, a dreary experience at the Naval Academy where morale was low because of our continued "incarceration" without leave and the uncertainties now beginning to come about what was really happening in the war. In January and February 1942, the concern built because of the lack of any concrete news from the Pacific. We had expected an immediate retaliation for the Pearl Harbor attack, but now there were only reports of a raid on Marcus Island, which our atlases showed was an out-of-the-way flyspeck in the Pacific of no apparent strategic interest to either side.

In December the Class of 1942 graduated six months early, and my class became seniors with a very abbreviated first-class year ahead of us. It would consist of only five months in which to enjoy the much-anticipated privileges of first-class midshipmen. By the spring of 1942 our anticipation of becoming ensigns had overcome the disappointment of losing Christmas leave and having reduced privileges as first classmen. My classmates now looked forward to getting out of the Academy, joining the fleet and going to war. Suddenly, academics, class standing, and midshipmen rank became relatively unimportant. We felt that our professional success would depend on our performance in combat in the fleet—which was true. The result was that many of us—including me—neglected our studies and midshipmen duties in favor of enjoying every available opportunity for shore leave and liberty as much as possible before being sent to the fleet in June.

DABNEY RAWLINGS ENTERS MY LIFE

In late February 1942 I agreed to double date with my roommate [Charles] Fred Gressard [Jr.] and his One-and-Only ("OAO") Betty, who was rooming with Dabney Rawlings at the Ogontz School in Abington, Pennsylvania.[11] I remember the weekend well, as it was one of the most delightful experiences of my young life. We had a great time that included my breaking the rules by wearing a tattersall vest under my blue service jacket, and spending Saturday and Sunday afternoons at the cocktail hour in a dive called *Annie's Alley* where we drank straight bourbon out of teacups—very much an offense against Academy regulations. The idea of being a first classman with a very pretty girl in a fashionable dump with my coat unbuttoned displaying a loud checkered vest and being stimulated by Old Grand-Dad: that was my idea of having arrived at maturity!

My first act Monday after the working day and during study hall was to call Dabney for a date the next weekend and the next. From now on I was on my own and Dabney was very good to make the trip by bus down from Philadelphia. It made my spring a wonderful escape from the drudgery of academics and the general despair of the news from our forces in the field in both Europe and the Pacific. At that time we were really taking a beating across the board. On one weekend in early March, I was able to get off and went to Washington, DC, to meet Dabney. After I picked her up on Saturday night at the Kennedy-Warren apartments, I chatted with her father while she put the finishing touches on her outfit for the evening. Capt. Norborne L. Rawlings, who was at that time one of the senior officers in the Navy's Bureau of Ships, told me of the terrible damage that had been done at Pearl Harbor in the attack on December 7. This was the first I had heard the real story of the debacle. Very few of us even in the military in the United States were aware that two battleships had been destroyed and almost all the other BBs sunk and resting on the bottom of Pearl Harbor when the day ended. That was very closely held information and an example of the censorship that existed in this country to prevent the morale of the citizens from hitting rock bottom, because none of the news was good.

GRADUATION

In April 1942 our class drew lots for our ship assignments. By drawing a number in a lottery, my priority of selection would be determined. Lower numbers got the first choices. My number was low enough for me to select a destroyer in the Pacific. I was grateful because some classmates were headed for battleships and cruisers that were not desirable assignments for junior officers, or to Atlantic Fleet units that would keep them out of the shooting war. We had been told that the larger ships were overloaded with JOs, and a new ensign reporting on board would probably end up as laundry officer.

10. Dabney Rawlings with her soon-to-be husband, Jimmy Holloway, on graduation day. Courtesy of Jane Holloway

About ten days before graduation I learned that my assignment had been changed. Apparently my destroyer had been sunk, and the only recourse was to assign me to a ship under construction. I would be in the commissioning crew. At that time, the naval construction program was approaching its peak levels and the shipyards were turning out destroyers and cruisers in great numbers. Unfortunately, going to new construction meant that I would have to wait two to three months before joining my ship. The Navy solved this problem by assigning a number of us who were headed for new construction to serve as instructors at naval schools being established in June 1942 at Harvard and at Dartmouth colleges.

The Class of 1943 graduated a year early on June 19, 1942, after a "June Week" (now called "Commissioning Week" and occurring in late May) of delightful activities that seemed unaffected by the war. June Week had traditionally been the period of celebration and relaxation for the graduating class with awards ceremonies (such as the letter "N" award ceremony for varsity athletics at which I received my varsity *N* for wrestling), parades, picnics, tea dances, formal balls, and time off, with visiting family and girlfriends at hand. The war had caused some changes, but most were easily accommodated. Of course, the sense of excitement at June Week was much heightened by knowing that this was the last "normal" activity we would participate in for some time, as virtually the entire class would be on its way to the fleet after two weeks of postgraduation leave.

In June 1942 our graduation speaker was a relatively obscure rear admiral whose identity I do not recall.[12]

CHAPTER 2

HARVARD AND BOSTON

TO MAN A FLEET that was expanding at a spectacular rate due to the amazing productivity of American industry—which by the summer of 1942 had been largely shifted to defense production—the Navy needed lots of trained manpower. The new ensigns produced by the Naval Academy in our class of 615 graduates would not go far in satisfying the Navy's requirements for a buildup to an officer corps of more than 50,000 as an initial goal. Officers with experience and specialties were needed to operate and maintain the ships that were coming out of the shipyards and repair depots. Also, the shore establishment required to support this massive fleet had to be staffed with specialists in engineering, management, finance, logistics, etc. Much of the officer requirement would be satisfied through midshipmen schools that trained college graduates for three months and produced what were known as "Ninety-Day Wonders."[1] These newly appointed ensigns then reported to the fleet for duty on board ships.

A second source of officers—with one of which I found myself involved—was the direct-procurement system, where an individual with a particular needed skill, such as an engineer, a scientist, or a businessman, would be given a direct commission as a junior officer. (There were even a few cases in which people of special abilities or prominence were brought in as midgrade and senior officers.) It was essential that all of these direct-procurement officers receive enough training as officers that they would know how to wear a uniform, how to salute and to understand the jargon of the Navy in its simplest terms.[2]

The U.S. Navy had arranged with Harvard University and Harvard Business School to host a number of wartime schools and training programs for both the Army and Navy. One component of this effort was the U.S. Naval Training School (Indoctrination and Communications). The first commanding officer was Cdr. C. A. Macgowan, who took charge in June 1942.[3]

The bulk of that organization was initially made up of eight members of the USNA Class of 1943, including me, all of whom were in limbo pending the completion of our new-construction ships building in shipyards on the East and Gulf Coasts. After graduating on June 19, I had forty-eight hours in which to get my affairs in order, say goodbye to my girlfriend, and report for duty at Harvard.

All eight of us ensigns arrived by train at about the same time. Within a day we found a place to live not far from the Harvard Yard in a rickety old building that had previously housed the "international" undergraduate students at Harvard. With the war there were no longer any foreign students, and the building was empty and available. One of our group of eight had married immediately after graduation and lived in a

11. Ensign Holloway
Courtesy of Jane Holloway

boarding house with his bride, but the other seven were bachelors. The day after we reported on board, Commander Macgowan called us together and told us our mission. It was to establish a school to train commissioned officers who had been directly procured from civilian life and have them ready to report for duty in the fleet in thirty days. Our students would number about four hundred and would vary in rank from lieutenant junior grade to lieutenant commander. None had any previous military experience. It was our job to organize them into military units, lay out a schedule, develop a curriculum and be ready to start on July 1, 1942. Funding was not an issue, but getting what we wanted could be a problem because of shortages resulting from the phase-out of civilian production and the progressive phase-in of wartime material.

Because all of the work would largely rest upon the eight ensigns, we decided to organize ourselves and drew straws for our positions of responsibility. One of us became the regimental commander, there were two battalion commanders (of which I was one), and there were eight company commanders. The three additional company commanders were three Naval Reserve Officer Training Corps ensigns who joined us late in June. Since we were ensigns and our students would all be senior to us, we decided to prohibit the display of naval rank among the trainees except when they went on liberty on the weekends. We decided that the trainees should spend the five weekdays in the Yard in order to encourage their doing homework and studying at night.

There was a parade every Saturday morning when the entire regiment of four hundred trainees marched from Harvard Yard to the Harvard football stadium, where we went through infantry drill for the benefit of the local citizenry. After marching back to the Yard the regiment was dismissed. The trainees could then put on their uniforms with their naval insignia of rank and leave at noon Saturday to meet their wives and family or do other things for the weekend, until time to report back at 8:00 p.m. on Sunday evening.

Since most of our trainees were mature men—lawyers, businessmen, accountants, etc.—with families, it is remarkable that there weren't more complaints about being stripped of rank and confined to the barracks during the week (except for two hours of liberty from 5:00 to 7:00 p.m.). But these were patriotic Americans who had volunteered to fight in the war, and they were wise enough to realize that their real hardships would probably come later. In place of the rank insignia, each of the trainees was given a little golden felt patch with the logo "USNTS [U.S. Naval Training School] HARVARD" to sew on the overseas cap.[4] The uniform of the day during the week was khaki trousers, khaki long-sleeve shirts, and the overseas cap with the colored felt patch.

A number of the trainees we received in that first class had a special background. These were affluent yachtsmen who owned vessels large enough to be donated to the Navy for use on inshore patrol to protect harbors and waterfront areas. These men donated their vessels to the Navy for the duration of the war. The Navy then painted the vessels grey, mounted .50-caliber machine guns or 20-millimeter, (mm) cannons, and, where possible, depth charges. Hull numbers were painted on the bows, and the ships were manned with members of the Naval Reserve. The owners who had donated the yachts then attended the Naval Training School at Harvard for thirty days, during which they mainly learned naval protocol, since their skills as ship handlers, navigators, and underway commanders were substantially better than those of any of our instructors.

We saw our first class through successfully. Amazingly enough, there were no untoward events. There was no graduation. Members of the class who had orders simply packed up and proceeded to their destinations. Others got temporary orders to a Naval Sea Frontier [coastal defense command] or some other holding spot where they waited in limbo until they were needed. Many were integrated into the Sea Frontier staff. Meanwhile, a new group of trainees had come in and these were a mixed bag. Some were to be there under instruction for two months, others for three months. This was no problem for us ensigns, because neither duration would be enough—in our view—to fully qualify them for duty on board ship. We simply added more books to the curriculum and assigned them forty to fifty more pages of reading per day in order to increase the length of the course another one or two months.

By September, when I detached, the makeup of the school staff had changed considerably. Additional reserve officers who outranked our eight Academy ensigns were being ordered to the Naval Training School staff, and many of them had considerable teaching or college experience in civilian life. As additional administrative officers were added to the staff, we Academy ensigns were increasingly relegated to teaching duties. We also encountered our first really serious problem. Up until this time we had simply trained the officers who had come to us without any thought that we would give them grades or qualify them in any sense. We simply did as much as we could to cram naval lore into them in the period of time they were assigned to us.

Unfortunately, some educator assigned to the Bureau of Naval Personnel (BuPers) in Washington wanted to formalize the course and establish standards, qualifications, etc., including attrition. So we were told to fail 5 percent of each class. This was utter foolishness. The officers who came to us were volunteers who had left their businesses or sold their establishments to serve as officers in the Navy. They had already been given commissions in the U.S. Naval Reserve and these commissions were not provisional or conditional. To fail these officers as graduates of a school that had no curriculum approved by the Navy, and had no authority to qualify an officer in any gradable respect, was simply not logical, reasonable, or, probably, legal. However, by November 1942 the Navy was growing so fast that some areas were out of control. Up until now the people running the Navy had been experienced career officers who understood the needs of a unique service. What was occurring, I believe, was an overstaffing of the Washington bureaucracy by people who were new to the Navy and had never been to sea. They were mostly bright and eager and wanted to busy themselves with something, even though it might be inappropriate for the Navy.

All of the Naval Academy ensigns at Harvard (and at Dartmouth, where a similar institution had been established) were frustrated by the fact that we were not at sea fighting the war. The fact is that there was no place yet to put us. Meanwhile, we were performing a valuable service at Harvard. The intense effort required in setting up the Naval Training School, the very high quality of the trainees, and their subsequent contributions to the wartime Navy made it a memorable but different World War II experience.

Also, we were having a good time. In the summer of 1942, the United States was not yet fully on a wartime footing and a lot of the social life in Boston was still very much alive. Many of the civilians tried to carry on with life as it had been in the prewar days, with parties and lavish entertainment as a way of salving consciences. The locally available military personnel were included in what had been rather exclusive affairs. Almost every night as we returned to our quarters at the International House, there would be a note on the bulletin board saying "three ensigns are needed for a wedding party" or "two ensigns are needed to volunteer for a reception." Though we may not have known our hosts, the affairs were usually fun, with pretty girls, lots of booze, and good food. Best of all, they were free.

Another interesting aspect of life as Harvard was that the Navy had very wisely left the Naval Training School as a part of Harvard University so that the maintenance of the buildings, the laundry services, and the cafeterias continued to be the responsibility of Harvard. This meant there was no wholesale transfer of funds, or the need to establish a whole new management system. It worked like a charm and should be remembered for any future situations of this nature. This also meant that the eight ensigns became members of the Harvard faculty. This didn't mean much at first, but when I received an engraved invitation to attend a faculty tea hosted by Dr. James Bryant Conant, the distinguished president of Harvard University, I realized it was a real thing. I was twenty years of age, and a member of the Harvard faculty![5]

To ease my frustration at not being on sea duty at war, I took advantage of a brief lull in our training to wrangle temporary additional duty (TAD) orders to Price's Neck, an antiaircraft weapons school that had been set up in Rhode Island near Newport.[6] There was training on maintaining and operating these weapons, but most of the time was spent actually firing .30- and .50-caliber machine guns and the 20-mm and 40-mm automatic weapons we would encounter on board ship. These training facilities were invaluable in preparing sailors right out of "boot camp" [basic training] for their shipboard combat duties. Price's Neck was one of the success stories in fleet training and readiness for World War II. It was there that gunners were taught to lead the target by use of the ring sight. In fact, the lead-computing gyro automatic weapons sight was first introduced through these training activities.

It was while I was on TAD at Price's Neck that I ran into my father, who at that time was a commander. He was assigned as Commander, Destroyer Division 23 (ComDesDiv 23), commanding a division of four *Bristol*-class destroyers based in Newport. We "made a liberty" together, father and son, commander and ensign. My father's staff communications officer was a Lt. Beverley Bogert, a Naval Reservist from the Harvard NROTC. Bogert's family owned one of the enormous houses on Bellevue Avenue in Newport, and he took my father and me there for an informal dinner party that provided a rare glimpse into the lives of the "Newport 400."[7]

In September I received orders detaching me from the Naval Training School at Harvard and sending me to the Fleet Training Command at Norfolk for duties under training in preparation for assignment to a fleet destroyer, USS *Ringgold* (DD 500). It was time for me to go. We eight ensigns had done our job at Harvard, and the new BuPers policy requiring attrition of the direct-procurement officers that we considered most unfair was creating unpleasant problems. We were glad to let our replacements, who were generally college professors in uniforms, handle these sticky issues.

PART II
USS *RINGGOLD* (DD 500)

CHAPTER 3

JOINING THE FLEET

TRAINING SCHOOLS

FROM BOSTON I took the train to Washington, DC, where I was able to get a couple of days' leave, enough to propose to Dabney Rawlings (happily, she accepted!) and then catch the overnight steamer from Washington to Norfolk. At the naval station there I checked into the BOQ [bachelor officers quarters] and was assigned to a large bunkroom with about forty other junior officers living out of footlockers and sleeping in double-deck bunks. In October and November, I attended several fleet training schools to prepare for my job on *Ringgold* as an assistant gunnery officer. These schools were truly excellent, very realistic and run by professionals. At firefighting school, the trainees would don foul-weather gear, man hoses, and enter a brick building that had been set on fire with pools of gasoline and black oil. These courses were run by former New York and Boston firemen (inducted into the Navy as damage-control petty officers) and were realistic to the point of our feeling real pain from heat and breathing smoke.

There was another week's training at the Dam Neck range, south of Virginia Beach, where we fired Oerlikon 20-mm and Bofors 40-mm machine guns at aircraft-towed sleeves, using a new gyroscope sight that was to enormously improve the close-in air defense of ships in the Pacific. At Dam Neck, time on the firing line shooting the guns far exceeded the classroom time learning the mechanics of their operation. There was no shortage of ammunition and the course was designed to make us comfortable in the noise and smoke of multiple machine gun installations.

The final week was on board a battleship, the ex–USS *Wyoming* (AG 17), that had been converted into an antiaircraft training ship. The main 12-inch gun turrets had been removed and the ship was equipped with 5-inch/38-caliber dual-purpose [air and surface targets] guns, Mark 37 directors with modern radars, and many 20- and 40-mm close-in weapons. *Wyoming* would get under way at 0800 every Monday morning with a new group of trainees and return to port at the Norfolk Naval Station Saturday afternoon in time for liberty. For the entire week during daylight hours we fired the 5-inch, the "40s" and the "20s" out in the Chesapeake Bay at aircraft-towed sleeves and an occasional drone. The Chesapeake Bay had torpedo nets rigged across its entrance to keep out German submarines so that the training could take place without concern for an enemy torpedo attack. All of the courses on board *Wyoming* were exceptional. They were well designed and they kept the trainees active at all times. It was real hands-on work with live ammunition and the instructors were true pros, having had some professional experience in their field plus the additional experience of working with the equipment every week of the year training students.

THE WEDDING

The date for my wedding was December 14 and I had gotten a week's leave beginning on the 12th before reporting to the precommissioning detail of *Ringgold* in the New York (Brooklyn) Navy Yard. The last bit of training was on board a converted yacht that was rigged for CIC [combat information center] demonstrations. Due to foggy conditions, it was late getting in and I disembarked in haste on the 10th. I was unable to make any reservations to get from Norfolk to Washington, DC, because of the enormous pressure on the transportation system due to moving troops to ports of embarkation, and for a while it looked as if I was going to miss my own wedding. At that time my family lived in Arlington, Virginia, and our neighbor was Lt. Cdr. Ned Hannegan, with two sons who would also serve in the Navy.[1] My father was at sea and Hannegan discovered my dilemma from my mother. He flew an SNJ trainer from Naval Air Station Anacostia in the District of Columbia on a training flight to Naval Air Station Norfolk where he picked me up with my one suitcase for a return journey. I must have been some sight riding in the open cockpit of an SNJ in blue overcoat and white cap cover.

Dabney Rawlings and I were married on December 14, 1942, in the Bethlehem Chapel of the Washington Cathedral. Neither of our fathers could be present (her father, a Navy captain, and mine a commander, were on assignments elsewhere).[2] I had a difficult time finding ushers because almost all my friends were deployed to the fleet or en route there. I rounded up a few whose ships had been sunk or were in Naval Hospital Bethesda recovering from wounds suffered in action. In a way, it seemed like a makeshift affair but that's the way things were during the war.

RINGGOLD'S COMMISSIONING

I reported to *Ringgold* in the Federal Shipbuilding and Drydock Company, a commercial shipbuilder located in Kearny, New Jersey, on December 17, 1942.[3] *Ringgold* was a *Fletcher*-class destroyer, one of the finest warship classes ever designed and produced by the U.S. Navy. *Ringgold* had a displacement of 2,050 tons, was 376.5 feet long and in that volume packed a tremendous offensive wallop. The main battery was five 5-inch/38-caliber dual-purpose guns in gunhouses, two quintuple torpedo tube mounts, six 20-mm guns and a 40-mm quad [four barrel] mount on the fantail, the open deck at the very stern.[4]

HOMEPORT: NEW YORK CITY

Dabney and I found a one-room apartment on the fourth floor of a walk-up on East 73rd Street.[5] It was as good as we could hope for on my salary of $200 a month with the housing shortage that then existed in New York City. Although the war had been in progress for a year, New York seemed little affected by any stringent rationing or shortages. The restaurants were well stocked. The nightclubs were booming. There was no shortage of prime beef or fancy scotch whiskey and the big department stores along Fifth Avenue had bursting inventories.

In our apartment, the bathroom had been equipped with a small icebox and an electric burner on a small table that served as our kitchen, and a single sink did double duty for shaving as well as washing pots and pans. We felt fortunate to have it. Our neighborhood was an old established part of Manhattan ethnically consisting of Italians and Jews, so there was an abundance of excellent grocery stores. A unique feature of that time was the absence of any supermarkets. When Dabney went shopping she went to the dairy store for milk and cheese, the butcher shop for meat, the greengrocers for vegetables, and a small grocery store for just about everything else. The shopkeepers were expert in their trade and personally waited on every customer.

The USO (United Service Organizations) in New York was well organized and conveniently available to anyone in uniform. We were able to get tickets in the evening to everything from grand opera at the Metropolitan to the latest musical revue on Broadway, all at virtually giveaway prices with good seats in the bargain. New York has always abounded in many small but very good restaurants, and they were not yet feeling the pinch of rationing or a reduced clientele. There were no reduced prices for servicemen, but with prudence and experience we learned where to go and what to order in order to enjoy these bistros on my small salary.

At that time I was a twenty-year-old ensign and Dabney had just turned nineteen. In New York the law was that a male had to be twenty-one to buy a drink but a female only needed to be eighteen. Usually I had no trouble ordering a scotch and soda, which was the fashionable drink at the time, but whenever Dabney thought I might have had too much she simply told the waiter to check my ID card. Then if I behaved myself she would buy a drink for me, which she could because she was of legal age!

Early on December 24, a crew of Federal Shipbuilding and Drydock Company workmen moved the ship from Kearny to the Brooklyn Navy Yard (because she was not yet in commission and the commissioning had to take place in a U.S. Navy yard). On December 24 at 10 o'clock in the morning, *Ringgold* was put into commission in a small but moving ceremony with a local rear admiral from the naval district being the presiding official.

I had the dubious honor of standing the first watch, from 1200 to 1600 on the 24th, which meant that I would also catch the midwatch from midnight to 0400 on Christmas Day. The commanding officer was a fine God-fearing man and declared liberty to commence at twelve noon on Christmas Day. So Dabney and I celebrated that Christmas with a tiny tree in our dinky apartment, but we had a magnificent Christmas dinner at one of the big New York hotels.

12. USS *Ringgold* (DD 500) at anchor off the New York Navy Yard in May 1943
Official U.S. Navy photo, courtesy James C. Fahey Collection, U.S. Naval Institute photo archive

For the first week it was two nights of duty and one night ashore. That seemed ridiculous in the Brooklyn Navy Yard, and was especially grim when our families were living in Brooklyn or Manhattan. The executive officer prevailed upon the commanding officer to relent and we went into a one-in-three watch rotation, with one night on board and two nights ashore.

BROOKLYN NAVY YARD

There we went through a complete predeployment overhaul. The first evolution after commissioning was surprising, in that the Navy Yard proceeded to rip out all of the attractive furnishings in the ship. In my youth and inexperience, I could not understand what was going on. All of the paint that had been so lovingly applied by the skilled artisans of the Federal Shipbuilding and Drydock Company had to be scraped off by our sailors. Apparently, battle reports from the fleet indicated that during the engagements off Savo Island the paint being used on our cruisers and destroyers was easily set on fire and made control of battle damage very difficult. Then all of the linoleum that had lovingly been put down with great skill and care by the specialists in the Kearny yard was ripped up. It too had proved to be a frightful fire hazard when *South Dakota* (BB 57) was badly shot up in one of the actions off Guadalcanal. Taking the linoleum up was only half the job; our sailors then had to scrape up—on their hands and knees—the vestiges of the very strong adhesive that had bonded the linoleum to the steel decks.

We did feel somewhat better when six more 20-mm guns were added topside. Almost every empty spot on the weather decks was being used for the placement of these Swiss guns, designed by the Oerlikon Company.[6] These weapons, according to the battle reports we were receiving, had been terrifically effective in the battle of the Coral Sea in destroying close-in Japanese aircraft. We were to learn that they were indeed marvelous weapons, practically jam-proof and simple and easy to maintain. They were a far cry from the 1.1-inch and the 50-caliber machine guns that the Navy's Bureau of Ordnance had developed in the 1930s and were installed on board our destroyers and cruisers at the time of Pearl Harbor.

Living conditions on board *Ringgold* in the Navy Yard were pretty bad. The ship had been designed to accommodate twelve to fourteen officers and we had thirty assigned. I slept on a folding cot as the third man in a two-man stateroom. Fortunately, we only slept on board on the days we had duty, which was every third day (and night). Some of our less fortunate compatriots in other destroyers in the yard were on a watch-and-watch basis. Why, we never knew. Perhaps their commanding officers wanted to look good in the eyes of the commodore [squadron commander]. I don't think the commodore was around enough to even know what they were doing.

Because the work was going on in the Navy Yard around the clock, there was always an enormous amount of racket from chipping hammers and acrid smoke and bright flashes from the welders. The ship was festooned with the cables providing compressed air, electricity, and acetylene to the welders, and the topsides and the compartments were grimy with grit and paint chips.

The work continued well into January. It was very cold on the Brooklyn waterfront and we had no internal heat in the living compartments in *Ringgold,* so we piled the blankets on as a substitute. With a new and inexperienced crew there were frequent accidents that would eliminate electrical power for hours, or—as happened on several occasions—oil spills that flooded the decks in the living quarters with two inches of sloshing black oil. What a mess. All the news we were getting from the operating forces was bad news. The Marines had landed at Guadalcanal in August and the struggle for the island had turned into a stalemate. In three major engagements off Savo Island, the Navy had been disastrously defeated.[7] No one wanted to complain about our living conditions under those circumstances. Our only wish was to get out of the Navy Yard and get to sea and take our part in the shooting.

RINGGOLD'S OFFICERS

The captain of *Ringgold* was an experienced destroyer officer from the Naval Academy Class of 1926. He was competent but not particularly bright, and we young officers thought that he was very, very old; he was probably forty-two or -three years of age but that was very old to us.[8] The "exec" was a lieutenant commander, Sam McCornock from the USNA Class of 1932; he was also an experienced destroyer officer who had postgraduate training in steam engineering. He had a delightful personality and a great sense of humor as well as a tremendous knowledge of the Navy and love of the service. He taught me much more in my months on board *Ringgold* about seamanship and navigation than I could ever have picked up in a classroom. I felt I owed a great deal to Sam McCornock as my first exec, not only for what he taught me in a professional sense but his generally pleasant nature as exec that could brighten everyone's day. He taught me that one could be tough-minded and achieve results, and still have a sense of humor and a pleasant disposition. I never saw Sam McCornock after I was detached from *Ringgold* in the fall of 1943, but he went on to command another destroyer at Okinawa with great courage and distinction.[9]

The engineer officer was Lt. Neal Almgren, an Academy graduate of the Class of 1939 who had been captain of the Naval Academy crew. Almgren had extensive experience in destroyers. He had gone to postgraduate school and had a degree in steam engineering. We were fortunate to have an officer of his training and his command ability as chief engineer, because that was the most difficult area in training a brand-new crew.[10]

The captain had planned for me, as one of his two Academy ensigns, to be the ship's communications officer. However, a classmate of mine, Ens. Earl Drissel Hackman, reported on board a week before me. Since the communications traffic was beginning to pile up and an officer was needed to decode a certain category of classified messages the exec put him in the slot of communications officer as a "temporary" measure until I arrived. By the time I showed up, Hackman had mastered the intricacies of entry-level communications officer training, and the exec decided to leave him there—to my eternal gratitude.

Communications officer had to be the most difficult job on board any ship. Most of the message traffic we got was encoded. Much of the decoding had to be done by hand, and further, certain categories of classification could only be decoded by commissioned officers because of the stringent need-to-know requirements. So every time that a high-precedence message came in—even if in the middle of the night—the communications officer was routed from his bunk and had to work his way up to the code room (a claustrophobic seasick-inducing closet). It was terrible. I'm not sure I could have survived that assignment.

Ensign Hackman did a good job. He was a nice guy but he hated communications and did not enjoy his time on board *Ringgold*, and he put in for submarines. He left the ship shortly after I did and finished his training in time to deploy on board a new-construction submarine at about the end of the war. I'm sad to say that his was the last U.S. submarine sunk by the Japanese in World War II.[11]

ASSISTANT GUNNERY OFFICER

My own assignment was as assistant gunnery officer/fire-control officer, which pleased me very much. Initially my battle station was in the plotting room, a crowded space in the bowels of the ship containing the electrical switchboards that controlled all of the guns and their control systems, plus the heart of the main battery, a large three-by-five-foot, three feet high, reinforced aluminum box—the Mark I Mod 0 fire-control computer. This was a true computer but it differed from present models in that all of the computations were done by mechanical devices rather than by electronic circuits. By tracking a ship or an airplane with an optical director, providing bearing and elevation, and with range provided by a synchronized radar, the computer could in a matter of seconds determine the target's course and speed and could predict its future position. The guns were then trained to fire at this predicted position and time the explosive projectile to explode at that point. Rudimentary as it was for air targets, it was still possible largely through volume of fire to knock down an aircraft. It was much more effective on ships and surface targets, because the element of elevation was eliminated. It was superb for shore bombardment, because the computer measured the ship's roll and pitch and took those motions out of the fire-control problem, enormously simplifying the work of the pointers and trainers in the gun mounts.

After several months as plotting room officer, I was promoted to machine-gun officer and I became responsible for the control of the 40-mm and 20-mm guns topside and the Mark 51 directors that controlled the 40-mm mounts. As far as I was concerned it was the best job that any ensign in the United States Navy could have. My battle station was on the Mark 37 director platform, an open-air perch surrounded by a railing that was on the level just above the bridge and just below the Mark 37 director itself. I was unencumbered by any equipment but attended by a sound-powered-telephone "talker" who received orders for me and the machine-gun battery from the bridge and the main director. The talker transmitted my commands by sound-powered telephone to the Mark 51 director operators, the 40-mm gun captains, and the loaders on the 20-mm guns.

From my position on the director platform I had a 360-degree horizontal view stretching from the horizon to the zenith in all directions. I was also within shouting distance of the captain on the wing of the bridge and the gunnery officer in the Mark 37 director standing in his hatch. This was far more comfortable than the confined space of the main plotting room. Not only did I have fresh air but also I could see what was going on. In a sea battle, sailors will tell you, only about 15 percent of the crew knows what's happening. Those were the people in the directors, on the machine guns, and on the bridge. The rest of the crew was in the engineering spaces, the ammunition handling rooms, inside the gun mounts, and damage-control parties within the hull. Furthermore, I really liked working with the 20- and 40-millimeters, because all of the rounds were tracered and it was very satisfying to see the bullets going out from the guns to exactly where you wanted them.

By the first week in January all of the hard work had been done in the Navy Yard to make the changes required when the action reports came in from the Southwest Pacific.

CHAPTER 4

TO SEA

ON JANUARY 7, 1943, I having bid Dabney farewell, the ship departed for its shakedown and training cruise. I'll never forget our departure. It was a clear cold day with relatively gentle seas for early February. As we came out of the Brooklyn Navy Yard and steamed down the East River, Manhattan showed in the sunlight to its best advantage. We passed the Statue of Liberty, which will always be a beloved landmark for the seafaring man. It is unique among the many ports I have traveled in around the world, and that copper lady is a symbol of home like no other that I have ever encountered.

We initially loitered for three days at the entrance of New York Harbor, anchoring at night in Gravesend Bay off Brooklyn following short underway periods in which we calibrated our radio-direction-finding equipment and "swung ship" for compass calibration. We then headed north to Casco Bay, Maine, by way of the Cape Cod Canal. We ran into some heavy seas for the first day or two, and about 50 percent of our crew were seasick, but no one was excused from their duties—they were just told to carry a bucket.

We spent about a week off the coast of Maine dropping depth charges, firing guns, and conducting high-speed runs. Casco Bay provided an ideal sanctuary for recently commissioned warships to gain their sea legs, and we didn't waste the opportunity. We trained with two other recently commissioned *Fletchers*—*Foote* (DD 551), Bath Iron Works–built, and *Beale* (DD 471). The latter ship had been constructed over in Staten Island at a Bethlehem Steel–run shipyard and was commissioned just a day ahead of us at the New

York Navy Yard. Together we worked on antisubmarine tactics and conducted flag-hoist drills.

From Casco Bay we steamed south with *Foote* and *Beale*. Mindful of the German U-boat threat, we zigzagged along the East Coast, slowing along the way on several occasions to investigate sonar sound contacts. A day or so south of Cape Hatteras the seas flattened and the temperature warmed. As *Ringgold* entered the Caribbean, kicking up a fine bow wave at twenty-five knots, the entire crew felt the pleasure of being sailors at sea on this fine ship. There was no sign of the war that was tearing the rest of the world apart.

We sighted a convoy, a slow nine-knot gaggle of a dozen rusty old ore carriers. They were escorted by older destroyers that with the introduction of the *Fletcher*s into the fleet were being relegated to convoy duties. The convoy continued north, zigzagging according to a prearranged pattern that resulted in a speed of advance (SOA) of only about six knots.

Arriving at Guantanamo Bay (Gitmo), Cuba, we underwent another two weeks of intensive training, where we worked with a World War I–vintage coastal submarine in realistic antisubmarine warfare training.[1]

The screen commander was a captain—a squadron commander [and so referred to as a commodore]. He kept the destroyers busy around the clock: for instance, exchanging stations, throwing a dummy over the side for a man overboard drill; having one ship fire its 5-inch gun to put a burst in the air and then requiring the others to fire a minimum of ten rounds at the burst. It was not like real war but it got the crew used to loading ammunition and shooting the guns. The machine guns had no targets to shoot at, so our own skipper arranged to have another vessel put an orange crate in the water. As we passed by, I would suddenly direct the 40s or the 20s to find it and shoot at it. It did not approximate taking on Japanese aircraft, but it got the gun crews familiar with handling ammunition on a rolling ship and feeding clips into the recoiling weapons as the guns elevated and trained in response to the motion of the ship and the bobbing of the target. We had a lot of minor casualties in the first week, broken toes when 5-inch shells were dropped, mashed fingers caught in breech mechanisms, and various scrapes and bruises from the concussion of the guns.

RETURN TO HOME PORT

After a series of inspections in the middle of February, we departed Gitmo and were under way again for New York.[2]

One aspect of these months is that we never knew where we were going to be the following week or what we were going to do. This port call was no exception. *Ringgold* made landfall off the sea buoy and entered the gate in the torpedo nets off New York City at first light. As we steamed into New York Harbor our first view was that of the Statue of Liberty. Again I have to say that sailors never cease to feel a thrill when the grand old lady looms on the horizon. When we got to the New York Navy Yard over in Brooklyn about eight in the morning, activity there was already at its height.

The most important project of this yard period concerned the topside armament. The quadruple 40-mm mount on the fantail was lifted off that first afternoon by crane, put on a truck and hauled away. The yard workers swarmed over the ship, electricians and steelworkers, with their cutting torches, welding machines, and metal benders. The project was to replace that 40-mm mount with three 20-mm mounts on the fantail, put a 40-mm quad mount on the after deckhouse with a Mark 51 director just forward of it, and install two 40-mm twin mounts, one on each side of the main deckhouse just aft of the wings of the bridge. Each of these twin mounts had its own 40-mm director. Then four more 20-mm mounts were added, bringing us up to a total of eleven individual 20-mm mounts with Mark 14 sights, one 40-mm quad, and two 40-mm twins, plus three Mark 51 directors that controlled the three 40-mm mounts.

We in the Gunnery Department complained a bit because we were required to keep people on board during this work, but it was clear that we would be much more of a fighting ship when we went to sea with this new installation. The original 40-mm mount on the fantail had always given us trouble. The fantail on *Fletcher*-class destroyers was wet in any kind of seaway. The drive that controlled the elevation and training of the 40-mm mounts was mechanical-electric drive and involved the use of vacuum tubes. The wet environment and the shock of gunfire gave us constant problems in keeping this mount operable. The new mounts were hydraulic installations produced by York Lock and Safe Company and were dramatic breakthroughs. In retrospect, I cannot say enough for the material support that we received. Those York drives saved many a ship from a kamikaze strike during the war.[3] I have never seen anything like the efficiency of those shipyard workmen in New York. The old equipment had to be ripped out, and the ship had to be made seaworthy again. The new installations had to be firmly attached to the ship's structure and then wiring installed between the fire-control center or plotting room, the gun directors, and the gun drives themselves. Also, all of our 20-mm mounts were equipped with Mark 14 sights and each 40-mm mount was controlled by a Mark 51 director.

A brief description of the Mark 14 is worthwhile. It was one of the secret weapons for the Navy during the war in the Pacific. In about 1938 or 1939, a young PhD physicist at MIT, the Massachusetts Institute of Technology, named Charles Stark Draper, came to the Navy Department. He had a plan for a lead-computing sight that would replace the enormous and complex electromechanical devices we were struggling with at the time, mechanical ring sights that were about as accurate as using the end of a rake. Dr. Draper's sight was about eighteen inches high, six inches wide, and four inches deep. There was a window in the top half of the sight in which an illuminated reticule—that is, a circle of light—would appear. The Mark 14 sight was fixed rigidly to the 20-mm gun itself. When the gun was swung to track an air target the lighted reticule would lag behind it in the window. The amount of lag was the amount of lead ["windage"] to be used when shooting at a target moving at a particular speed. A system of gyros measured the swing of the gun and with the distance of the plane from the gun itself put in the target's speed was determined and the amount of lead computed. All of this was done with two switches, an on/off switch and a little dial in which the assistant gunner, the loader, set the approximate range of the target. The simplicity of the sight mechanism was remarkable, the construction was rugged, and the maintenance was practically zero. I always considered Dr. Draper's Mark 14 gun sight one of the marvels of our weapon laboratories.[4]

The Mark 51 director was simply a Mark 14 sight rigidly attached to a set of handlebars that could be elevated and depressed and swung right and left just as a 20-mm gun might be. But instead of being attached to a gun it simply transmitted those movements to the gun sight of the 40-mm mount it was controlling, and the gun barrels followed the motions of the gun sight, as the director operator maintained his lighted reticule on the target.

BACK TO SEA

After this post-cruise availability of about two weeks *Ringgold* was under way again in mid-March, under less than pleasant conditions: cold and sleety with strong winds, high seas, and reduced visibility. We were through the submarine nets by midmorning in the open sea headed south in company with *Beale* and *Schroeder* (DD 501) with orders to steam to Norfolk to rendezvous with the new carrier *Essex* (CV 9).

From Norfolk, we escorted *Essex* south to Trinidad in the British West Indies. Our destination had been simply described as "Naval Operating Base Trinidad." Once under way, the chief quartermaster unrolled the charts that had come on board with a secret cachet. The reason for this secrecy was the military installations located in the

Gulf of Paria and the operations being conducted there. The Gulf of Paria is a rough rectangle about a hundred miles east/west and forty miles north/south, with good deep water throughout. There are two entries into the gulf, both straits about ten miles in width: the "Dragon's Mouth" to the north, from the Caribbean Sea, and the "Serpent's Mouth" to the southeast, which opens into the Atlantic Ocean. With these two entrances closed off by submarine nets and the approaches heavily mined and the channels kept secret from all but the U.S. operating forces, the gulf itself was an ideal operating area where carriers could steam, exercise their air wings and practice underway replenishment and emergency drills without danger of attack by a German U-boat.

Thus, like Casco Bay, the Gulf of Paria provided a large haven for workups and the added advantage of year-round temperate weather. With the pressure to get new big-deck carriers out to the Pacific theater, Trinidad and Paria Bay would play a critical role in efforts to ready our naval aviators for the fight. During a couple of days during the five-day transit we had the opportunity to observe flight operations, and my interest in that line of work only strengthened.

After a couple of days in Trinidad, *Schroeder* and *Ringgold* steamed back north at high speed, arriving in New York before the end of the month. In contrast, *Beale* steamed west for the Panama Canal and eventual duties with the Pacific Fleet. Unfortunately, my reunion with my recent bride would be short. After a long weekend at the New York Navy Yard, we again steamed past the Statue of Liberty and eventually anchored in Sandy Hook Bay to await the departure of a transatlantic convoy.

"TRANSLANT"

Ringgold loitered for about twelve hours in the vicinity of the sea buoy and then joined up with a large convoy coming out of New York. We became part of its protective screen, which consisted of eight *Fletcher*-class destroyers.⁵ Fortunately, maneuvering was restricted to zigzagging in a circular disposition. The convoy was making only twelve knots, so all of the screening ships quickly got into the swing of things.

When I next came on watch I was briefed by the exec, who was also the navigator, on our plans. We were headed for North Africa where our convoy would deliver logistical support for the Allied forces there.

CASABLANCA, NORTH AFRICA

Our timing seemed to be excellent. When the convoy arrived, the channels through the minefields had been cleared and marked. The ships in the convoy, mostly merchant ships still wearing the stack markings of their parent companies, were able to proceed directly to anchorages and quays for their offloading. After three or four days of patrolling the approaches, the submarine nets had been rigged and *Ringgold* and several other destroyers were able to anchor in Casablanca Harbor and put liberty parties ashore. As we came into the port area the scene was a shock. The French battleship *Jean Bart* had sunk alongside her pier, hit by a salvo of 16-inch shells from a U.S. battleship. Next to her were a cruiser and several destroyers that had also been mangled by the fire of American warships. The French navy liaison officer who came on board *Ringgold* was friendly enough in providing us with pilot services, but it was easy to detect an underlying feeling of resentment that the United States had found it necessary to destroy the French navy in Casablanca.

Ringgold's first night in port I was assigned shore patrol duty and rendezvoused with the local French gendarmerie, some U.S. Army MPs [military policemen], and a Navy lieutenant commander who was the senior shore patrol officer. Our instructions and briefings were minimal. Our main mission seemed to be to keep the sailors out of the bawdy houses. All that did was infuriate the local French ladies of the evening and disappoint our sailors. As it turned out the red-light district was so extensive and our shore patrol forces so few and unmotivated that the night life in Casablanca pretty much went on as it always had.

As a shore patrol officer I had an opportunity to ride in a jeep and see much of Casablanca, a lovely town with a climate much like Southern California surrounded by smaller suburban villages. Houses in the suburbs were handsome cottages on green lawns with palm trees and well-tended gardens blooming with flowers. Downtown the atmosphere was dominated by a strong flavor of the Mediterranean style, but with a strong input of the Arabic, with bright tiles and light pastel shades everywhere. On the main streets in Casablanca were railed porches on the second floors, which housed cafes. It was a pleasant experience to take one's luncheon or dinner on the second-floor deck that stuck out over the street so that one could see the sights of the city, the French, the Arabs, the taxis, and the camel carts. It was quite noisy but very well ordered. The French seemed to know how to run a colony. Amazingly, there was very little sign of any ground fighting. All of the damage seemed to have been confined to the barrage of heavy naval gunfire that had torn up the naval base section of the port of Casablanca.

In less than a week *Ringgold* was outbound again.[6] This time only six destroyers, all *Fletcher*s, headed westward escorting a smaller convoy of empty cargo ships and troopships evacuating casualties from the fighting in North Africa. Some two weeks later, on May 8, *Ringgold* returned to New York, slipping into the harbor at midday, with the Statue of Liberty picking up the full rays of the sun. It had been a good cruise for us and demonstrated the wisdom of the policies of the naval planners. It was clear that *Ringgold* was not yet ready to fight a night action against the Japanese, but with every day at sea we were becoming more proficient, and already the crew had gained confidence and a slight swagger. We had seen for the first time up close the results of war, in the terribly torn carcasses of the French ships. Because of our entry into the ETO (European Theater of Operations), the crew was entitled to wear that campaign ribbon. The *Fletcher*-class destroyers had returned to CONUS [continental United States], leaving the older classes in the ETO. The *Fletchers* were destined for the more arduous warfare tasks of the western Pacific.

VETERANS' RETURN TO HOMEPORT

Our return to New York was rather triumphant. We wore our uniforms ashore. Mobilization had progressed to the point that there were very few males in civilian clothes either on the streets or in the cafes or bars at night. The fact that we were wearing the American Defense ribbon and the ETO ribbon made us something of heroes. The movie *Casablanca* with Humphrey Bogart and Ingrid Bergman had hit the theaters in Manhattan, and all the bands were playing a tune from that movie, "As Time Goes By" (famously beginning, "You must remember this, a kiss is just a kiss . . ."). The fact that we had just returned from Casablanca made us the heroes of the moment.

The privations of war had not yet hit New York. The prime beef was still in the window of Ronnie's Steak House on Sixth Avenue, and there was plenty of scotch in the bars. The United States was still not winning the war and what was needed was encouragement and heroes, and that was the part we got to play. Even in the most cynical and sophisticated nightclubs, the hat-check chicks would not take a tip from me when I picked up my naval uniform cap after an evening of dinner and entertainment. America was still getting used to the fact that it was at war, and that sons, boyfriends, husbands, and fathers would be away a long time, maybe forever. But since virtually all Americans were involved, there was no single group that any of us felt especially sorry for. We were all in it up to our necks.

Meanwhile, in the New York Navy Yard, *Ringgold* had a five-day availability in which the shipyard workers again swarmed on board with their cutting torches, welding rods, and chipping hammers. Many of the changes involved increasing stowage of ready ammunition topside. Battle reports from the Pacific indicated that enormous quantities of ammunition were being expended in very short battle encounters. Our ships were getting in trouble when Japanese aircraft attacked because they had to bring up ammunition from below, a time-consuming process.

Departing from the yard, *Ringgold* headed up past New York's East Side through Hell Gate and out into Long Island Sound to practice ASW [antisubmarine warfare] off New London, Connecticut, with the same submarine we had worked with down in Gitmo. After a short call at the submarine base at New London, we were under way once again, this time for Delaware Bay with orders to rendezvous the next morning with *Belleau Wood* (CVL 24), which would be transiting the Delaware Capes. We were to escort *Belleau Wood* to Norfolk providing her submarine protection.[7]

The next morning after the midwatch, from midnight to four, I turned in and been in my bunk only for an hour when a messenger told me to report to the bridge, that I had the watch. I complained that I had stood the midwatch and was not scheduled again until the "12 to 16" [noon to four]. The messenger said in salty sailor talk I better get up there that things on the bridge were all fouled up. I dressed quickly, pulled on my foul-weather gear and walked on the bridge. The captain said, "Holloway, relieve Lieutenant Elmore as officer of the deck. Lieutenant Elmore, go to your room. You're in hack" [punitively restricted to his stateroom].[8]

Lieutenant Elmore was a second-tour [i.e., this was his second ship] lieutenant and had been a top-watch stander [formally qualified as an officer of the deck under way] before reporting to *Ringgold*, so obviously he had stepped on his "Irish pennant" and upset the skipper. I approached Elmore to get a turnover of the watch. He mumbled that we were trying to rendezvous with *Belleau Wood*, and the ship's characteristic book on the bridge showed *Belleau Wood* to be a former passenger liner converted to a transport. However, the only ship in the vicinity was a strange looking vessel with a flat top and no superstructure at all. In the low visibility we were having trouble reading flashing-light signals from this flattop, and it was impossible to make out her signal flags much less read them. Fortunately, just then I recalled reading in an intelligence report only several days before a reference to a new class of U.S. carriers being commissioned and shortly to be going to sea. These ships were 20,000-ton aircraft carriers being constructed from cruiser hulls. Since carriers were traditionally named for battles it occurred to me that this strange-looking flattop vessel could be the new USS *Belleau Wood*.

Making this presumption, I told the commanding officer that I intended to close the strange vessel on the suspicion that it was our objective. At least, we could read her signal flags, question her with flashing light, and even read the name on the stern. We slid by the carrier on an opposite course at about five hundred feet and as we got closer were able to read signal flags on her mast instructing us to take a screening station ahead. *Ringgold* swung around her stern and even in the gloom we could see *Belleau Wood* painted on her transom. By now we had established communications by flashing light and were reading her signal flags, so station keeping a thousand feet ahead presented no problem. At this point the exec joined me on the wing of the bridge, and I asked him who had the four-to-eight OOD [officer of the deck] watch. He replied "It looks like you do." I said, "But I'm not qualified for top-watch." He said, "You are now." So that is how I became qualified as an officer of the deck under way on a fleet destroyer. It was also an example of how confused the situation could get with new ships with new crews and heretofore unseen profiles joining the fleet on a daily basis.

We escorted *Belleau Wood* to Norfolk and after refueling at Craney Island headed back out in company with *Stevenson* (DD 645) and *Stockton* (DD 646) to form a screen around the recently commissioned battleship *Iowa* (BB 61), which was returning to the New York Navy Yard, where she had been under construction over the previous three years. Besides the three triple 16-inch turrets, the ship bristled with 5-inch twin mounts and scores of 20- and 40-mm batteries. Of course, I had no inkling that my father would have command of that capital warship in the not-so-distant future.[9]

CHAPTER 5

SIDETRACKED

OFF AGAIN TO TRINIDAD

AT THE END OF MAY 1943 we got under way en route to the Virginia Capes, where we met two other *Fletcher*-class destroyers and *Princeton* (CVL 23).

The weather en route to Trinidad was relatively good, and the carrier and its three escorts proceeded at high speed south to the Caribbean, zigzagging because of the continuous serious threat of German U-boats. Our task group navigated to arrive at the northern end of the Gulf of Paria at sunrise. That gave us daylight for navigating the approaches through the minefield and then entering through the many submarine nets that were stretched across the Mouth of the Dragon entrance. We arrived at the Gulf of Paria low on fuel, although we had replenished black oil once from *Princeton* during our transit.

Traveling at between twenty-eight and thirty knots had caused enormous fuel consumption, and that was a lesson that has stayed with me my entire career. *Ringgold* was down to about 25 percent of burnable fuel remaining when we arrived at Trinidad and made up to the fueling pier at the commercial port. That night, having topped off our fuel supply, we moved to the Naval Operating Base (NOB), where at one of the several piers was a destroyer tender flying the command pennant of a Navy captain who was senior enough to be known as "the commodore" [see chapter 4]. At eight o'clock the captain and some of the key officers from *Ringgold* reported to the tender for a briefing on our future operations in the gulf, which would be mostly training. Because I was machine-gun officer and much of the training would involve gunnery, the gunnery officer, Lt. [Lyttleton Brockenbrough] Ensey, took me along.

In the midst of all that was going on, I was promoted with virtually all of my classmates to lieutenant (junior grade) on May 1, 1943, by an ALNAV (message sent to all activities worldwide in the Navy).

GULF OF PARIA, NAVAL OPERATING BASE TRINIDAD

The Gulf of Paria operation was a remarkable setup, in my view one of those brilliant support functions that did much to hasten our nation's victory at sea. The whole underway training concept at an advance base showed a remarkable amount of ingenuity, imagination, and common sense. It certainly contributed much to building the readiness of our crack carrier strike forces during the war.[1]

When a carrier is launching or recovering its air wing, it must maintain a steady course at a relatively high speed (twenty-five knots or more) into the wind for sometimes as long as an hour. Between launch and recovery operations the carrier must run downwind at high speed to give itself the necessary sea room for the next launch and recovery. During these flight operations and underway replenishment drills with oilers, ammunition ships, storeships, and destroyers, the carrier as well as the underway replenishment group could be fatally vulnerable in submarine-infested waters. Without such a safe haven as the Gulf of Paria the carrier shakedowns would have required an enormous operational support force of antisubmarine destroyers and aircraft, and these forces were desperately needed for the convoys in the operating task forces in the Atlantic. By the same token, the *Essex-* and *Independence*-class carriers were urgently needed in the Pacific for the campaigns of fast carrier task forces that were becoming the principal offensive forces, along with the amphibious forces, of the Navy's drive westward across the Pacific. An *Essex-* or *Independence*-class carrier spending three weeks operating around the clock in the Gulf of Paria could have its crew and its air wing combat ready immediately when she joined the Third Fleet or the Fifth Fleet after a high-speed run to the western Pacific from the Panama Canal.[2]

NOB Trinidad did not amount to much. It had one pier for maintenance support of the destroyers and a second pier for refueling. The destroyers and the oilers refueled from the pier and the carriers refueled from the oilers. Generally, there were never more than two carriers shaking down at the same time, and therefore seldom more than two or three destroyers needed for their escort. Consequently, the destroyers would moor at the piers in the evenings, where a third of the crew was granted liberty. The destroyers remained at sea with the carrier when they conducted night-flight operations, but the air wings had so few night-capable aircraft that these night-flight operations were infrequent.

There was a small officers' club at the head of the pier that sold beer, Australian "scotch" whiskey, and rum. Across the street from it was a much larger and better-equipped enlisted club that was stocked with good Cuban beer and very good Trinidadian rum. An emergency airstrip had been hacked out of the jungle by the Navy's CBs [construction battalions, "Seabees"] in the vicinity of a rum distillery that provided housekeeping support such as fresh water and electricity, but very little of that. Each day a small group of sailors from the NOB would take a couple of trucks with radios and emergency aircraft support gear out to the airstrip to take care of any planes that might have to land due to an emergency either with the aircraft or on the carrier.

There was an initial problem when several crews got into the distillery's rum supplies and, unused to the effect of 150-proof spirits, rendered themselves "inoperative" for the entire period of their daily duty. The chief petty officers (CPOs) got this problem under control quickly, but then a second difficulty arose. The dive-bomber pilots started declaring an emergency landing at the strip and then loading a case of rum in the back seat of their SBDs. This problem was discovered when two of the pilots got too drunk to land their aircraft on the return flight, so further steps were taken to minimize the impact of the high spirits on the operational training schedule.

There was also the opportunity for our ship's people to go to Trinidad's Port of Spain with a special liberty pass for an overnight in that city. However, this was not popular and most of the crew found it easier to hit the local bar at the end of the pier and a few of the shanties that had grown up around it during the limited liberty that was granted. Trinidad had been an exotic winter vacation resort for the English for many years, and there were several resort hotels not far from the NOB (ten to fifteen miles away).

One of these, the Macqueripe Beach Hotel, was taken over by the Navy as an officers' club. It was an absolutely gorgeous spot; the hotel was situated on a steep cliff at the inlet end of a fiord [an indentation about two thousand feet across and seven hundred feet deep] about half a mile in length. The hotel's fiord was on the ocean so the water was of ocean purity and there was a lovely white sand beach at the bottom of the cliff that the hotel overlooked. There were the normal conveniences for swimming, cabanas afloat, a shark net, and a rather long set of stairs. However, the young officers who frequented the Macqueripe Beach Club were not interested in swimming. It was the booze they were after. The side of the hotel facing the fiord featured a large patio, a handsomely tiled floor, and a lovely freshwater fountain in its center. A balustrade separated the patio from the cliff drop-off to the sandy beach below; the patio was essentially a dance floor, ringed with tables and a well-equipped spic-and-span bar.[3]

It was a magnificent spot and had been one of the favorite European watering holes in the late 1930s. Much of the time it was a delightful quiet spot to have a cocktail and dinner and observe the lush jungle flora that surrounded us, the trees abounding in all kinds of tropical blossoms with more orchids than I have seen before or since. Twice a week this idyllic atmosphere was shattered when liberty was granted to the pilots in the carrier's air wing. These young men were on their way to a war in which the attrition among carrier air wing pilots was running better than 25 percent, counting both combat and operational losses. They were being pushed hard and conditioned to be fearless, and that fearlessness extended to "Demon Rum," good behavior, the shore patrol, and their senior officers in that order. It was a pretty wild bunch.

I did meet one notable character among them, an F4F Wildcat pilot named Nile Kinnick. Nile Kinnick had won the Heisman Trophy in 1939 as a running back from the University of Iowa. He was about five feet, ten inches tall and weighed about 175 pounds when he played for Iowa, and he was the best football player in the country that year. I had first seen Kinnick at the Naval Academy when he was visiting a number of colleges on a war bond tour. To me Kinnick was very impressive: blonde hair, blue eyes, and very soft spoken and reserved, but with a very powerful physique for his size.

I ran into him at the Macqueripe Beach Club one Saturday night when his colleagues from the air wing were tearing the place up. A group of ensigns had just thrown one of the squadron commanders in the fountain pool in the center of the patio. Kinnick was sitting at a table on the edge of the patio nursing a beer and enjoying the fun. He had a good time watching the antics of his squadron mates but never did I see him actually take part in the skylarking and roughhousing. A week later at the "Saturday night massacre," as the air group party at the Macqueripe Beach Club was known, I was told that Kinnick had been lost during a training flight. He was a fine young man and his loss hit his squadron mates pretty hard because he was very popular and much admired. However, losses like this were part of the "hazards of naval aviation" at that time during World War II, when more Navy pilots were being lost in operational and training crashes than in combat.[4]

The main objective of the operations in the Gulf of Paria was to "shake down" the carriers and their air wings. As I have pointed out, the conditions were ideal and the benefits to the effectiveness of the fast carrier task forces in combat were enormous. It was also a great benefit to the destroyers that were assigned as escorts to the carrier shakedown operations, because every day, seven days a week for ten hours, we were able to practice key ship-handling maneuvers and conduct underway training that would have been unavailable to us if in a convoy or steaming singly. Each morning *Ringgold* would get under way from the NOB pier without the benefit of a tug. It would then join up with the carrier and then race around the ocean at twenty-five or thirty knots plane-guarding and screening the carrier as it conducted practice maneuvers and flight operations.

For me it was four hours as OOD maneuvering the ship with little direct supervision. The captain normally sunbathed in the morning and napped in the afternoon. The exec was too busy below attending to ship's administration and supervising engineering drills to spend much time on the bridge. Nevertheless, the captain, like most destroyer commanding officers, seemed to have a sixth sense that told him when conditions in the formation were getting dicey and this special sensitivity seemed to be at its maximum when a young and inexperienced OOD had the watch. Fortunately, I seemed to know when to call the skipper because things were getting tight and when I could handle it myself, and I was seldom the object of the skipper's wrath.

After three weeks of operations in the Gulf of Paria *Ringgold* was relieved by another new-construction destroyer that like us had escorted its newly commissioned carrier for shakedown. Our ship and *Terry* (DD 513) then escorted *Belleau Wood* north to Delaware Bay and then we turned south for one final stateside availability in the Norfolk Navy Yard. Upon our arrival on July 4 at the Portsmouth, Virginia, shipyard facility, Dry Dock 6 was filled and ready for us and with the aid of four tugs we were quickly docked. The dry dock was then pumped dry.

The first order of business was to check the underwater hull, the propellers, the struts, the rudders, and the sonar dome. This was to ensure that the original workmanship at the shipyard had been good and that *Ringgold*'s experience at high speeds and in heavy seas had not damaged these installations.

We did not know where *Ringgold* would be ordered after this yard period, whether the Atlantic or the Pacific Fleet, but we were ready to go. The ship was well shaken down and in excellent material condition. The building yard had done a good job in her construction; the Norfolk Navy Yard still retained the experienced and talented workforce that had established its reputation over the years as one of the finest naval shipyards in the country. After clearing the yard, we shifted over to the Norfolk NOB and embarked on one-day sorties to conduct full-power runs and fire at target sleds. With everyone satisfied that we were up to snuff, we departed for our homeport of Brooklyn.

HOMEPORT IN BROOKLYN

As soon as I could get off the ship after our arrival in Brooklyn, I headed for the Hotel St. George in Brooklyn Heights and rented a room. That is virtually the only way one could make a long-distance call in those days. It would take from one to three hours to get a long-distance call through from Brooklyn to Washington, DC, where Dabney was staying with my family, and it was just not possible to tie up a pay phone or an extension in a bar or club for that long.

The only real way to get from Washington to Brooklyn was by train. No one had enough gas coupons for a trip by car that long and furthermore we didn't have a car. I don't think Greyhound ran more than one or two buses a day because of the gasoline shortage, and the waiting lines at the terminal would dissuade all but the hardiest. In any case, Dabney arrived at the St. George forty-eight hours after I did, along with most of the other wives. However, we husbands were not there to greet them. *Ringgold*, along with *Stevens* and *Hudson*

(DD 475), got tagged to escort *Iowa* up to Casco Bay for shakedown. After two days under way, we once again passed under the Brooklyn Bridge for a three-day in-port period. The skipper informed us that we would be heading for the [Panama] Canal and points west when we got under way. He made us promise we would not divulge the details of our schedule to our wives but would understand if we were able to intuitively let them know that we were finally on our way. Interestingly enough, there were no emotional farewells among the crew, certainly nothing to compare with the weeping and distraught wives and sweethearts I saw during Korea and Vietnam. It is probably because everyone else was going off to war and we accepted this as our responsibility as members of the United States Navy. The difference was that nobody knew when we would get back—if we did get back. We realized that the most probable reason for our return would be as survivors from a sunken or battle-damaged *Ringgold*.

DEPLOYING TO THE PACIFIC

We got under way from the Brooklyn Navy Yard with another *Fletcher*-class destroyer on a pleasant day in late July 1943 and said farewell to that grand old lady, the Statue of Liberty, accelerated to twenty-five knots after passing through the submarine nets and the minefields, and headed south to Delaware Bay. There we rendezvoused with both *Belleau Wood* and *Princeton*, which had sortied from Hampton Roads en route to the Pacific.[5]

The run down to Panama was uneventful and we arrived at the Atlantic terminal of the Canal at Cristóbal on the morning of July 26 and tied up to Pier 6 to refuel. Passing through the Canal that afternoon we moored at Pier 6 in Balboa. The following day *Ringgold* granted liberty to the crew commencing at noon and expiring at midnight. As this would be one of our last port calls at a civilized city, the crew pretty much made the best of it.

Panama was a wonderful place for liberty. The Panamanian culture is dedicated to having a good time: lots of rum, Latin American dancing, and attractive Latina hostesses. The clubs in Panama are worth a comment. They had large open dance floors with circular or horseshoe areas around them for dining and imbibing. There were usually two bands, one playing popular American jazz and the other providing the best in Latin American rhythms. The music never stopped, the drinks never slowed down, and there was always a hostess inviting you to dance or asking you to buy her a drink. Of course, her drink was actually tea but they said it was scotch, and the buyer paid a hefty tariff for the opportunity to treat the lady to a drink.

As far as I could see, nobody got in trouble. It was truly a colorful scene because many Army officers stationed in the Canal Zone were attired in their mess dress, black tie with white shirt, short jacket, and long high-waisted trousers. All of the naval officers wore service dress white with its high-collared white jacket. That was the only warm-weather uniform we had. (The day of the "tropical white long" [with long trousers but short-sleeve shirt, both white] had not arrived.) So we all had a night to remember in Panama, as we turned out at noon the next day to get *Ringgold* under way and join the other ships forming up in the Gulf of Panama.

As we exited the Canal on the Pacific side we paused for several hours in the fleet anchorage while a small task force assembled. These were several destroyers, a cruiser, and the carriers *Princeton*, *Belleau Wood*, and *Lexington*. By the next morning we were under way operating together as if we had spent the past six months in one another's company. This was the advantage of the Navy Signal Book. This made a great impression on me and I have been a devoted believer in standardization, particularly in operations and maneuvering, ever since.[6]

TRANSFERRED FROM *RINGGOLD*

In early August 1943 the task force arrived in Pearl Harbor and *Ringgold* was berthed at the NOB. As was customary, a great deal of radio traffic of lower precedence—administrative material—had been sent to the radio station in Pearl Harbor for mail or messenger delivery to arriving ships. In that first batch of mail was a message from the Bureau of Naval Personnel detaching one Lt. (jg) J. L. Holloway III USN from *Ringgold* at the first available port (which would be Pearl) to proceed without delay to report to Commander Destroyer Forces, U.S. Atlantic Fleet as prospective gunnery officer of *Bennion* (DD 662).

Commander Conley, our CO, was upset at this and wanted to remonstrate with BuPers but the exec, Sam McCornock, explained what had happened. In *Ringgold*'s last quarterly Readiness Report of Officers, I had been listed as qualified for "Head of Department, Gunnery." With shipyards launching *Fletcher*-class destroyers in ever increasing numbers, there was a demand for experienced officers and men in the commissioning crews, and anyone who was qualified as a head of department was immediately vulnerable for transfer and reassignment to new construction.

Consequently, I was summarily detached and put ashore. All of my worldly belongings were stuffed in a large rugged canvas seabag with the overflow in a small handheld cloth suitcase that we referred to as our "Ditty Bag." We had a little goodbye party at the officers' club, but it was a very informal thing and a third of the officers had to remain on board with the duty. Also, the "O Club" was so crowded and noisy that any personal things we might have wanted to say at a farewell dinner were virtually impossible. Two days after my detachment I went down to the waterfront to watch *Ringgold* get under way.

I was living in the basement of a BOQ that was under construction, assigned the top bunk of a three-bunk rack in a room with about twenty people, with the only running water and head [bathroom] facilities at the officers' club two blocks away. That is how crowded things were at the Pearl Harbor Naval Base at that time. Awaiting transportation to CONUS, I learned that the wait could be as long as two weeks. All of us traveling under orders similar to mine (returning to join new-construction ships) were directed to travel by surface transportation—a troopship or freighter returning to the West Coast. Each morning we would have breakfast at the consolidated mess and then at 0800 check in with the Transportation Office, to be told nothing was available that day and to come back tomorrow. Most of us invested in a pair of swimming trunks and lay by the pool or caught a bus to one of the beaches around the island and worked on our tans.

SUBMARINES

One day I was standing on a corner near the main gate of Pearl Harbor NOB wondering what I could do to kill time that day. A jeep stopped for the light and immediately I recognized the driver, Lt. (jg) Lawrie Heyworth, one of my closest friends and a classmate at the Naval Academy. Lawrie had gone to Submarine School and had been sent to one of the newer diesel submarines operational in the Pacific theater.[7] He motioned for me to jump in, which I did, and he asked where I was going.

When I told him that I was just killing time in Hawaii waiting for transportation to CONUS, he said, "Well, join me for the day." His boat, the submarine *Finback* (SS 230), had just returned from a war patrol—Heyworth's third—and the crew was undergoing "rest and recreation" (R&R), which was an integral part of the submarine program. He explained that when *Finback* returned to Pearl Harbor after a war patrol, the seagoing crew moved off, lock, stock and barrel, with all of their belongings and luggage, and an in-port crew with the same numbers of officers and men moved on board. While the in-port crew maintained the boat and oversaw the overhaul work, the crew returning from the war patrol were given rooms at the Royal Hawaiian Hotel, two officers to a suite. It was Honolulu's premier resort hotel before the war and had been taken over by the Submarine Force Pacific Fleet for the purpose of providing R&R facilities to its submariners.

After a brief trip to the submarine base to pick up another submarine officer from the seagoing crew, Lawrie drove us to the Royal Hawaiian Hotel. The Royal Hawaiian was a pale pink color and dominated Waikiki Beach just west of Diamond Head. The Royal Hawaiian had never looked better; its peacetime staff had been retained and, except for a bulletin board in the lobby with a bus schedule to the Sub Base, it looked the same as it must have when American tourists arrived by steamer from the West Coast of the United States. I helped Lawrie with his suitcase and his golf clubs, which had been left in storage, and we stopped by a sitting room in the hotel where Lawrie introduced me to other members of his crew. Four or five of us in our short-sleeve shirts had a drink of fine scotch whiskey.

When the round had been completed, I spoke up and said, "Gentlemen, the next round of drinks is on me." There was a startled silence and then a great guffawing, because I was not aware that all of the liquor and amenities were free, paid for by the Submarine Force Pacific Fleet. I contrasted this grand lifestyle of the submariners on R&R with our own pathetic attempts to get together a little party of *Ringgold* officers in the madhouse of the O Club, and realized these guys really had it good. Then on reflection, I realized that there were few people in the war that were as much at risk as submariners.

By the end of the war some 20 percent of U.S. submarines deployed on war patrols had been lost. That meant one out of five submarine crews were lost in action. They deserved what they were getting at the Royal Hawaiian, or at least we thought so at the time.[8] There had been horrendous losses in destroyers at the beginning of the war and would be later at Okinawa; had the latter already occurred we might have found them approaching the submarine experience. Of course, the people who really took the losses were the Marines. I always wondered how the U.S. Marine Corps in the Pacific could sustain its momentum from one campaign to the next with the savage losses that Marines had to absorb at the hands of the fanatical Japanese defenders.

RETURN TO CONUS

After about ten days of waiting, I boarded *Long Island* (CVE 1) with about fifty other officers homeward bound.[9] *Long Island* was to have been a merchant ship but had been completed as an escort carrier. Then, because of its relatively small size even for an escort carrier [or CVE, of which she was the Navy's first] and apparently some instability in a seaway, it was relegated to the role of an aircraft transport.

I bunked in a room with about forty junior officers, this time in a tier of bunks four high. We were fed in the wardroom but it was cafeteria-style and the food was not very good. Not much attention was paid to the transients, which was understandable because we were on our way to "civilization," or so it was presumed. After a week of boredom broken only by all-night bridge and poker games in the wardroom we arrived at Alameda. Incidentally, I am not a card player so I spent most of my time trying without success to find a good book. The library was almost entirely paperbacks, action stories and dog-eared with pages torn out, especially those that had any interesting or salacious passages.

PART III
USS *BENNION* (DD 662)

CHAPTER 6

BACK TO SQUARE ONE

SAN FRANCISCO NAVAL SHIPYARD, SAN FRANCISCO, CALIFORNIA
IN MID-1943 Dabney's father was commanding officer of the San Francisco Naval Shipyard (aka Hunters Point Naval Shipyard). Capt. Norborne Lewis "Rim" Rawlings was an "Engineering Duty Only" officer, and EDOs commanded naval shipyards.[1] He had been there for about three months, having been transferred from the Bureau of Ships in Washington, DC. The Rawlings lived in spacious quarters built after the Navy took over Hunters Point from its civilian operators and converted it into a naval shipyard in 1940.[2]

The yard was overflowing with Navy ships, most there for repair of combat damage. Some were in much worse shape than others. There were even a couple of British cruisers and destroyers that had been badly bombed at Crete and in Malta and had been towed to the U.S. West Coast because our East Coast yards were so full. Now, with our own battle casualties increasing from engagements in the Pacific, there was a tremendous press to get the British ships out of the yard, and their crews seemed rather reluctant to go. I suppose that was understandable because the United Kingdom was in its fourth year of the war against the Axis.

While visiting the Rawlings, I had the opportunity to see some of my Naval Academy friends, including classmates who were serving on battle-damaged ships, and it was an education for me to listen to their experiences. Most of these officers were not around very long. They were sent back to new-construction ships and their places taken by reserve officers and others coming out of shore duty.

Since I was not in a "survivor" status, I did not get the thirty days' delay in reporting (DELREP) afforded to people who had come off battle-damaged ships, but I did get two weeks' leave, more than I had hoped for. Dabney and I stayed with her parents in the shipyard and found it very pleasant. Several times we went to San Francisco, where the fine restaurants seemed to be unaffected by the war; now, they entertained returning and departing people in uniform. I estimate that 80–90 percent of the male patrons in a place like the Top of the Mark—a famous "watering hole" in the penthouse of the Mark Hopkins Hotel, on the heights of Nob Hill—were in uniform.[3]

Dabney and I were able to get a Pullman reservation through the Naval District Travel Section. (Virtually all travel at this point was being controlled by the services.) It took us a week to get to Washington, DC, where we spent a day or two with my mother. She was living in Arlington, Virginia, across the Potomac, while my father was deployed in command of a destroyer squadron operating off the East Coast.[4]

We took a cab to Baltimore and then went on the overnight steamer to Norfolk, where I was to check in with the precommissioning detail of the *Bennion*. We checked into our cabin on the steamer and had a delicious dinner of Maryland seafood. When we got up at seven the next morning the ship was already tied up at the pier.

Housing in Norfolk was almost impossible to find. Fortunately for us, Dabney's mother's family was from Norfolk, and we were able to stay in a spare bedroom with her aunt and uncle for several days before we found a vacant house out at Virginia Beach, about thirty miles from NOB. Houses at Virginia Beach were available, but they were summer cottages. Most had no heat and there were few services (e.g., electricity, water) at Virginia Beach. Bus lines were gone, like other public transportation.

I checked in to NOB Norfolk and was immediately assigned to attend Radar School at Virginia Beach, which was fortunate for me logistically. Our cottage was right on the beach at 77th Street.

Happily, it was equipped with a large iron potbellied stove, and there was an ample supply of firewood just outside the kitchen door. There was also a woman's bicycle in the garage that the elderly ladies who had lived in the house used for their exercise. I rode the bicycle from 77th Street to the Radar School at the Cavalier Hotel—the only high-rise resort hotel in Virginia Beach—at 42nd Street.[5]

Each morning and evening I rode thirty-five blocks to and from the Radar School, and it was a chore. On about the sixth day of my commute a pedal broke as I was pumping, and I was thrown into the ditch on the right-hand side of Atlantic Avenue with the bicycle on top of me. I left the bike and hitched a ride, and that evening hitched a ride back to where the bike crashed, and I walked it home. From then on I simply got out on the highway and used my thumb. Had I complained, my instructions would have been to move into the BOQ where I could catch a Navy bus to work. I preferred taking my chances so that I would have some time with my wife, living on the economy. Somehow Dabney was able to find transportation to the one grocery store open on the beach and she kept us supplied with food. We had to eat at home because there were no restaurants at Virginia Beach and a trip to Norfolk was a long haul and the food being served was of poor quality and preparation. The good food and professional cooks had gone to war.

The Radar School at the Cavalier Hotel was another example of the Navy's ingenuity in setting up training commands with the available civic infrastructure. Bedrooms facing the ocean in the seven-story structure were converted into radar control rooms and radars mounted on the roof facing out to sea. Aircraft from NAS [Naval Air Station] Oceana located about five miles away would fly patterns off the coast. The radar training consisted of detecting simulated enemy aircraft and controlling simulated friendly fighters to intercept the enemy aircraft.

There was a heavy curriculum of classroom work where we were trying to get the hang of this new science of radar. We had only

13. USS *Bennion* (DD 662) under way during World War II. Note dazzle camouflage. Official U.S. Navy photo, courtesy James C. Fahey Collection, U.S. Naval Institute photo archive

seen the word for the first time during our first-class year at the Naval Academy so this was truly new technology. *Bennion* would have three radars: an air-search radar; a surface-search radar; and a fire-control radar (mounted on the main-battery director). The Radar School had courses for senior officers to teach them how to best use radars. Junior officers were expected to know enough about radar to employ it as officers of the deck or as gunnery watch officers. Enlisted radar operators and maintenance men going through training had the benefit of a very friendly environment and a lot of excellent instructors.

Bennion was scheduled for commissioning before the end of 1943, only three months away. Drafts of men from other ships and from boot camp were already arriving in Norfolk with orders to report to the *Bennion* precommissioning detail. All personnel ordered to report to a precommissioning detail were immediately assigned to the Atlantic Fleet Training Command (TRALANT) and formed into cadres for their particular ships. Whenever possible, *Bennion*'s precommissioning detail carried out training and evolutions as a group, but because men were arriving all the time they had to be assigned to training activities on the basis of weekly quotas. It is unfortunate that all couldn't go through the training on weapons, fire fighting, damage control, etc., as one group.

All *Bennion* enlisted personnel were berthed together in one set of barracks, under the watchful eye of petty officers who would serve in *Bennion* as supervisors. Officers had a different situation. There were far fewer of them than enlisteds, and many officers, particularly those who were second-tour or were being trained for a technical specialty, were required to be in Boston where the ship was being built, to help inspect the installation of the equipment for which they would be responsible. Generally speaking, brand-new ensigns reported to the Fleet Training Command in Norfolk, lived in the BOQ (but not together as a *Bennion* unit), and attended the various schools as the courses became available.

GUNNERY TRAINING AT DAM NECK

Wisely, perhaps even prior to the war, the Navy Department in Washington had acquired three sites along the Atlantic Coast to be used as gunnery training facilities. Price's Neck was in Rhode Island, Dam Neck was at Virginia Beach, and there was a third site at Jacksonville, Florida. Each of these gunnery training sites had similar characteristics. The sites were on the seacoast in uninhabited areas. At Dam Neck a large cement hardstand had been laid down. On it were arranged in a long line facing the ocean 20-mm Oerlikon guns, Bofors 40-mm guns, and 5-inch/38-caliber mounts. These were the weapons the destroyer and destroyer escort [smaller, slower than destroyers, specialized for ASW and convoy protection] crews needed to be trained to operate. There was also a section of 3-inch dual-purpose weapons and some old World War I–vintage

5-inch/51s that were used by the Armed Guards—the Navy crews assigned to merchant ships.

My interest as prospective gunnery officer was in those weapons we would have on board *Bennion*: 20-mm machine guns, 40-mm machine guns, and 5-inch/38 dual-purpose weapons. The 5-inch guns were controlled by a Mark 37 director mounted on top of a low building housing the Mark 1 computer, in a compartment made to look like the gunnery plotting room of a destroyer.

The course of instruction at Dam Neck was a minimum of a week long, and all of personnel assigned there for training lived in Quonset hut barracks and ate in a consolidated mess. There were good classrooms, where instructors would tear down the various weapons to show the gun crews the theory of operation and how to deal with malfunctions. Then the sailors, usually with the officers mixed in as part of the gun crew, would practice loading, training, and elevating a gun to track sleeves being towed overhead by aircraft.

The gun crews then graduated to the firing runs. Utility squadron aircraft towed sleeves at the end of very long towlines. The tow planes would proceed to sea about ten miles, turn around, and fly perpendicular to the coast on a course that would take them right over Dam Neck. Each run would come in at a different altitude, all the way from a thousand to ten thousand feet. Guns were controlled by a range commander in a tower with a very loud announcing system backed up by klaxons to signal cease-fire.

Normally, the order to open fire was not given until the tow plane was overhead, so that it would be very difficult for a student to mistake the tow plane for the sleeve. At "Commence firing!" all of the guns would bang away until the target was at an elevation of about seventy degrees when the range commander would order "Cease firing!" All guns would train "fore and aft" and an assessment taken of jams, fingers caught in breech mechanisms, men thrown off the quickly turning mounts, etc. The brass was quickly policed and put in containers to be hauled away. The crews remanned the mounts and within five minutes another sleeve was under fire. This went on for hours at a time. It was of utmost importance to have the gun crews become accustomed to the noise and the racket of the guns and the platforms moving under them while they did their jobs. There was nothing to duplicate this cacophony of sound and movement except by doing it.

It was impressive to see the skill levels improve in just a day's time as the sailors got used to operating the guns with live ammunition. Occasionally a sleeve would get shot down, not so much because of the accuracy of the shooting but the volume of shot that would somehow cut the towline. This didn't happen very often but there was tremendous enthusiasm when it did occur. I often thought that the tow pilots might have had some sort of rig to release the towline every two or three days just for morale reasons.

Normally all seamen and other deck ratings were put through the one-week course, as were the deck-specialist line officers [i.e., "unrestricted" line, eligible for command at sea]. For gunner's mates and fire controlmen there were three-to-four-week courses that got into the maintenance of the guns and related equipment. It was unfortunate that there was not more time available for our gunner's mates and fire controlmen, but they were needed in Boston to supervise the installation of the mounts in the ship.

FIREFIGHTING

Another training course that had gotten even more realistic was firefighting. At each of the major NOBs there had been built a large, low, sturdy concrete structure that was fitted out with hatches and ladders and gratings and false boiler fronts similar to those in the interior of a ship. Students would be divided up into groups, with no distinction of rank, officers included. These were called "hose teams."

As we entered the area where the fire was the hottest we could see the flames of the burning oil and gasoline in the bilges. The technique was to shift to a spray rather than a steady stream to deprive the flames of oxygen and extinguish the blaze. The firemen instructors also had us hit the source of the fire with a full force of a hose stream just to teach us that was the wrong technique: the powerful stream simply stirred up the petroleum and spread the fire and produced even greater heat.

A new product was being distributed to the fleet called "firefighting foam." A heavy, thick, liquid mixture was injected into the water of the firemain [ship-wide piping system charged with seawater]; this would result in liquid foam being sprayed by the hose nozzle. This liquid foam created a blanket over the petroleum fires and, by depriving it of oxygen, extinguished the blaze. There were some tricks and techniques involved in laying down the foam blanket and we were given ample opportunity to learn them.

Our instruction also included training in the care and handling of the firefighting equipment and how to operate such items as the foam generators that injected the foam mix into water from the firemain. We also learned to operate the "Handy Billy" pumps that could be lowered over the side into the ocean to pick up firefighting water when damage had ruptured the firemains.

Every member of our crew went through the basic firefighting course, because one never knew in battle when, regardless of assigned position, one would have to become part of a firefighting and damage-control team. The standing damage-control parties, which consisted mostly of engineering ratings, received extra instruction in firefighting, damage-control equipment and damage-control techniques such as shoring [supporting weakened bulkheads with timber, carried for the purpose] and plugging shell holes.

OTHER TRAINING ASHORE

Each NOB also had an antisubmarine "attack trainer," a mockup of a destroyer pilothouse with a sonar station, a helmsman station with engine-room annunciators, and the proper sound-powered phone circuits. The attack trainer simulated a sonar contact on a German U-boat, and the conning team working with the sonar operators would maneuver their phantom ship to cross just ahead of the submarine and drop depth charges so they would bracket or strike it. Of course, there were no submarines or depth charges, but the sonar sound was realistic and the maneuvering of the ship was captured on graph paper for all the world to see how well or how poorly the conning officer and his bridge team had done. The record of the runs was sent back to the ship's commanding officer for his review, so we knew that we would be held to account for our performances on the attack trainer.

Unfortunately, once an officer and his teammates got the knack of the attack trainer it was fairly simple to make a good run, after which the benefits of the training diminished. Nevertheless, whenever destroyers were in port for more than two days the local training commander would order the destroyers to send up their teams to keep the attack trainers occupied. All of us on board ship became a little bored before our destroyers moved far enough forward in the combat zone; there were no attack trainers in the fleet anchorages. Still, the attack trainers were valuable. Although they lacked the sophistication of today's simulators, they were somewhat realistic and they made up for the fact that in the Pacific a destroyer might go an entire twenty-four-month tour without ever pinging on a real submarine. The attack trainer ensured that all of the ships' ASW teams were up on the techniques and capabilities of the current destroyers with their sonars and depth charges.

I attended all of the schools in the Norfolk area—and there were considerably more than I have described here, such as in aircraft recognition, ship recognition, principles of radar, and basic maneuvering-board [for rapid approximation of relative-motion solutions] refresher training. We were kept busy and the quality of instruction was good, although I am sure that the instructors must have gotten bored with the number of times they had to repeat their training for the new destroyer crews.

PRECOMMISSIONING DETAIL

Having completed all of the mandatory schooling and a good many of the elective courses, I was told to report to the *Bennion* precommissioning detail in Boston in mid-November 1943. I rode to Boston by train and checked into the BOQ at the Boston Navy Yard, which was quite pleasant, and for the first time I was treated better than a Naval Academy midshipman in terms of berthing and mess. I was very impressed with our commanding officer, Cdr. Joshua Cooper, a Naval Academy graduate from the Class of 1927 with a reputation as a fine naval officer and a fine leader.[6]

The Bureau of Naval Personnel [as the Bureau of Navigation had been renamed in 1942] had assembled an experienced and competent crew for this soon-to-be commissioned destroyer. All officers above the rank of ensign had served at sea in destroyers in the specialties (e.g., gunnery) to which they would be assigned in *Bennion*. This was due in part to the fact that the large influx of officers and enlisted men that occurred in 1941 had qualified at sea and in combat and were now being sent to more senior positions in new-construction destroyers. Some officers reporting to new construction were coming from battle-damaged ships or combatants that had been lost. They were young enough to be sent back to sea in basically the same jobs they had left rather than being assigned to shore-duty billets. Not many surface officers who returned from the combat zone below the rank of lieutenant commander went to shore duty. Junior billets in the shore establishment were being filled by junior officers who had been commissioned with a specialty in engineering, law, food management, etc. They could fill staff billets ashore in those support areas better than a combat veteran.

The executive officer was Lt. Cdr. Jon Bernard "Red" Balch, of the USNA Class of 1939, who had served as the executive officer of a destroyer escort and would go from *Bennion* to command his own destroyer—*Remey* (DD 688). The chief engineer, a critical job on the newly commissioned ships, was Lt. Phil Teeter, an NROTC graduate. Teeter had won the Navy Cross for conspicuous bravery when his previous destroyer, *Smith* (DD 378), was badly shot up. He had been an engineer on that vessel and had stayed below, fought fires, repaired machinery, and plugged bullet holes and was instrumental in helping to save the ship.

A new dimension had been added in the officer corps: CPOs with fifteen to twenty years' experience were being commissioned as ensigns and sent to destroyers to be assistants in their areas of expertise. I was the gunnery officer of *Bennion*. One of my assistants had been a chief gunner's mate before his selection as a "limited duty officer" (LDO). My assistant for the torpedo battery had served as a chief torpedoman's mate. An especially valuable assistant was a former chief fire controlman who would serve as the plotting-room officer, the position that I had initially been assigned to on *Ringgold*. All of these LDOs were extraordinary men; they not only knew their business in a technical sense but were mature enough that they wore the mantle of officer responsibilities with pride and assurance.

About a week after checking into the BOQ, I took a day off and house-hunted. With the help of a very capable and sympathetic Naval Housing Office, I was able to rent an apartment at 273 Beacon Street, a very elegant address in Boston. It had been a handsome townhouse of some Boston Brahmin, four stories of rooms that included servants' quarters. Each of the floors had been converted into a separate apartment. Ours was on the second floor.[7] Our living room had a large bow window that overlooked Beacon Street, which had not changed much and still had many elegant homes and "watering spots."

When I had been living in Boston in the summer of 1942 while attached to the staff of the Naval Training School at Harvard, Boston had been a very exciting place for a young bachelor. It abounded then with truly excellent restaurants such as Durgan-Park, Locke-Ober, the Union Oyster House, and The Grill at the Parker House, to name a few.[8] These were world famous before World War II. In the summer of 1942 these eateries and the nightclubs, featuring the big bands of Benny Goodman, Tommy Dorsey, Stan Kenton, and Artie Shaw, were still doing a big business. There was still scotch whiskey along with premium cuts of beef and always excellent seafood available.

In the fall of 1943 all that had changed. There were few young bachelors to be seen, and the people in uniform were mainly sailors attached to Navy ships undergoing overhaul or operating out of Boston. Most seemed largely preoccupied with their shipboard responsibilities, which kept them on board for most of the day and evening. When they did go ashore the Navy people pretty much congregated in the waterfront bars or the clubs in the Navy yard. The fine restaurants such as Locke-Ober, Durgan-Park, and the Union Oyster House were only half-filled at dinnertime, catering to an elderly clientele and without the fine foods that had made them so notable. The Wig-Wam, which had been a center of jazz for New England that attracted hordes of college kids as well as the local Bostonians, had closed. All of the band players had joined the military and were now playing in marching bands.

So there was little social life for our ship's company except for bachelors, who found plenty of action within blocks of the Boston Navy Yard main gate. The rest of us were just happy to go home and be with our families. The wardroom officers saw very little of one another after working hours; time was too precious. The married men wanted to be with their wives and families. Consequently, there was very little social life among the wardroom officers after working hours.

Commander Cooper very thoughtfully allowed the liberty sections (two out of three) to go ashore at noon on Thanksgiving Day, to have an old-fashioned midday Thanksgiving dinner. Dabney and I went to Scholl's Cafeteria, an upscale cafeteria that was renowned for providing lots of food, very well prepared at reasonable prices, in a settled atmosphere. Since turkey, yams, rice, oysters, and the ingredients of "Minced Pie Pops" were not yet on the rationing list, the cooks at Scholl's were able to do their usual magnificent job. I remember that Thanksgiving as a truly pleasant occasion during one of the sadder times of our lives, when our country was only just beginning to recover from the defeats of the first years of the war. Although there was no timetable as to when the conflict would be over, the news got better almost every month. *Bennion* was commissioned on December 14, 1943, in the Boston Navy Yard. [9]

CHAPTER 7

PACIFIC BOUND

COMMENTS ON THE NAVY'S EXPANSION

BY THE SUMMER OF 1943, eighteen months after the conflict had started, America's shipyard mobilization was beginning to hit its peak in production. Existing shipyards had been enlarged and modernized, new shipyards had been constructed, and the tooling for ship production lines had been installed. Workers had been found and, through training and experience, had become proficient in shipbuilding skills such as riveting, welding, electrical work, and painting. At the time our ship was completed at the Boston Navy Yard, that facility was delivering one new destroyer, destroyer escort (DE), or landing ship tank (LST) every day and a half each week.

Manning this enormous influx of new ships joining the operating forces became a terrific problem for the U.S. Navy. Initially, when there were few new-construction ships joining the fleet, those vessels were manned by drawing down experienced regular officers from the shore establishment and sending survivors from battle-damaged ships back to sea. These veterans became the experienced nucleus in ships to lead the new ensigns and activated reserves that were coming out of the manpower pipeline. Officer manning was partly met by promoting CPOs to LDOs, partly by the "Ninety-Day Wonders" from the V-7 program, which, started in 1940, ran college-educated candidates through "midshipmen schools" that were set up on such college campuses as Columbia, Northwestern, and Notre Dame.

The Navy's real problem was manning destroyer escorts, which were coming out of the shipyards in great numbers and were equipped with fairly sophisticated sonars, ASW weapons, and 3-inch/50-caliber dual-purpose guns, with their attendant fire-control systems. The challenge was to take the ship's company, 90 percent of which had never been to sea before, and make its members knowledgeable in such evolutions as getting under way, anchoring, mooring to a pier, coming alongside an oiler or an ammunition ship for replenishment, and maneuvering in formation while attacking submarines or defending themselves from aircraft. It was a great deal for these young Americans to learn, and time was very short.

As a consequence, in early 1943 the Navy Department set up a "DE-DD Shakedown Group" in Bermuda. The purpose was to create a dedicated training organization that would transform a new-construction destroyer or destroyer escort in four to six weeks from two separate entities—a crew on one hand and a ship on the other—into a single entity that would be USS *Neversink*. Furthermore, this training had to be undertaken at sea in a realistic environment, but an environment in which these new crews in their new ships (with all their attendant shortcomings) would not become prey of the German U-boats that were infesting the Atlantic.

Consequently, the group was located at Bermuda, with the permission of our ally the United Kingdom, because those tightly connected islands provided a large sound in which the entire training group could be anchored or berthed in the evenings. Importantly, access to the sound could be closed by torpedo nettings to keep submarines and their torpedoes out. During the day DDs and DEs operating adjacent to Bermuda would hold down the threat of U-boats. These were destroyers and DEs nearing the end of their four to six weeks' training and now had an effective antisubmarine capability that could threaten a U-boat once that submarine was detected.

It was also decided that this shakedown would be dedicated to just that purpose; liberty aspects of the four weeks in Bermuda would be minimized—in fact minimized to the extent of being nonexistent. It seemed unfortunate that with this beautiful island only a thousand yards away from the anchorage, the sailors were kept on board. But it was important for several reasons. The first was that liberty was certainly a distraction and the training would be better assimilated each day by clear heads and fresh minds. Second, the numbers of sailors in the shakedown group would absolutely overwhelm the villages, including Hamilton, the capital.

COMMANDER, SHAKEDOWN GROUP

The officer selected to set up the shakedown group was Capt. James L. Holloway Jr., USN, my father. He had developed a reputation as an expert in operational training from his days in the Navy Department during the 1930s, when he was assigned to the Gunnery Section, Fleet Training Division. Fleet Training Division was a component of the staff of the Chief of Naval Operations.

Immediately after the war started, Holloway, then a commander, had gone to sea as a destroyer division commander in charge of four 1,630-ton *Benson/Gleaves*-class destroyers [two nearly identical classes]. Within four months he had been promoted to command of a squadron of eight destroyers (two divisions) and was responsible for the screening force during the attack and invasion of North Africa, Operation Torch. It was from his command of Destroyer Squadron 10 that he was ordered to Washington on temporary duty to develop, for Secretary of the Navy James Forrestal, a plan for training the DEs. In three weeks Captain Holloway assembled his staff and left for Bermuda with Forrestal's directive to get the program going in a hurry, using whatever shortcuts he considered necessary to achieve the highest effectiveness in the shortest time.

The basic concept was one of simplicity and directness. Destroyers were added because they too would benefit from such a shakedown period, but with more mature and experienced ships' companies the new-construction destroyers would need only four weeks instead of the six weeks provided to the DEs. When the ships left the States they would already have on board training packages that essentially scheduled every hour of every one of their thirty days at Bermuda, so that the CO could make up his own training plan and the XO the "plans of the day" to maximize benefit of the training.

UNDERWAY REPLENISHMENT

One significant change to past practice was a new policy of disregarding any damage to DEs or oilers in collisions while coming alongside to replenish. In prewar days underway replenishment was considered a very dangerous operation only to be undertaken under extreme circumstances. A collision between a destroyer and another ship with only fifty to seventy-five feet of clearance between the two, traveling at between seventeen and twenty-four knots, would do substantial damage to both vessels. Also, a collision was not good for a commanding officer's career!

Heretofore, the Navy had engendered an attitude in its commanding officers of approaching underway replenishment in a tentative fashion, very carefully. It was a long-drawn-out evolution, involving a great deal of anxiety. However, action reports coming back from the Pacific made it clear that expediting underway replenishment was absolutely essential. Destroyers were having to come alongside burning carriers to evacuate casualties, alongside ammunition ships while under attack by enemy aircraft to replenish their antiaircraft (AA) ammunition in order to survive, and alongside oilers to receive fuel during typhoons to avoid fuel states so low as to cause (and did cause) the destroyers to capsize.

Consequently, at the training group the COs were immediately told that such minor damage as dents in the sides of either ship, lifelines torn away, davits ripped out, and other things of that nature would be looked upon as simply the wear and tear of training. The training group maintained a group of expert welders who would visit damaged ships during the night to repair them and make them look like new the next morning. This approach allowed the young and relatively unexperienced COs to be bold and to develop their ability to conduct approaches with confidence. Though many feared that the policy would result in carelessness and a lessened sense of responsibility on the part of commanding officers, what actually happened was that the COs developed confidence and an enormous pride in their shiphandling, their ability to get alongside quickly and safely and get the job done very smartly.

SHAKEDOWN CRUISE

Bennion departed Boston early on January 11, 1944, for an overnight trip to Bermuda, steaming alone at about twenty-five knots. The entire trip was under overcast skies so our navigator was never able to use celestial navigation and had to rely on dead-reckoning fixes factoring our course and speed over time for our entire trip. We reached our estimated time of arrival (ETA) of midday on the 12th, but Bermuda was not there. The XO, Lieutenant Commander Balch, was the navigator and he was terribly abashed by this, but the captain—the very wise skipper that he was—did not make an issue of it.

Normally various aids to navigation would have been employed, such as tuning on the radio stations in Bermuda with a radio-direction finder, but all these stations were off the air because of their potential use by U-boats in fixing their own positions in the vicinity of Bermuda. So the navigator and the captain did something I had never seen before on a surface ship. They initiated what is known as an "expanding-square search," in which the ship steams the four cardinal headings of north, east, south, and west on legs that become successively longer. We had not very long to steam before Bermuda, which lies very low on the horizon, came into view. We were able to transfer to piloting navigation using visible charted features and arrived at the gate in the submarine net only a few hours late, which was no problem for the people at the Training Group. Their philosophy was: That is why you came out here—to be trained, and navigation is one of the areas in which you will have an opportunity to increase your proficiency. They were especially pleased that the ship had executed an expanding-square search, an evolution that is not often undertaken at sea. (Later in life I did this many times flying airplanes, where navigation was not good and speeds were fairly high.) We went through the gates at six o'clock that evening and were immediately instructed to berth outboard of the flagship.

With lines lashing the two ships together, the captain was instructed to report on board the flagship immediately with his exec to call on the commodore [squadron commander]. The flagship was a destroyer tender—*Altair* (AD 11).

The next morning the training group meeting got under way. The meeting was a weekly affair involving all ships undergoing shakedown, plus the commanders or their representatives of the units providing services. These were training submarines that would operate against us, twin-engined Army Air Forces bombers converted to tow planes to haul the banners that we would shoot at with 5-inch and automatic weapons; and the Training Group "ship riders." The latter were experienced petty officers and commissioned officers who would ride *Bennion*, not so much to teach but rather to observe and then critique each evening when we had returned to port. These teams gave us every opportunity either to do well or to mess up. The effort and degree of success was clearly up to us.

These weekly meetings were an opportunity for the ships undergoing training to complain about lack of services, to request additional services, or to make known their material and mechanical problems so that they could be repaired and the ships could continue their training program. My father had been detached from command of the DD-DE Shakedown Group about two months before *Bennion* got there. He had been relieved by Capt. Dashiell L. "Dash" Madeira, a rather stocky man with a lot of energy and a rather loud presence.[1] At *Bennion*'s first weekly conference I accompanied my CO, because much of the training had to do with gunnery, and gunnery officers were included in virtually all the training conferences.

Captain Madeira, who liked to be called "commodore," was aware of the fact that the son of the officer he had just relieved was on board *Bennion* for training. Representing one of our group of new ships attending the weekly conference for the first time was an officer out of the Class of 1941 who was short, overweight, and balding. On this occasion he was wearing a khaki uniform that was in very poor press and that he had substantially outgrown around the middle. Since he was an Academy graduate most of us knew him and were aware that he was not a front-runner among his contemporaries. He was two years senior to me and just being ordered as a gunnery officer for the first time, although his duty had been entirely in destroyers.

At promptly 0830 the orderly shouted "Attention!," and the commodore made his entry, very brisk and businesslike. He looked around the room and immediately walked over to the officer whom I have just described, grasped him by the hand and said, "You must be young Jimmy Holloway!" I was only about four feet away but Dash Madeira had said this in such loud and positive tones that everybody in the room heard him. When the officer who had been misidentified replied, "No, sir, I'm Lieutenant Schultz," Dash looked somewhat startled and snapped back, "Well, isn't Lieutenant Holloway in this group?" My commanding officer then said, "He's right here, sir," and the commodore came over and with somewhat less enthusiasm shook my hand. It was very embarrassing to me to be singled out, particularly since I was just a lieutenant (jg) and the junior officer in the room amongst the representatives of the ships under instruction. Furthermore, the fact that Dash had identified this less than sterling character as "Young Holloway" made me wonder what sort of tales had preceded my arrival in Bermuda.

Madeira was known as a "captain flogger." That is, he seemed to make a practice of finding one or two of the weaker skippers or perhaps a CO for whom he had taken a dislike and rode him during the entire shakedown period. It was a form of bullying that I have always abhorred. Madeira was "greasy" in his relationship with seniors but was a consistent violator of that major premise of good leadership, to "praise in public and censure in private." He did it just backward. For some reason he jumped on Commander Cooper; it must have been something that went back to their earlier days together in the Navy. He was very unpleasant to Cooper, and Madeira's first matter of business in the conference was to state that he understood the captain of *Bennion* had some reservations about the shakedown program and that he had better get those squared away or *Bennion* would be in a lot of trouble. He did not bother to explain his words or elaborate on them or even give Cooper an opportunity to speak, all of which was probably for the better.

We younger officers wondered why the command of the DD-DE Shakedown Group would be put in the hands of an officer so obviously lacking in the fundamentals of good leadership. After many years of thinking about this and other similar situations that I encountered over my years in the Navy it seems to shake out like this.

- During World War II the demand for experienced officers was relentless, considering that the officer corps had grown by more than 1,000 percent in a matter of two years. Consequently, officers who in peacetime, competing with their contemporaries for promotion, probably would not have been selected for captain, were picked for four stripes because the Navy needed experience. Madeira had done all the things necessary in the Navy for promotion to captain, including having commanded a destroyer and a destroyer division—not with any particular distinction, but he didn't get in serious trouble either.

- Officers who had the experience and were recognized as leaders with reputations for being able to get things done were not assigned to take over these training jobs but were sent forward to command the major combatants in the fleet, especially the Pacific. That is where the real demand for professionalism and leadership was.

- Perhaps the best rationalization of these circumstances is presented in Herman Wouk's book *The Caine Mutiny*, which points out that these officers were not incompetent, just inferior to their contemporaries. Wouk observed that in spite of their lack of impressive ability, they nevertheless fulfilled a desperate need that the Navy felt to have commanding officers and managers in responsible positions who at least knew what had to be done and what they were doing.

The activities during our thirty days—and it was exactly thirty days—in the shakedown group were without letup, including Saturdays and Sundays. Each day the destroyer would get under way at first light and proceed out through the torpedo nets and the minefields, often coming under simulated attack by one of the training submarines as the ship sortied from the anchorage to exercise ASW and sonar crews in that demanding situation. After that the ship riders might disable the electrical system, forcing the ship to go to emergency power. Once that was restored there would be perhaps a simulated fire in a forward magazine. All these emergency drills came without previous warning that a particular drill would take place. During the thirty days virtually every emergency that had occurred in the fleet, plus some that had not happened but probably would in the future, were thrown at us. Sometimes thirty men were pulled off their stations and told that they were dead, wounded, or otherwise incapacitated; personnel adjustments had to be made on the spot to keep the ship moving and the systems going. Periodically, the ship riders would do such things as shut down the galley, so that we spent twenty-four hours eating slabs of baloney between slices of bread spread with white margarine.

I think we must have had at least one man-overboard drill every day and put the whaleboats in the water at sea every other day. Once or twice daily we would rendezvous with another ship. It might be a destroyer coming alongside to pass mail, or an ammunition ship to replace the 5-inch, 40-mm, and 20-mm rounds we had shot the day before against the air targets that were constantly being presented to us for live firing. We took on board no supplies or fuel in port at Bermuda. All the ammunition, food, "small stores" [basic personal items], and fuel we required was delivered to us at sea, and most of the time the replenishment ships themselves had new crews that were just learning how to do their jobs. We were all learning together. The result was that we would become so proficient that these logistical tasks could be carried out with a small fraction of the crew, while the ship was at General Quarters at night under an air attack. This would be a situation we would often encounter in the Western Pacific.

One important training byproduct that we received (but perhaps not as much as we should have) was experience of the exhaustion that affects men in combat. Our Navy learned early in the war that exhaustion can be a critical factor in winning or losing. At the battle of Savo Island three American cruisers and an Australian cruiser in one task force were sunk in a matter of hours by a Japanese surface force at night because the Allied forces had worn themselves out—or been worn out—by remaining at General Quarters constantly for more than twenty-four hours. I remember that subsequently on *Bennion*, during the Leyte campaign, giving the crew some rest was one of our biggest concerns, particularly when the kamikazes made their first appearance. Often we did not go to General Quarters until the "bogeys" (enemy aircraft) were within five miles of our ship. I recall one occasion when we were alongside an ammunition ship transferring 5-inch ammunition with bogeys overhead being chased by F4F Wildcats from *Kaiser*-class carriers [CVEs] off Samar.[2]

On February 11, 1944, Captain Madeira came on board *Bennion*. In a very cordial and jovial way he told us we had not only completed our shakedown but had done well. He considered *Bennion* fully ready to go on to the war in the Pacific. For all the many criticisms, he had done the job that was needed of him, and in spite of his previously critical attitude, we appreciated the warmth of his farewell and best wishes for the war ahead.

RETURN TO BOSTON HOME PORT

We returned to the Boston Navy Yard for eleven days to have some repairs made to essential equipment. We also received new equipment, which was constantly being developed and installed on our ships every time they entered a Navy yard. We offloaded much of our 5-inch ammunition and received a new type of projectile, which was so hush-hush that there were armed guards with machine guns standing by the trucks delivering it from the ammunition depot. This was the so-called Magic Stuff, 5-inch antiaircraft ammunition with proximity (or variable-timed, VT) fuzes. Instead of the former timed fuzes exploded by clockwork devices in the nose of the projectile, the VT shells had a fuze that sent out a radio signal. When a radio return gained certain strength, it indicated that a bogey was close enough for the shell to explode with a good probability of damaging it.[3]

Three days after taking on board the VT ammunition and completing the installation and testing of some new radio equipment, *Bennion* was under way for the Pacific. There were no teary farewells, no wives seeing the ship off. We had all said goodbye that morning after breakfast and went to the ship and got her under way.

Our first stop was the Philadelphia Navy Yard at midday on March 1; we put in overnight to offload some workmen and their tools and equipment. They had ridden the ship from Boston to complete installing radio and electronics equipment that would enable

Bennion to function as a fighter-direction ship. We were under way at first light. We steamed into Delaware Bay to rendezvous with *Bataan* (CVL 29), another light carrier built on a cruiser hull at New York Shipbuilding in Camden, New Jersey, and then fitted out at the Philadelphia Navy Yard. *Bennion* would be escorting *Bataan* to Pearl Harbor.[4]

The trip to Panama was uneventful until we approached the Canal. I was OOD when, as we approached the gate in the submarine net, our sonar operator called out that he had a submarine contact. The junior OOD happened to be the sonar officer and his immediate reaction was that it was a valid contact, so I sounded General Quarters and made preparation to drop depth charges. The captain, as if magic, appeared beside me in his pajamas. Without interfering, he just listened to what was going on while I made all preparations to intercept the submarine's course and drop depth charges. I was about ten seconds from firing the Y-guns and releasing the depth charges when the skipper said, "I have the conn, we will not drop depth charges. Repeat do not drop depth charges or fire Y-guns."[5]

As we moved over the contact and left it in our wake, the sonar was no longer able to pick it up. Josh Cooper, ever considerate of his subordinates, said, as I recall it now, "Jim, I apologize for interrupting you while you had the deck, and I took the conn. However, I was aware that other destroyers approaching the Panama Canal have also picked up sonar contacts in this area that have turned out to be nonsubmarine. They are the hulks of merchantmen sunk earlier in the war by the German U-boats. I have access to special intelligence that you have not seen. In my judgment that was not a submarine, although I must agree that it sounded like one. I felt that to have dropped depth charges right here at the entrance to the submarine nets would have thrown the Panamanian Sea Frontier command into a real tizzy. Consequently, that's why I countermanded your order to drop." He was a real gentleman and it was easy to understand why his officers were inspired to do their best for him.

TO THE MARIANAS

We proceeded with *Bataan* to San Diego, arriving on March 16 for two days of minor maintenance and replenishment and then departed with *Bataan* for Pearl Harbor in what would be a speedy five-day transit. Upon our arrival we learned that we had gotten there too late for the recently completed invasion of the Marshall Islands and air raids against the Marianas.

Bennion would eventually be assigned to the Fifth Fleet, which "stood up" on April 26, 1944, under the command of Adm. Raymond A. Spruance [see chapters 8 and 9]. Our particular task force would carry the landing force to the next objective in the Pacific, wherever it might be. Rehearsals for that landing commenced immediately even though we did not know what the assault objective was. We simply worked with code names that disguised the actual location and identity of the objective. Most of the time we could come in periodically for liberty. For several weeks *Bennion* and other surface combatants rehearsed operations such as ASW and antiaircraft defense of the troop transport ships and spent many hours simulating shore bombardment at one of the Hawaiian Islands. However, we were able to fire live rounds under very realistic circumstances at the island of Kahoolawe, off Maui. Our gunnery department learned that shore bombardment was quite a different fire-control problem than shooting at ships and aircraft. In some ways it was more satisfying, in that we could see our rounds impact and tell whether the target was destroyed. On the other hand, much of our fire was "indirect," fired into a defiladed area ashore not visible to the ship where the troops and the forward controllers said that numerous enemy were.

Pearl Harbor began to fill up with transports, converted passenger ships, and amphibious ships from new construction and previous campaigns in the Pacific, plus other assault shipping. Grey-painted Liberty ships were laden with trucks and boxes of food and ammunition that they would offload with their own cranes and kingposts into landing craft carried by the force.

Then, we all got under way for the lagoon at the recently captured Kwajalein Atoll in the Marshall Islands, where the invasion force was being assembled. After we got under way from "Kwaj" we learned our ultimate objective would be the Mariana Islands of Saipan, Tinian, Rota, and Guam. The Japanese had moved into these islands, having captured Guam from us early in the war. With Guam the Japanese had inherited a fine harbor, at Apra.

Of second-highest importance was Saipan, which the Japanese had seized from Germany during World War I. It was occupied by about 30,000 Japanese soldiers and also construction battalions, which were converting Saipan into a major forward base. Tinian, five miles southwest from Saipan, was a smaller island, not as suitable for development as a base, but the Japanese had garrisoned it with ten thousand troops to defend it. Rota was just a small islet, very mountainous but useful as a radar base and lookout station. The southernmost island of Guam would be the most difficult of the Marianas to recapture, because of its larger size and its very rough terrain.

CHAPTER 8
THE MARIANAS CAMPAIGN

PLANNING

THE ROSTER OF THOSE TASKED with the oversight of and planning for the invasion of the Marianas was replete with famous American naval commanders. Adm. Chester W. Nimitz directed the overall strategy from Hawaii as the Commander in Chief, Pacific Fleet. Adm. Raymond A. Spruance was commander of the Fifth Fleet. Vice Adm. Richmond Kelly Turner commanded Task Force 52 (TF 52), the assault force. TF 58, the fast carrier striking force, was commanded by Vice Adm. Marc A. "Pete" Mitscher.[1] TF 58 would support the seizure of the Mariana Islands by striking Japanese forces at sea and ashore well in advance of the assault on the immediate objectives of the amphibious operation. It was then to hit targets in the Philippines as TF 52 prepared to assault the beaches in the Marianas. The forays of the fast carriers against Japanese installations in the Philippines led to the decisive air battle of the Philippine Sea, which can be considered the action that broke the back of Japanese carrier aviation. It was in this battle that the F6F Hellcat proved itself to be more than the equal of the Japanese Zero.

This would be a good time to describe the organization of the Pacific Fleet and the task force scheme that was normally standard for these Pacific operations. As noted, at the top of the command chain was Commander in Chief, Pacific Fleet; Admiral Nimitz had relieved Adm. Husband Kimmel in that billet after the Pearl Harbor attack. Spruance and William F. Halsey alternated as fleet commanders; when Spruance and the Fifth Fleet were conducting operations, Halsey and his Third Fleet staff were in Pearl Harbor working up the next major operation. The ships were essentially the same, turning without pause to the next assault with "mirror-imaged" task designators. The Marianas campaign had been assigned to Spruance and the Fifth Fleet. The heavy hitter of the fleet was TF 58, the carrier striking force, under the command of Vice Admiral Mitscher. This force consisted of four task groups. Each task group comprised two to three fleet carriers (i.e., a large carrier built as such from the keel up) and two light carriers, or CVLs, which were flattops on cruiser hulls carrying a smaller complement of aircraft. (CVLs are not to be confused with CVEs, or escort carriers. The latter, initially converted merchant ship hulls, were limited to about eighteen knots and carried one squadron each of Wildcats and TBMs. CVLs had a maximum speed of over thirty knots and could keep up with the fleet's major combatants—destroyers, cruisers, battleships, and fleet carriers of the *Essex* and *Enterprise* classes.)

In addition, TF 58 included fast battleships, such as *South Dakota*- and *Iowa*-class capital ships constructed just prior to or during World War II. Filling out each fast carrier striking group were three or four cruisers, and about a dozen destroyers. The function of the destroyers, cruisers and battleships in the TF 58 organization was defense of the carriers. Because of the high speed of the units, submarines were not considered major threats, and it was not anticipated that, given the long range of the carriers' aircraft, Japanese battleships and cruisers would be able to come within gun range of any of our fast carrier striking force units.[2]

TF 52, the assault force, was under the command of Vice Admiral Turner, one of the Navy's most experienced amphibious commanders, who also had a top-notch reputation as a naval tactician and planner. TF 52 included transports embarking two Marine

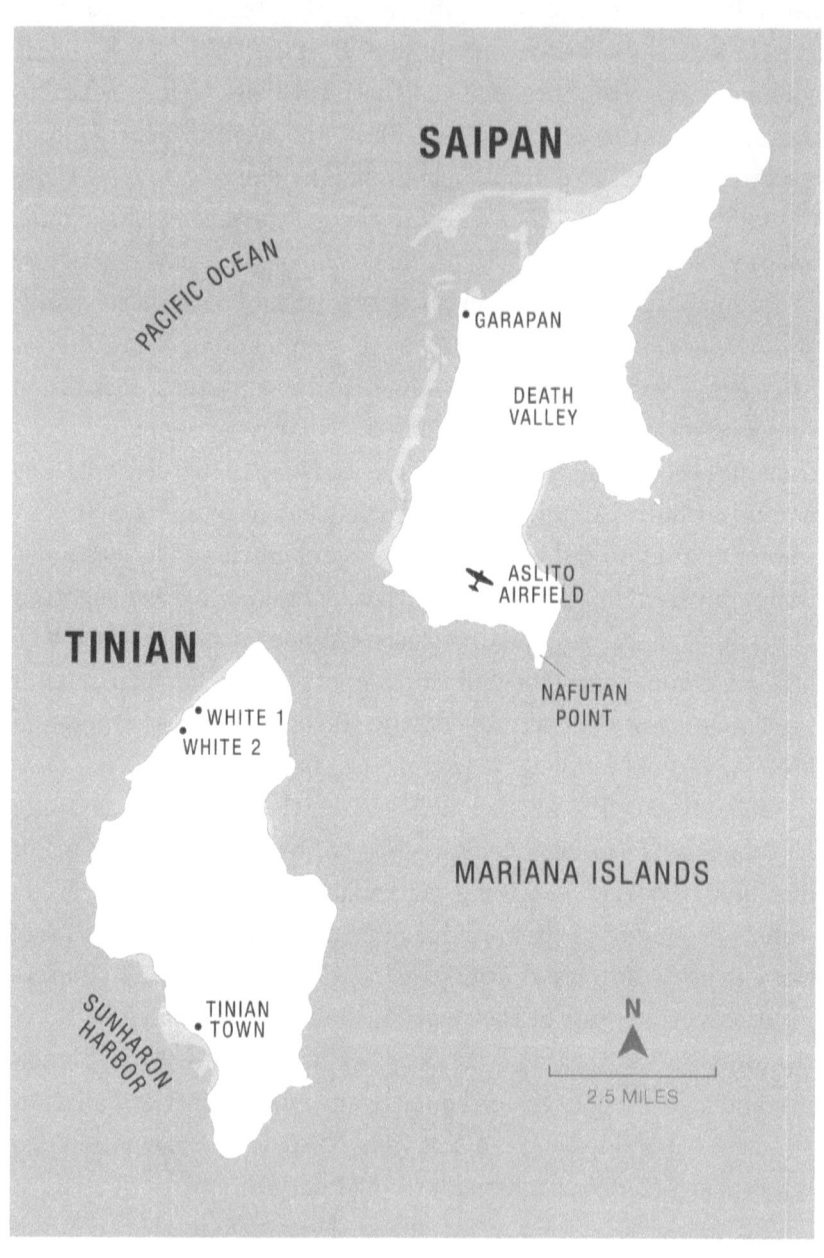

MAP 1. MARIANAS ISLANDS: SAIPAN AND TINIAN

divisions, the 2nd and the 4th, the latter under the command of Lt. Gen. H. M. Smith, known to his troops as "Howlin' Mad" Smith. Their initial mission was to seize Saipan. After its capture they would use Saipan as a base from which to launch an amphibious assault across the Tinian Channel to land on the beaches at Tinian, five miles south. There was a reserve task group that embarked the U.S. Army's 27th Infantry Division along with two Army regimental combat teams. TF 52 included the amphibious transports (converted commercial cargo ships fitted out to carry troops) and LSTs, which would land over the beach the heavy tracked vehicles, such as tanks and bulldozers, as well as large trucks with prepackaged ammunition and supplies. There were also more than a dozen supply ships loaded with combat consumables to support the troops ashore. These included food, petroleum products (including oil and lubricants), ammunition (both artillery and carried weapons), and medical supplies, plus tentage, toothpaste, and everything else needed to support an invasion force of over 60,000 American troops (two Marine divisions totaling 45,000 men and the Army 27th Division with 16,000 soldiers).

The amphibious ships and supply ships of TF 52 were screened—provided with antiaircraft and ASW protection—by destroyers, of which there were two squadrons of nine each plus a "bobtailed" squadron of six, for a total of twenty-four. The destroyers would fill numerous roles. During the transit to the assault area they would form a circular screen around the transport and support force. Once the transports anchored in the transport and support area the destroyers would be dispersed to other duties. One squadron would remain in the transport area for close protection. The other would be dispersed on radar picket duty north and south of Saipan to warn of incoming enemy air raids. The bulk of the destroyers would be used for shore bombardment, both preparation "fires" prior to the landings, and then as floating field artillery to provide close support "on call" for the troops ashore engaged with the Japanese.

The final component of TF 52 was the fire-support group. This task group was to conduct heavy bombardment prior to the landings and support major ground offensives. It consisted of seven battleships, four of which had been sunk on December 7 in Pearl Harbor and since resurrected—refloated, repaired, modernized, completely overhauled, manned with new crews, and sent forward. They lacked the electronics and speed, by several knots, needed to operate with the fast carrier striking forces. Their big guns (two of the battleships—*Maryland* [BB 46] and *Colorado* [BB 45]—were equipped with 16-inch rifles, the others with 14-inch) could be devastating to targets ashore.[3]

These old battleships (OBBs) had trained extensively in Hawaii in shore bombardment at Kahoolawe in the Hawaiian Islands, and some of them had seen action during the invasion of the Marshall Islands. Along with these seven battleships were six heavy cruisers and five light cruisers. These were generally prewar-built ships that lacked the stamina and sophisticated fire-control equipment of the new-construction cruisers in TF 58. There were a total of twenty-six destroyers in TF 52, more than half of them modern *Fletcher*-class ships. Additional TF 52 surface ships included fleet tugs to tow battle-damaged vessels. There were also four-stack destroyers that had been converted to high-speed assault transports (APDs) for the underwater demolition teams (UDTs). Some four-stack destroyers had been converted to seaplane tenders, their internal spaces rearranged with tankage for high-octane aviation gasoline (thereby making them probably the most hazardous vessels afloat). There were some LSTs converted for special use for the assault and for the resupply phase.

Casualties, always of concern to the ground force, had been very carefully thought about. After treatment by corpsmen in the field, casualties were to be carried to collection points on the beach, from where they were moved on board a beached LST for medical attention from surgeons and other doctors. From the LSTs, which rotated onto the beach and out to the transport anchorage, casualties were shifted to transports that had been fitted out with operating rooms and rudimentary wards.

Intelligence indicated that there were about 32,000 Japanese troops on Saipan. Some of them were reputedly the finest in the Japanese order of battle (including the division known honorifically as the "emperor's own"), Japanese marines, and other experienced units that had fought in China. Also, Saipan was the first territory for which American troops would fight that could be considered Japanese; this gave the defenders great incentive to resist. Inhabitants of Saipan were treated as Japanese citizens. They were loyal to the emperor, which meant that they could cause problems behind the lines as the troops went forward. The commander of the Japanese forces was one of Japan's better generals.[4] Subsequent information indicates that he believed his forces would have not much trouble preventing the U.S. force from landing. If it did gain a foothold on Saipan, he would be able to chop it to pieces and drive it into the sea. Furthermore, his view was somewhat reflected in Tokyo, where the Imperial General Staff felt that Saipan could be held. After the first indications of a U.S. assault, the high command began sending reinforcements and a relief force to the Marianas.

The original plan for the assault involved the 2nd and 4th Marine Divisions with over 20,000 Marines landing on the southwest coast of Saipan, securing a beachhead, and then capturing Aslito Airfield near the middle of the island. That would cut Saipan in half, thus separating the two groups of Japanese defenders. A secure beachhead and control of the air and surface threat would ensure the security of the transports and supply ships while they put the troops and combat consumables ashore. The Army's 27th Division then would conduct an administrative landing (i.e., unopposed by enemy fire). The 27th Division would move into line abreast of the Marines. Together they would push northward to take the northern half of Saipan. That would be the most difficult part of the campaign, because of a towering landmass, or mountain, Mount Tapochau, that dominated the topography and in which had been dug all kinds of earthworks to slow the advance of the infantrymen, such as trenches, caves, tunnels, and hidden gun emplacements.

As had become standard, the invasion force had its own carrier support in the "Taffy" groups, each of which was centered on one or two CVEs operating FM-2 Wildcat fighters.[5] The FM-2 Wildcats were critical to the defense of the invasion force, as they represented the only air cover for the amphibious and replenishment ships, which had minimal self-defense capability. These slightly armed CVEs and amphibious ships were defended by destroyers such as *Bennion* and by the combat air patrol (CAP) of Wildcats under the radio control of designated destroyers, one of which was *Bennion*. Only three of the task force's destroyers were equipped for fighter direction. This capability had been built into *Bennion* just prior to her departure from Boston. It consisted of converting the division commander's cabin and head into a small CIC-like room able to support two fighter/director officers, two talkers, and banks of very-high-frequency (VHF) voice radio equipment with which to communicate with the fighters.

SAIPAN ASSAULT OVERVIEW

The operation kicked off on the June 11, 1944, when the F6Fs, TBMs, and dive-bombers of TF 58 pounded Japanese installations on Saipan that had been identified by Navy PB4Y Liberators. These reconnaissance planes had overflown the island the week before on a very dangerous mission to get the latest photography. The Navy PB4Ys had flown from bases more than a thousand miles away through areas regularly patrolled by Japanese fighters to get this essential data. After three days of strikes, joined on the 13th by shore bombardment from the fast battleships and new cruisers, two of the four task groups of TF 58 proceeded northward toward the Volcano Islands to pound Japanese bases there in order to deter the sending of reinforcements. The surface ships of TF 58 dealt Saipan a wallop as they went by on June 13, but according to historical records their bombardment was not very effective. Their gunners had not been trained or had not practiced shore bombardment. As a result, the shore defenses were essentially intact when TF 52 arrived to conduct its prelanding bombardment and then close-in fire support.[6]

On June 14, TF 52 arrived and seven older battleships commenced bombardment from about four thousand yards out to sea. The destroyers went in to a thousand yards to hit with their 5-inch guns "emergent" targets—that is, "targets of opportunity," not preplanned but picked up "by eyeball." Almost immediately *Braine* (DD 630), a *Fletcher*-class destroyer, was hit by counterbattery fire from nearby Tinian and sustained a number of casualties. However, her CO kept her in position, firing away at the Japanese guns that were shooting at him, until he received orders to retire.[7]

The American fire was very deliberate. Each of the "heavies"— battleships and cruisers—fired its main-battery guns one round at a time, noted the fall of the shot, and then adjusted fire to register on their assigned target. Each had a ship-based floatplane to spot their gunfire. These OS2U and SOC pontoon aircraft were carried on battleships and cruisers and launched by catapult to fly over the objective area. The parent ship told them by radio when it had fired a round or a salvo, and by measuring time of flight the spotting aircraft was able to identify its ship's round as it exploded in the target area. With the number of ships firing at about the same time in adjacent areas, this took considerable coordination. However, these battleships and cruisers had spent much time training with their observation aircraft, because shore bombardment was going to be their principal mission in these operations. Mission time for the spotting aircraft was roughly three and a half to four hours. After that the spotting aircraft landed in a relatively sheltered area on the leeward side of Saipan close to a four-piper destroyer converted to aviation gasoline tanker and assigned to refuel the cruisers' and battleships' floatplanes. After the final flight of the day—spotting was impractical at night—the OS2Us/SOCs landed beside their parent ships, were hoisted on board, and placed on the ship's catapults for maintenance, refueling and rearming, and maintenance in preparation for launch at first light the next morning.

Occasionally a Wildcat or a TBM from a Taffy carrier squadron was pressed into service as a spotting aircraft. However, it was apparent to us on *Bennion* from listening to the exchange of transmissions on the gunfire spotting web that this was relatively inefficient. Carrier pilots had not been trained for spotting, and they had not worked with the fire-control people on the battleships and cruisers before. The clumsy old pontoon seaplanes, as ridiculous as they might appear circling the beach and dodging the flak, were by far the most effective means of adjusting fire in the absence of gunfire liaison people ashore with the troops. In any case, the carrier attack aircraft were not available until after the Marines hit the beach.

Bennion's initial assignment for the invasion was as part of Task Group 52.15, a protective screen for one of the transport groups.[8] We arrived off Saipan during the dawn hours of June 15, 1944, and our mission was "preparation" gunfire against any targets of opportunity that might develop.

INVASION: OVER THE BEACH

When the sun came up on June 15, *Bennion* had a front-row seat to observe the initial exchange of gunfire between our bombardment group and the Japanese defenders. We were immediately impressed at how handsome an island Saipan appeared to be. It was mountainous in the north, hilly in the middle and flat at its southern end. The entire island was covered with vegetation, ranging from cane fields in the flat areas to semitropical trees and shrubbery over the rest of the island, with the exception of some craggy areas near the tops of the two small mountains.

14 & 15. Destroyers conducting shore bombardment at Saipan in the Marianas
Official U.S. Navy photos, courtesy Fred Freeman Collection, U.S. Naval Institute photo archive, and Naval Heritage and History Command

Of special note were the underwater demolition teams (UDTs). A day before our arrival, their swimmers climbed out of the water onto rocks and reefs, planted explosives, then swam back out to sea. Next they detonated these charges to clear the way for the amphibious craft that would be moving to the landing beaches with Marines on board.

An interesting footnote on the UDTs relates to Cdr. Draper Kauffman, who graduated with the Naval Academy Class of 1933 but could not be commissioned because of bad eyes. Kauffman then volunteered to serve with the British in London as a bomb-disposal officer; there he became an expert in demolition and bomb disposal. To Kauffman goes credit for developing, virtually single-handedly, a concept: the tactics training, and operations of the UDTs in the Pacific in World War II.[9]

Bennion, together with the other eight destroyers of DesRon 56, screened the transport formations from possible Japanese

16. Underwater demolition team members working just off Saipan Beach. Note men paddling a rubber raft. Photographed by Cdr. Bonnie Powell.
Naval History and Heritage Command

submarines. At the same time, *Bennion* controlled a CAP of six to ten FM-2 Wildcat fighters launched from the Taffy groups of CVEs assigned to provide air cover for both Task Force 52 and the landing force.

As the gunnery officer, my duty station during General Quarters during the amphibious assault was in the Mark 37 director. There I alternated between using the naked eye to take in the big picture and focusing on the beach through the range finder, which had ten-power magnification. The range finder and director operators had the best view of the island of anyone on *Bennion*. It was easy to pick out the farmhouses, which were Japanese style, and the villages of Japanese houses made of bamboo and paper design with their shingled roofs. We could very clearly see any individual who might be moving from his dwelling to an outhouse or barn and could see the cattle in the fields as they strolled around, oblivious to the whistling of the shells passing over them.

H-hour was 8:30 a.m. An hour and a half before the assault was to begin, the bombardment group cut loose with virtually unrestrained fire, and overhead the Wildcats and TBMs from the Taffy group assaulted the beach and the areas just behind it with bombs and rockets, delivered in forty-degree dives. As we watched a TBM was hit by antiaircraft fire, burst into flames, lost its left wing, cartwheeled through the air trailing fire smoke and pieces, and crashed into the Japanese positions just beyond the beach.

THE ASSAULT

To our east and north were the Saipan beaches, virtually obscured by smoke and dust from the impact of 14- and 16-inch shells and 500-pound bombs. To our north and west almost as far as the eye could reach were the ships of the invasion force. The transports were anchored, and Marines were climbing down their sides on netting into LCVPs (landing craft vehicle, personnel). As each landing craft filled up with Marines it departed for a rendezvous area where the LCVPs circled, emitting great clouds of noxious exhaust fumes that combined with the choppy waters to make most of the Marines seasick.

Interspersed among the transports were LSTs, under way "with no way on" (stopped, not anchored). Their bow doors were open, and they were launching amphibious tractors (LVTs, sometimes called "amtracs"), armored vehicles that could float and, ashore, protect their occupants. The LVTs drove down the ramps of the LSTs. From the well decks of landing ship docks (LSDs) now issued LCUs (landing craft utility). Each of them carried a Marine tank plus several smaller caissons or jeeps loaded with ammunition and supplies that would be urgently needed on the beach. As we looked out at the ocean to the west, we saw a sea dotted with fifty large commercial cargo ships, amphibious ships, and support vessels. It was hard to realize that this force carried roughly 42,000 Marines not yet landed plus their vehicles, armor, ammunition, water, food, and medical supplies for the next fifteen days. It all had to be gotten ashore in twelve hours, sorted out, and delivered to the fighting men up forward. What a job.

At 0820 it was clear to us in the director of *Bennion* that the landing would be on time. We could see hundreds of landing craft disposed in three or four lines parallel to the beach behind the line of departure (LOD). The LOD was marked by two patrol boats anchored two miles apart and identified by very large banners as the two ends of the starting line. As if by magic, suddenly all the roar of artillery ceased. There was one more attack by Navy dive-bombers and strafers, then silence from the roar of aircraft engines also. The landing craft passed over the LOD, and the invasion of Saipan was under way.[10]

As we watched and listened, we heard now the staccato fire of automatic weapons and the crump of artillery and mortar rounds as the Japanese on the beach fired their rifles and machine guns and their artillery and mortar batteries let go. The shot was clearly falling amongst the landing craft—we could see the splashes. They didn't look very dangerous until we saw the first hit, which kicked up a lot of debris and black smoke from the stricken LCU, which circled out of control in the approach lane. As we watched we could see another landing craft, an LCVP, steer erratically or go out of control, an indication that the coxswain had been hit or had for a moment been disconcerted by the enemy fire that was kicking up the water around the boats.

There were eight landing beaches, designated by numbers and colors; each landing craft had to land at a specific beach. We saw that the tide was setting the entire wave to the southward. It was with some relief that we realized the coxswains recognized this and were headed for their designated areas. There was normally a naval officer in each landing craft responsible for navigating the boat into its proper landing spot, because tide and wind could blow it off course. Also, there was a natural reaction, when your assigned landing area was bristling with machine-gun and artillery fire, to attempt to "cheat" a little bit and get on the edges of that landing beach rather than steam right into the mouth of the cannons. From our position it appeared that the landing was going well.

We could see the numbers of craft coming into every one of the landing beaches were balanced, which indicated that no beaches would be overcrowded or areas in the front neglected. As the boats came in they were required to follow certain lanes, because the UDT personnel had blasted paths through the coral for the deeper-draft landing craft, such as the LCUs and landing craft infantry (LCI) rocket-firing ships, to enable them to get into water shallow enough to discharge their loads.

Sitting in the director watching with high-magnification glasses the Marines hit the beach was a heart-wrenching experience for me, sitting in the relative safety of the director. We were ready to provide whatever help we could with our 5-inch guns, but these men we could see coming down the bow ramps of their landing craft were staggering under heavy loads on their backs. It was not only their personal gear but also the disassembled pieces of machine guns and mortars. We watched them struggle up the beach in sort of a cross between a dogtrot and fast walk, with their rifles at the ready or at the hip firing away at the fringe of the tree line on the land side of the beach. We knew that what these people were doing would take the lives of many of them. In the director, we were relieved to see most of the Marines make it across the open beach and into the shrubbery of the tree line. We watched the second and third waves come ashore with the jeeps, the trucks with ammunition, the tanks, and the amtracs. It was about this time that *Bennion* was directed to proceed to the other side of the island. As we left our vantage point at the southern terminus of the landing beach I observed artillery shells and mortar rounds falling on the beach in the vicinity of the trucks and stores and dumps that were already being piled up ashore—an ominous sign.

JAPANESE AIR ATTACKS

Late on June 15, the main body of TF 52 retired to the west. Here our mission was mainly fighter direction of the Wildcats over the amphibious ships to protect that force from Japanese aircraft moving into the area from Mindanao, Yap, Guam, and even Tinian.

That evening four enemy planes, likely from Tinian, made it over the transport group. *Bennion*, along with nearly every other ship in the vicinity, let loose a barrage of AA fire. Our war diary would record that there was no evidence that any of our ships had success in bringing down these intruders. However, there was also no report of any damage to the transport group. We expended forty-eight rounds of "AA common"—our first shots fired in anger.

Early the next morning we again went to General Quarters (GQ) as a "lone wolf" overflew the transport group. We fired ten rounds without apparently scoring a hit. With sunrise, the transport group moved east to continue landing Marines. Late in the afternoon transports carrying the expeditionary force reserve (TG 51.1), under Rear Adm. William H. P. Blady, arrived. No time was wasted in getting elements of the Army's 27th Infantry Division ashore.

That evening the transport group again retired to the west, but then we chose not to loiter but instead to circle around both the islands, Saipan and Tinian, I suppose to evade any Japanese submarines that could have been directed to our staging area. In fact, during that night the attack transport *Waters* (APD 8) detected a submarine and was joined by *Goldsborough* (APD 32) to form a hunter-killer group that steamed toward a reported periscope sighting off Saipan's Cape Obian. Meanwhile, *Bennion* took station again off the landing beaches for air defense and air control.

That evening we observed sporadic air attacks, but most were directed toward the fast carriers and were thwarted. None came within the range of our 5-inchers.

Japanese air attacks on the 17th were so heavily attrited during their approach and their retirement that, as was clear from the lack of air activity on the 18th, they could probably not mount another attack of that size. At first light on June 19 we were surprised to see the transports and supply ships raising their anchors and getting under way. *Bennion* rejoined its colleagues in DesRon 56 and took station in the task force screen as the transports with their wounded and the only half-unloaded merchant ships proceeded through the Tinian Channel and retired at best speed in an easterly direction.

BENNION ON PICKET STATION

The reason for our departure was twofold. First, the air attacks had been alarming. Second, TF 58 ships had made contact with a large Japanese force approaching Saipan from the northwest, out of the Philippines, and the two forces were just beginning to exchange blows. The 18th was the first day of heavy fighting in the battle of the Philippine Sea, which concluded on the 19th in a major U.S. victory.[11]

While Japanese and American aircraft from opposing carrier forces engaged at sea, the fight ashore continued. On June 18 the Marines and elements of the 27th Division broke out of the beachhead and in a decisive move they cut the island in half, reaching the eastern shore of Saipan at Magicienne Bay. As the Marines and soldiers paused to consolidate, the Japanese in the southern end of the island who had been cut off by the Marines' bold advance to the east coast had to be cleaned out. This turned out to be much easier than anticipated; elements of the 27th Division, facing what had been anticipated as a foxhole-to-foxhole struggle, met minimal resistance. Few of the expected Japanese were there, most having exfiltrated before the Marines sealed the southern end of the island, some going by small boat or swimming around the Marine lines on the east coast.

Aslito Airfield had not been badly damaged. Within a day, the Marine engineers had the runways patched up sufficiently so that the Marine liaison aircraft—similar to Piper Cubs—were able to operate. Two days later the first tactical aircraft arrived, Army P-47s. There was some concern on the part of the Army Air Forces, and the Navy as well, that there would be mistakes in identification, because the P-47 Thunderbolt resembled the Zeke version of the Japanese Zero in many ways. However, very clear "rules of engagement and approach" were established whereby the Army aircraft approached and departed Aslito in certain corridors. Also, warship crews were given a crash refresher course in aircraft recognition. I don't recall a single incident of a P-47 being shot down by "friendly" forces.

Early on June 21 the "Retirement Group," as we had been labeled, returned to Saipan, where the two divisions, Marine and Army, faced a tough struggle as they advanced northward. Anchored off landing beaches near Charan Kanoa, the transports continued to offload materiel for the troops ashore and to back-load casualties. The transports were anchored in assigned positions and destroyers were detailed to an ASW patrol and to an antiaircraft barrier.

In addition, many LCUs fitted with machine guns patrolled the anchorage. To that was added automatic-weapon fire, which seemed to be effective against low-flying Japanese planes, most of which were twin-engined land-based naval aircraft, mainly Bettys.

During this last week in June *Bennion* would shuttle between the picket station, fifty miles south of Saipan, for the nighttime and the gun line to support troops ashore. For the remainder of this chapter I will focus on our picket station duties, where we were to give advance warning to TF 52 of incoming bogeys. Gunfire support for the ground forces ashore will be covered in the following section.

Ammunition was of vital concern to Commander, TF (CTF) 52, because resupply had to come from Pearl Harbor some two thousand miles away. As a consequence, gunfire support of the troops ashore assignments was rotated among all the destroyers so that no one ship would run out of ammunition. Some had to be retained for the ship's self-defense in case of a breakthrough of Japanese surface forces or against a determined attack by Japanese aircraft.

Bennion's magazines held about 2,500 projectiles of various categories and the same number of powder cans. The distribution of projectiles was approximately as follows:

- Ten percent VT fuzed (variable timed fuzed), the fuze being a small radar that detonated the shell at its closest proximity to an aircraft. This was also known as "proximity fuzed ammunition." It was used only against air targets.

- Five percent star shells. This percentage was increased as the campaigns in the Pacific progressed, because of the need by the troops ashore for illumination to counter Japanese night infiltration and suicide attacks.

- Five percent armor piercing (AP). This was a holdover from the days when it was expected that our destroyers might engage Japanese armored warships at close range.

These rounds were being phased out and replaced with "AA common," which proved more effective, even against large Japanese warships, in knocking down the topside gear such as radars and periscopes, and destroying the secondary and machine-gun batteries.

- The balance of the projectile load was AA common. This 5-inch projectile weighed about fifty-four pounds, was loaded with TNT, and had both nose and base fuzes. The nose fuze was a mechanically timed device that would cause the shell to explode at a certain elapsed time, which for gunnery purposes meant a certain range from the firing ship. It was used for air bursts against air targets or occasionally, because of the devastating shrapnel effect, against troops in the open field. The mechanical fuze was constantly being set as the projectile was in the hoist just before being removed and loaded into the gun, so that at least the second round fired would detonate very accurately at the predetermined range. If the shell was to be used for shore bombardment, the nose fuze was set on infinity; the base fuze was actuated by inertia caused by the shock of the shell hitting the target, which during close support was in many cases the ground. When AA common was used against surface targets, again the nose fuze was set on infinity and the base fuze was used. That gave about a hundredth of a second's delay, which allowed the shell to penetrate into the body of the hostile ship before exploding.

It was very important that ammunition be properly managed and the proper kind of shells loaded for the assigned mission. A certain number of star shells and VT shells were kept in the upper handling room of the gun mount where they could be loaded in a hurry, since that kind of ammunition was most often used in emergencies when the ship was fighting in self-defense.

Late in the afternoon on June 25, we departed to the transport area and vectored out to Picket Station 6 on a bearing of 235 degrees true from Point Lola on Tinian at a distance of fifteen miles.

Bennion was equipped with the standard *Fletcher* fire-control system: a Mark 37 director with a Mark 12 radar. [At that time the so-called Banana Peel radar antenna had not been retrofitted to the director.] The fire-control radar, known as the Mark 4 or "FD," on the Mark 37 director was excellent for range and could be locked onto a target to give constant ranges. However, its bearing accuracy was good only to within a degree. Elevation accuracy had the same amount of error, except at very low elevations. Above seven degrees the accuracy was only plus or minus two degrees, not good enough to bring down a low-flying aircraft. Unfortunately, most of the aircraft that would attack us came in low at night, when we needed radar control. [There was no high-altitude level bombing, and the Japanese did not attempt dive-bombing at night.] Their tactics were to come in at three hundred feet or below and either drop a "stick" of bombs [several at once], in what the Aussies called "skip bombing," or attack the surface ship with a torpedo.

Our operations plan in *Bennion* was as follows. At a half hour prior to sunset, the ship would go to GQ, the crew having been fed. Usually within an hour the first bogeys would show up, our air-search radar would track them, and we would report their movements by radio to CTF 52's command ship at Saipan. Our CAP, usually from four to sixteen Wildcats, would stick with us until sunset and then streak for their home carrier (one of the CVEs) to land on board before the end of evening twilight.

Speaking of being fed, on board *Bennion* we officers had "sumptuous" dinners served with immaculate silver on white tablecloths in the wardroom by stewards in white jackets. The dinner might consist of fried slabs of bologna cut three quarters of an inch thick to resemble filet mignon, together with reconstituted powdered potatoes and with a heaping plate of canned spinach (from New Zealand, where they had not yet learned the art of canning). We had reasonably good bread, baked on board, but ruined with the pure white-oil margarine designed in an Army laboratory so that it would not melt in the ambient temperatures of the tropics. Nor would it melt whatever heat was applied to it! It was referred to as "wax" by the galley, but we in the wardroom mess referred to it as "the butter."

Having gone to General Quarters at twilight, we slowed our speed to fifteen knots having arrived at our picket station to the south. The crew was tired, having been at GQ much of the day, and now we would be up all night. We had to do something to ease this routine. Here's what we did. We relaxed our General Quarters regimen when there were no bogeys on the screen and allowed the men to go to the heads—that in its own way was difficult, because with Watertight Condition Zebra set most of the overboard drains were closed. Also, a few people were sent to the galley to pick up buckets of coffee and take them back to the battle stations, where each member of the crew seemed to have his own coffee mug. That cup of Joe was essential for alertness. Also, when we were in transit the ship went to Condition Three, in which two sections were secured from General Quarters and only one third of the main battery was manned. Until we began picking up bogeys about half the men on each GQ station would doze while their companions remained alert. No one ever asked for permission to do this—nor was it ever suggested that it was permissible—but by now our crew members were totally responsible and understood what their duties were, and they were the best judges probably of how to husband their energy during these twenty-hour alerts.

We were informed that there would be no friendly air cover for us that night. We were on our own. About 2000 the activity began with Japanese aircraft coming up from the south, initially at between ten and fifteen thousand feet and not showing any interest in *Bennion* or the picket station. Thus that first night at Picket Station 6 proved uneventful, and at dawn we steamed back to the transport group and then were sent back around the east side of the island for naval gunfire support.

At 1530 we were detached from our fire-support station and proceeded to our previously assigned picket station. The senior fighter/director officer burst out of his control room just as I was being relieved as officer of the deck to go below for chow. That officer reported to our captain (who was in his chair in the pilothouse) that we were being assigned an Army P-61 night fighter that evening. A squadron of Army Air Forces P-47 Thunderbolts had been operating out of Aslito for the past week, and sufficient auxiliary night lighting and communications had been installed on the single runway to permit operations by the P-61s at night.

The Army night fighter would report to *Bennion* for control. We could expect to have night fighters at our disposal from sunset to sunrise, as the squadron gained familiarity with the operations and the crews became qualified for night operations out of Aslito. It was a primitive arrangement at this airfield, with the runways and support facilities within range of Japanese artillery. However, the shooting from the Japanese was only sporadic, because the Marine 2nd and 4th Divisions had already secured the southern heights of Mount Tapochau, the dominating terrain in the center of the island, from which the most effective Japanese field artillery fire had been directed.

While there had been little enemy air activity on the 25th, on the nights of the 26th and again on the 27th as many as a dozen Bettys made it to the transport area. These attacks on TF 52 came from the south. These aircraft and those in subsequent raids appeared on *Bennion*'s radarscope as they overflew the island of Rota—a mere forty-five miles distant—which they were evidently using for a navigation landmark. Typically in these raids the first bogeys showed up about an hour after our CAP had departed; sometimes they flew directly over us, on other occasions they seemed to jog around us. They knew we were there but their orders apparently were to get the transports and "softer" ships at Saipan. There would be some exceptions. Normally, there would be two or three raids in the early evening and for some reason we never seemed to pick them up on their return flights. Perhaps they were flying to the north, or perhaps there were no survivors.

On that first night one Betty was brought down by a cargo ship when the plane ran into the freighter's cargo mast. With a great display of fire, the plane crashed into the sea.[12]

For us GQ sounded at about 1730 and it was dark by 1800. At 1830 CIC reported that "Black Widow 21" was overhead at ten thousand feet and had reported to *Bennion* for control. It was just in time. By 1930 we had our expected blips on the southern horizon at about 16,000 yards as the Bettys arrived on schedule. That aircraft was taking part in one of the seven different raids we tracked coming from the direction of Rota in the hours after dusk leading to midnight. On two of those raids we were able to vector the Army fighter against the approaching bogey, chasing the enemy plane out of the area. The Japanese on Rota perhaps having determined our role as the fighter-director ship, during the fifth raid about an hour before midnight a lone aircraft turned to attack us. When this bogey came within 6,500 yards we let loose with our main battery, expending fifty-eight rounds of AA common in short order. We recorded no hits, but at four thousand yards out the enemy pilot turned away and retired toward Rota.

At about 2100, however, we were tracking an apparent Betty, a single inbound plane that at about ten miles to our south changed course to head in directly for us. The Betty started its cat-and-mouse maneuvers of flying toward us then turning ninety degrees to stay just outside of our gun range, drop to a low altitude, and then pop up again on a different part of the horizon. This Betty, however, seemed to know what it was doing; after the third aborted approach it dropped down so low we had it only intermittently on the horizon and headed straight for us. The commanding officer increased our speed to twenty-five knots to make us a fast-moving target, and of course we had been at General Quarters for the past two hours. The Betty settled down at what appeared to be about five hundred feet and did not deviate from its course directly toward *Bennion*.

This time we had no friendlies in the area to worry about. When at 16,000 yards I reported that we were locked on with fire-control radar and tracking, the commanding officer authorized me to commence firing when I felt the Betty was within a reasonable range. When the Betty had approached to within three miles it made a distinct turn to the left, which was surprising, because that had it running parallel to our course and enabled all five guns to continue to bear. By now we could see the outline of the Betty as a black blob in our ten-power range finder optics and actually see the flickering of the exhaust from her inboard engine. We opened fire. Suddenly we saw our own shells exploding in the plane's vicinity and given the small field of our optics we knew those bursts had to be very close.

Almost immediately, we saw a larger flicker of flame and then a streak of orange fire that must have extended fifty feet behind the Betty, which was now clearly identifiable from the light of the gasoline flames. Our main battery continued to pump out 5-inch shells, because we did not want this one to get away. There was another burst of flames, due to probably an explosion of a gas tank on board, and showers of sparks and burning pieces joined the trail of gasoline flames. Then suddenly the Betty hit the water and our director, which had been tracking the plane at a high rate of traverse [sideways movement], suddenly overshot—the Betty had suddenly stopped on impact on the water. We trained back to see nothing but a slick of burning fuel on the water that petered out in less than a minute. *Bennion* slowed to fifteen knots and approached the site of the crash, for no reason other than to mark its spot geographically. We saw nothing but an oil slick and some identifiable debris in the water before the presence of two more bogey blips on the radar consumed our attention.

There were other enemy aircraft in our vicinity that night but no others came within firing range or seemed to be interested in making an attack on the picket ship. This was *Bennion*'s first kill of the war and I cannot say that there was any special feeling of exhilaration; we were just grateful that we had destroyed the Betty and not vice versa. We would later believe we had actually shot down at least three others in these night encounters, when we fired on approaching Bettys, could see our shells bursting, and the radar blips disappeared from our radarscope while the target was still inbound. But the rules of the game were that the plane had to be seen hitting the water or ground.

No time for celebration—just before midnight another bogey came within eight thousand yards by the time we came up with a good firing solution. Our five 5-inch/38s. pumped out 106 rounds of AA common before the enemy aircraft came within seven thousand yards and decided to hightail it out of there with a steep climb. This bogey then proceeded northward, where a P-61 under the control of the command ship *Rocky Mount* [one of several such conversions from merchant ships] was vectored to make the interception. On our air-search radar screen we watched the two blips merge and then disappear. I suspect there was a sudden loss of elevation.

Things quieted down past midnight, and at dawn we returned to the plotted position of the crash. As a demonstration of the excellence of our quartermasters' dead-reckoning track, we found some debris in the water, including of all things a toilet seat that the crew begged the captain to let them recover. Josh Cooper felt that a scatological trophy was better than none at all so we put a whaleboat in the water, recovered it, and the crew made a picture frame of it with [Emperor] Hirohito's portrait in the center.

We again steamed back to Saipan to moor off the invasion beaches to go alongside replenishment ships and take on fuel and stores. It was a pretty wild time for the transports and the supply ships in the support shipping anchorage area. They continued to offload supplies from the cargo ships, send them ashore, and backload personnel casualties into the transports. That evening we again returned to Picket Station 6.

It did not take long for a bogey to appear. Just before 1900 *Bennion* directed an apparently successful interception; we watched two blips on our screen merge and stay merged for seven minutes. But alas, our pilot could not spot his enemy, as the aircraft were at different altitudes. A half hour later we vectored our assigned aircraft against another bogey. Again blips merged—this time for six minutes—again no contact. Minutes later we picked up an enemy aircraft returning from a run over Saipan and he chose to come at us from due north. At 2015 with a good computer solution at six thousand yards we commenced fire, rapidly expending sixty-two rounds of AA common. A bit unnerving—as we fended off this bogey a second intruder overflew us, having approached at low altitude. He went on to complete his return leg to Rota.

A well-organized flight of Bettys passed over *Bennion* at about 2100 and arrived at the transport anchorage in time to be greeted, thanks to timely warning, by an effective barrage from the screening destroyers, and in spite of a great deal of activity, no U.S. ships were hit.

An hour later we detected a pair of aircraft closing from a distance beyond Rota, likely a raid from Guam. At 2142 we took the inbound bogeys under fire. One turned left and made a beeline to Rota. I think we nailed the second one. We expended eighty-two rounds. Fifteen minutes later we picked out a low flyer only three thousand yards out. Another forty-five rounds of steel failed to bring down this enemy aviator, who overflew us without firing a shot.

For the rest of the evening and into the early morning, our FD radar tracked Japanese aircraft heading to and from Saipan. No further runs were made on us. At daylight we again returned to the transport area to replenish our ammunition and other stores. On the evening of June 28 *Bennion* was assigned to the outer screen of the transport group to provide ASW cover. That night, I recall, when an air raid did come the transports produced enough smoke to obscure the landing area. Raiding Japanese aircraft were not able to achieve any success and I believe one of our shore batteries was able to knock down one of the attackers. We did not expend any AA rounds that night. Before dawn on the 29th, however, we did fire three depth charges at a dubious undersea contact—not that we had fixed a location but instead to disrupt a possible attack. Another destroyer and destroyer escort, having hunter-killer experience, rushed out to continue the search but came up empty.

That day we refueled in the morning and resumed our ASW station in the afternoon. At 1552 we made an underwater sound contact at 1,900 yards. Twelve minutes later we dropped eleven depth charges over the side at a medium depth setting. We continued to search, only to conclude we again may have killed off a lot of fish.

The next twenty-four hours, the last day of the month, proved uneventful. In the evening we again detected incoming bogeys. A P-61 was vectored to intercept one flight of three aircraft and from my perch in the fire-control director I watched one of the bogeys burst into flame and spiral down to the ocean surface. Nine raids materialized that evening but none of the enemy aircraft came in range.

From then on the size of the raids coming up from the south diminished, but what was worse for *Bennion*, the aircraft began showing a greater interest in the picket ships. By early July the Japanese planes were not only slipping around our position but attempting torpedo attacks on us. Such was the case during the early hours of July 2, *Bennion* having returned to Picket.

Two Bettys arrived and first laid a pattern of floats in the water in a straight line in our vicinity. Then a second Betty dropped five or six flares in what appeared to be a line about ten thousand feet up. Neither of these seemed to have any significance in terms of their orientation, nor were they in our immediate vicinity. Of course, *Bennion* was maneuvering at twenty-five knots all the time these aircraft were laying out their patterns. Finally, after about forty-five minutes of flying various courses just outside our effective gun range, the two Bettys dropped down to a low altitude, and it was clear that they were homing in on *Bennion* either by visual means or by their rudimentary radars.

Our air-search radar was continually sweeping, giving us a picture of all the air activity in our vicinity, but the fire-control radar could only track one bogey at a time. Therefore, I would swing the director around to engage the most threatening target, maintaining a lock on that plane so that if it did initiate an attack we would get a fire-control solution on it well before it got into torpedo-launching range.

We were taking our cues from our combat information center, where air-search radar was tracking the two sets of bogeys, which were flying around our ship in ever-tighter circles. Now the picture began to get slightly confused. CIC usually provided the range and bearing of the most threatening bogey to the Mark 37 director operator. He would train our fire-control radar to that bearing and attempt to pick up the target. Sometimes we could and sometimes we could not. Transferring target information from CIC's search radars to the fire-control systems was an imperfect science. This was because the search radars had no height-finding device and could supply simply a compass bearing.

The Mark 37 fire-control radar had a very narrow beam both in bearing and in elevation, so our technique was to swing to the bearing CIC gave us and then elevate and depress the fire-control radar on that azimuth, direction, in an attempt to pick up a blip. The problems were threefold. The first was the resolution of the air-search radar was accurate only to within three or four degrees. Then there was the difficulty of having no elevation or altitude information. Finally, the fire-control radar had distinct gaps in its ability to pick up a target (such as, we might be blind between ten and thirteen degrees elevation and between twenty and twenty-four, and perhaps from forty to forty-five). These gaps in our coverage were due to reflections of our radar's "side lobes" from the surface of the water, which would cancel out returns from aircraft.

Consequently, during the night we knew the Japanese were out there, we saw their flares and float lights, and sometimes we could track them and get a good lock-on and other times we were just probing like a finger in the dark hoping for a green blip on the oscilloscope. All this resulted in tension between gunnery and the bridge, because the bridge personnel could hear the engines of the planes coming in. They would ask us if we had a lock-on. Quite often we did not, and of course the question was, "Why not? You have a radar and optics but you can't locate the target while we can hear him with our own ears?" Fortunately, I had explained the situation to the captain, who was astute enough to understand and not harass us unduly. Other destroyer gunnery officers I talked to who had more nervous and less tolerant COs confessed they came close to screaming imprecations back through the 21MC, the loudspeaker intercom between the director and the captain's station.

On this occasion, when the two bogeys had drawn their noose within six thousand yards, we opened fire. We could not visually see any hits, and the air-search radar quickly tracked what we determined to be Bettys circling at a distance of 20,000 yards. Having probed us, the two bogeys turned and came right at us flying parallel about a thousand yards apart at about three hundred feet off the ocean surface. Our main battery took both aircraft under fire when they closed within six thousand yards and continued to fire as the two pilots turned away. The nearest target suddenly vanished from the scope of our FD radar, and lookouts claimed they could see a pall of smoke on the water. Meanwhile, our fuzed shells were detonating upon hitting the water, and we observed the second Betty machine-gunning what they mistook for our gun flashes. This aircraft escaped, and we observed it fade from our radar at a distance of twenty miles. During those early-morning hours our main battery of five guns expended 180 rounds. We were spared having to fire additional rounds against another Betty coming from the north as a P-61 had been scrambled and chased it out of the area.

The next day we returned to the transport area for antisubmarine screening and then returned to our picket station for what proved a quiet evening. The following morning, on July 3, we headed back early to escort the light cruiser *Cleveland* (CL 55) to an assigned position off Saipan where her armament of 6- and 5-inch guns could be brought to bear against the retreating Japanese ashore. We were then vectored back to Picket Station 6 having received intelligence that the Japanese had massed aircraft at Yap and Palau for a desperation raid against TF 52. Back at our post west of Tinian, our fighter-direction team maintained control of a changing combination of some twenty-eight FM-2 Wildcats and P-47 Thunderbolts, a potent blocking force. The raid never materialized.

After spending another quiet evening at our picket station, we spent our nation's birthday back at the transport area on ASW duty and then hightailed it back to Picket Station 6 expecting the Japanese might oblige us with an evening of fireworks. Again, a quiet evening, and at 1500 the next day we were relieved by the destroyer *Bryant* (DD 665) and dispatched to Picket Station 5, which placed us twenty-one miles east southeast of Aquijan, a tiny island off the tip of Tinian.

Our reward for shifting picket stations would be an immediate pickup in activity. On the evening of the 5th we tracked and reported on two raids targeting Saipan, five to seven inbound bogeys on the second raid and perhaps three to five on the outbound leg.

The following night would be particularly memorable. At about 2000 we picked up a bogey at a distance of six miles at an altitude of about five hundred feet. Our Mark 37 radar operator had a good lock-on in train (azimuth) and an off-and-on lock-on in elevation (which was to be expected) and excellent ranges. All this information was automatically being fed to *Bennion*'s Mark 1 computer in the plotting room. The target was tracking directly inbound, headed for *Bennion* at the speed of about 270 knots that was characteristic of the twin-engined Betty. I reported to the captain that we were tracking the target, had a lock-on and a solution, and were ready to fire. However, this time I recommended we not open fire until the target reached a range of four thousand yards or turned away—whichever occurred first. At four thousand yards we would be able to sense that the attackers were committed and in any case would not have an opportunity to take evasive action.

At about four thousand yards the CO said, "Do not fire. I say again, do not fire." My finger loosened on the brass pistol handle that held the trigger that would set all five main-battery guns blazing away in automatic at a rate of about fifteen rounds per gun per minute. By now the bogey was at two thousand yards headed right for us. *Bennion* was making a very sharp turn toward the target in order to force a last-minute adjustment in his torpedo or bombing run, and at one thousand yards I held the bogey visually. It was a moonless night with heavy tropical cumulus clouds covering 70 percent of the sky, so the bogey appeared even in our ten-power scopes as just a dark blob blocking out stars as it moved between clouds. I called the bridge on the intercom, something that I did not normally do. I also went through the sound-powered telephone talkers but I wanted the captain to hear my voice, because I recommended that he clear the main batteries to open fire immediately, that the bogey was definitely headed for an attack on *Bennion*. The captain came back without any excitement but in a positive voice that I well understood was based on a firm decision on his part: "Negative, negative. Do not, I repeat do not fire any weapons"—and that was that. As the bogey approached, it was apparent that it would fly almost directly over *Bennion* and at an altitude of three hundred feet. Even in the darkness we could identify the aircraft. More than that, we could identify *both*, because directly behind the Betty was a distinctive, twin-boom P-61 Black Widow night fighter! Had we fired, we would I hope have brought down the Betty but more probably the P-61.

This had been a close call. We came very close to shooting down a friendly. In war many people on both sides are killed, mostly by the enemy but a few by "friendly fire." That is a tragic reality of war. My Naval Academy roommate, Fred Gressard, was serving as assistant gunnery officer on the original *Fletcher* (DD 445), the "name ship" of the class, a ship whose performance and survival in the early days of the Pacific War were legendary. In 1942 off Guadalcanal, during the hectic operations around the island when the Japanese surface forces were blowing U.S. cruisers and destroyers out of the water and Japanese battleships were shelling Henderson Field on a nightly basis, *Fletcher*'s CO ordered the gunnery officer to commence firing at a plane crossing the stern of the destroyer that the gunnery officer had identified as friendly. The CO believed it was making a run on *Fletcher*, and the plane was shot down.

It was a Marine SBD Dauntless dive-bomber with the wheels lowered making an approach for a landing on Henderson Field. It was the wheels-down configuration that convinced the commanding officer that the plane was a Japanese Val dive-bomber, which had fixed landing gear. The captain of *Fletcher* was so overwhelmed by his guilt that while his superiors chalked it up to the "fog of battle," he had a nervous breakdown and had to be relieved of his command of *Fletcher*.[13]

It taught us on *Bennion* a lesson. After all the bogeys had gone home and our fighter cover—one lucky P-61—had returned to the Aslito airstrip having shot down the Betty, the captain called me down to the bridge, where the CIC officer (the ship's exec) and the fighter/director officer joined us. What we had to do was to develop procedures whereby the fighter/director officer kept CIC better informed about the locations of friendlies under his control. CIC could then maintain an up-to-date plot of both friendlies and hostiles in the area and ensure that the gunnery people were never directed to engage a target on the bearing of a friendly aircraft.

As the evening progressed, CIC tracked the progress of several small raid attempts on Saipan well beyond our range. And then, just before midnight, we picked up a bogey at fifteen miles distant closing at a speed of 170 knots. At seven thousand yards I could see the bogey through the director optics. At five thousand yards we opened fire—our shells burst short. Seeing what he was in for, the pilot banked hard right and dove, picking up speed, and then cleared the area. We stopping firing when he was beyond ten thousand yards, having expended seventy-eight rounds.

Dawn on July 7 brought us back to the transport area, where we replenished our ammunition and turned over spent shell casings to the ammunition ship *Mazama*. We then relieved *Bryant* at Picket Station 6 and that evening tracked what we could only think were "hecklers" aiming to keep the crews of TF 52 ships from getting a good night's sleep. We got off eighteen rounds at one of these bogeys that came to within ten thousand yards, with nominal effect except that the aircraft turned toward Rota. Some of these probing bogeys were shot down by our night fighters. However, one bogey on his return flight before midnight approached well within gun range. When this aircraft passed to within five thousand yards of us, we opened fire, quickly discharging seventy-five rounds of AA common. This pilot banked right and cleared us, making for Rota. At twelve miles distant he suddenly disappeared from all our radars.

As the ground forces ashore made progress to reach the northernmost tip of Saipan, we would continue patrolling at our assigned picket station until *Bryant* relieved us on the morning of July 9. We then headed to the transport area to get a gulp of black oil from the tanker *Gemsbork* (IX [miscellaneous] 117) and then we were sent on to the other side of Tinian to Picket Station 5, where for the next two evenings there was no activity. On July 11, we switched back over to Picket Station 6. Two days later we had orders to shift to Picket

Station 4 due east of Saipan. This would lead to our witnessing one of the more horrific events of World War II.

After reprovisioning on the morning of the 13th, we made our way to the picket station on a clockwise route around the north end of the island. When we came to the vicinity of Marpi Point at the northern tip of Saipan, we were absolutely appalled at what we saw. First, there were bodies in the water, becoming increasingly numerous. From the director I could count probably fifty bodies within a two-hundred-yard radius of the ship itself. These were civilians—men, women, and children—and also soldiers. We had to steam right through this floating human debris; we could identify the soldiers in their khaki uniforms, the women's long hair floating on the water, and the civilians in their traditional farmer's garb. About every fourth or fifth woman had a small child or a baby floating near her. We wondered where this sudden mass of human detritus came from, and as we got to Marpi Point it became clear.

Marpi Point is a mountain that comes down to the water's edge in a rocky cliff two or three hundred feet high. At the top of the cliff there is a gentle slope up to the blunt peak of Marpi Mountain and a road running around the cliff's edge. On the road stood numbers of civilians, entire families; they would walk to the edge of the cliff and stand there. Then as we watched a man would leap over the cliff, probably the head of a family. Children would be pushed, and then the mama-sans would follow. Maybe a dozen people would go in in a fifteen-second period, then the next group would arrive at the edge and stand there, probably making up their nerve to jump and then they too would join their ancestors.

Our only explanation was that the Japanese civilians had been told that the Americans were absolute savages and would torture and rape any civilians that they captured. We had this from our intelligence people, who had picked up leaflets written in Korean that had been distributed to the villagers. We already knew for a fact that the Japanese troops on the island had been told that the

U.S. Marines were the most savage and toughest fighters in the world—that in order to be able to enlist in the Marine Corps a young man had to prove that he had murdered a member of his family.

Bennion did not pause at Marpi Point. We continued at about seven knots, avoiding as much as possible the clusters of bodies in the water. We did not want to suck up any of these human remains into our seawater intakes. The thought of them going into our evaporators to make feedwater and potable water was sickening. We were not shot at, nor did we shoot. There was no point in firing our guns at the villagers. They were going to do what they were going to do. It was not possible to reason with them, apparently, nor did our people ashore have the time or the inclination to attempt to do so. They were having a tough enough time killing off the Japanese soldiers, few of whom up to this point had surrendered. All had determined to die fighting.

BENNION GUNFIRE SUPPORT AT SAIPAN AND TINIAN: "THE FOG OF WAR"

During the Saipan operation, we on *Bennion* were never too sure what was going on except in operations in which we were involved. Then we were told what to do, who to do it to, and who would be supporting us. Other information on how the battle was going we picked up from broadcasts copied by our radio crew. They checked every source from Tokyo Rose (which was preposterous) to the U.S. news, to listening to the tactical nets and gleaning information from conversations between commanders ashore and afloat.

It became immediately apparent to the American commanders, Turner and Smith, that Saipan could not be secured on schedule unless the reserves were committed. Therefore, on about June 20 the Army's 27th Infantry Division, the floating reserve, was administratively offloaded (not in the presence of the enemy) over the assault beaches. The 27th Division was a former National Guard outfit that had not been reconstituted since its initial deployment to the

Pacific, and things had not gone too well with the division in its previous operations.[14]

The problem according to postwar analysis and unit histories was not the GIs but the officer leadership. It was basically nonprofessional military organization, with officers down to company level mostly National Guard people who—according to this analysis—had received their promotions largely by patronage. The commanding general (CG) of the 27th Division was Maj. Gen. Ralph Smith, U.S. Army. After landing the 27th was moved up to where Marine Lieutenant General Smith put his three divisions (the 2nd, the 4th, and 27th) in line abreast across the southern end of the island. The Marines had driven to the east coast of Saipan by D+4.

On the 23th of June Lieutenant General Smith kicked off a drive to the north with all three divisions abreast and the 27th Division in the center. This was the first major offensive on the island, and the Marines and the Army were fully prepared for combat with their artillery, tanks, and support forces all ashore and operating in support. From the beginning the 27th Division fell behind. The Marines moved out on schedule at 0800, and regiments of the 27th got bogged down. That division never caught up, leaving a wide gap between their western flank and the Marines' eastern flank through which large numbers of Japanese infiltrated the first night to attack the rear echelons of both the Army and the Marines. The Marines were able to tighten up their perimeters and kill off the infiltrating Japanese, but not so the 27th. On June 24 "Howlin' Mad" Smith went to the senior Army officer in the chain of command and told him he was relieving Major General Smith and wanted the senior Army general in the area to take command. That is what happened: the incident reverberated in Washington. While some thought the Army had not done as well with their troops on the ground in the Pacific as the Marines, the Army believed that Major General Smith had been made a scapegoat. In the end, the powers that be stood firm and said if we're going to win this war we have to take this kind of decisive action to ensure that we have the right people leading our young troops.[15]

While the 27th Division drive was stalled, the Marines had taken the high ground at Mount Tapochau and were getting ready for the final drive to take the northern half of the island.

Bennion was ordered by CTF 52 to take a position at Fire Support Position 5 to relieve *Renshaw* to respond to calls for fire. As *Bennion* proceeded to her new station, in Magicienne Bay on the east side of Saipan, the purpose became understood.[16] *Bennion*'s CIC was now up on the frequencies used by the NGLF (Naval Gunfire Liaison Force). Each component of the Marines down to company level had a naval gunfire liaison officer, who was in communication with a control ship off the beach. When a company commander required artillery support in order to accomplish his objective, he could call on either the "organic" Marine field artillery, or a Marine tank, or naval gunfire. At this point, the heavy artillery was being landing ashore and not yet positioned, and tanks were scarce. Virtually all that was available was naval gunfire. Therefore, by D+3 the gunfire-support group was getting many requests. These were parceled out immediately to the ships that were available in the area.

Bennion joined several other ships redeployed to the east side of the island, where they could fire effectively on the undefended rear areas of the Japanese defenders facing the Marines coming at them from the west. Taking station about two thousand yards offshore in safe water with no visible reefs, *Bennion* established communications with the NGLF ashore and stood by. That first day on the line proved quiet, no targets were identified.

On the following day we were hooked up with naval gunfire liaison officer (NGLO) 51, and he did give us some targets to go after. However, by the close of business that afternoon, we had expended a mere twenty-eight rounds of AA common.

After several days conducting ASW patrols, on July 1 we received orders to go back on the gun line at Fire Support Area 5, where over a five-hour span from late morning into the afternoon we were given twenty designated target areas on the northeast quadrant of the island: machine-gun emplacements, gun batteries, troop concentrations, an ammunition dump, and a command post.

That day, with a floatplane off the heavy cruiser *Indianapolis* (CA 35) spotting the fall of our shot and radioing back corrections, our guns expended 942 rounds of AA common. The good news was a "Well done" from the Marines ashore for badly bloodying a Japanese company in Purple Heart Valley. But immediately after we received a scorching dispatch from the gunfire coordinator on the CTF 52 staff: we had been allocated only four hundred rounds for that mission and 5-inch ammunition was getting tight. Somehow, we had failed to get the word that we had a quota for the mission. But no one got in trouble professionally over our expenditure.

For the next week the Marines and soldiers fought to secure the northern half of the island. Desperate, the Japanese decided to direct a massive "banzai attack," a desperate human-wave assault, at regiments of the 27th Division now on the western coast. The Japanese essentially surrounded them and were driving them into the sea. This breakthrough had occurred on the night of July 6, and on the 7th *Bennion* with two other destroyers were dispatched to give fire support to the flank of the line of three divisions abreast.

We arrived at first light and were at General Quarters. I was in the director scanning the scene with my binoculars when I was surprised to see a number of individuals on the reef that extended out from the island. I got on the ten-power range-finder and as daylight increased realized that these were generally Caucasians, with the taller and rangier physiques of Americans. What we were seeing were the remnants of an Army battalion that had been overrun by the Japanese when they had encircled elements of the 27th Division and driven some back. Some had no place to go except to swim out to this reef; the others had been killed in the pockets of resistance.

When the GIs saw the destroyers they knew we were friendlies and stood up to signal us of their predicament.[17]

In doing so they also signaled the Japanese and were again taken under fire. By this time these troops were completely unarmed, many without even their helmets, crouched down in the water or the surf in the passages through the reef. Since it was impossible for the destroyers to get close enough to Tanapag Reef to bring the troops directly on board, our captain, Commander Cooper (who was the senior officer present), immediately called on one of the amphibious units to send a combination of LCVPs and LCUs that would provide transportation and firepower to extract the 27th Division GIs. Meanwhile, Josh Cooper put both *Bennion* whaleboats in the water with two sailors armed with Springfield rifles and sent them in to do whatever they could do to evacuate these poor devils. About this time *Bennion* began drawing artillery fire and was forced to maneuver. We did not leave the area but simply changed our position constantly, watching the artillery shells land in the spot we had vacated only thirty seconds before. About this time two things happened. First, our alert director/range-finder operator spotted the enemy battery that was shooting at us well dug in on the near side of a hill and therefore vulnerable to our guns. We were then able to take it under direct fire, laying our crosshairs on the artillery pieces and firing AA common fuzed to explode at the range of the target. Second, and almost simultaneously, the "amphibs" arrived. With the LCUs' heavy machine guns firing to suppress the small-arms fire and *Bennion* banging away at the artillery position, all the GIs who had made it to the reef were pulled off. I considered this to have been a very dicey operation, involving the hazards of enemy artillery, small-arms fire, and the forces of nature, the surf pounding the reef.

The push by the 2nd and 4th Marine Divisions to Marpi Point began the next day and took about a week. Although the sector was essentially secured in five days, it was necessary to destroy, with flamethrowers and satchel charges, Japanese survivors holed up in caves. We on *Bennion* were able to see, with our ten-power optic, American flags implanted by the Marines over Marpi Point and Mount Tapochau days before Lieutenant General Smith declared the island secure.

TINIAN OPERATION

There was no rest, however, for the Marines. The island of Tinian five miles across the Tinian Channel had to be taken. The plans were very carefully made; Marines from "Howlin' Mad" Smith's staff and naval officers from Vice Admiral Turner's staff going over every line of the operations order to ensure that the lessons learned in taking Saipan would be applied to the assault on Tinian. *Bennion* and other destroyers having been slated to give critical naval gunfire support, the CG of the 2nd Marine Division contacted CTF 52 to suggest that the commanding officers and gunnery officers of the destroyers that supported his division come ashore to confer with his naval gunfire liaison officers as well as battalion, company, and platoon commanders. All would gain better understandings of what the targets might be and what kind of fire would be most effective.

On July 18 *Bennion* came off radar picket duty and anchored in the transport area off Charan Kanoa, a former sugar-mill town. Other destroyers of DesRon 56 also dropped their "hooks." Each destroyer put a whaleboat in the water, which carried all the gunnery officers and most of the COs to a cement jetty coming out from Charan Kanoa. There we disembarked and were met by the operations officer and the chief of staff of the 2nd Marine Division. There were only about a dozen of us.

Some COs had been reluctant to leave their ships, but ours, Commander Cooper, had complete faith in the XO, Red Balch, and in the ability of the gunnery department to function temporarily with both the captain and the "gun boss" (me) ashore. Several COs and gunnery officers from another destroyer squadron were also present.

I was surprised to encounter my next-door neighbor from Arlington, Virginia, William Smedberg, then a captain and commander of DesRon 23.[18] Commander Cooper and I were assigned a jeep and a driver. Our convoy was escorted by armed riflemen and several jeeps mounting machine guns. Though the Marines had reached the northern tip of the island a week earlier, there were still pockets of resistance. We headed up from Charan Kanoa and cut through the torn-up turf to a battalion. For a destroyer sailor this was really a unique opportunity to see up close how these Marines lived and operated.

We first visited the battalion commander, a lieutenant colonel identifiable only because his foxhole was six feet deep and eight feet long, so that both he and his radioman could get in there together should any shooting occur. He was writing a letter home when we arrived. I must say I came close to choking up when I realized the sort of casualties that the Marines had paid for this dirty little piece of real estate. About fifty yards from what had been an MLR (main line of resistance) was one of the most gruesome sights of my life. In a little grove the bodies of Japanese troops were piled up awaiting burial.

The bodies were piled about five feet high, which was the height to which two Marines could loft a Japanese carcass on top. The bodies were arranged like cordwood. The pile was about a hundred feet long, and I estimate that at least six hundred dead Japanese soldiers were stacked very neatly in this one area.

A noncommissioned officer (NCO, a sergeant) offered to take Commander Cooper and me to the military crest [with not necessarily the highest elevation but the best fields of fire] from where we could look across the former no-man's land as he pointed out the vacated Japanese positions. As we were following the NCO in a loose line (we had been instructed not to bunch up, so there were just the three of us close by), I stumbled over the body of what was obviously an American soldier—identified as such by his helmet and webbing [pack straps, ammunition belt, etc.]. His face had pretty well been destroyed by the weapon that had brought him down. I called out to the sergeant, who said he would get a graves registration man up right away to register the GI as a killed in action and pull the identifying information off the "dog tag" around his neck. The sergeant also said that the remains would be brought out, put into a body bag, and properly disposed of. A little farther on we had to stop and bypass an area where a squad of soldiers from the 27th Army Division were practicing with a bazooka rocket launcher, firing rounds at a burned-out pillbox.

Our small party paused for a moment to watch. The Army GIs all appeared to be privates, with nobody really in charge. They were practicing with the bazooka, but we noted that the rounds were not exploding. Our Marine sergeant guide said we would take a wide berth around the blockhouse, because those unexploded rounds could be very dangerous, just to stumble over one could cause it to explode. As we left the group the Marine sergeant shook his head and muttered under his breath something about "them GIs." I did notice an enormous difference in the appearance and the apparent discipline of these Army men compared to the Marines, all of whom were clean shaven and were either in clean clothes or were washing their skivvy shirts in their helmets.

We got up to the military crest of the Marines' position where we had a fairly good view of what the Marines had faced when they kicked off their drive north.

We did not stay very long with the Marines because they needed the time to themselves to prepare for the upcoming assault on Tinian. We had informative discussions with the NGLOs, some of whom we would be working with. Commander Cooper and I rode back to the stone pier at Charan Kanoa.

With another landing operation imminent, at Charan Kanoa the landing beaches were under the control of the Navy; the "beachmaster," a very tough and well-tattooed Navy commander, was running the traffic with an iron hand and absolute precision. First, no boats were allowed to linger on the beach. They arrived, their cargo was immediately moved ashore, and the boats got under way, either for another load or to lie off until one load was ready. The materiel never remained on the beach. Working parties would immediately surround the ammunition, food, medical supplies, water, or whatever and move it into the tree line. There it could not be left subject to observation and fire by rogue Japanese mortar fire. When we arrived at Charan Kanoa a Marine with an Aldis lamp flashed a message to *Bennion* requesting they send the gig in to pick us up.[19] The gig crew had been standing by, and we could see them clear the side of *Bennion* almost immediately.

That night we returned to our picket station to the east of Saipan and after an uneventful evening were ordered back to the waters off Charan Kanoa, where a "secret mailgram" awaited. We were soon under way and by 1030 we were at our initial position. The nature of the "mailgram" was unsaid—that *Bennion* was to get in very close and provoke shore battery fire from the Japanese, because that was virtually the only way we could pinpoint their very well camouflaged gun positions. Because of the destroyer's close proximity to the beach line—we were virtually up against the reef—we in the director had the closest perspective of the target area. That morning we occasionally saw cars hustling down the country roads, kicking up quite a bit of dust. We immediately took them under fire with our 5-inch guns and either destroyed the vehicles or drove them into permanent hiding. We leveled various structures using AA common shells. Secondary explosions [detonations of explosives inside set off by the shell] occurred following hits on two houses, so we believe we eliminated two ammunition depots. We lobbed 5-inch white phosphorus (WP) incendiary shells against the wooded slopes, attempting to ignite forest fires that could expose enemy emplacements. Though the "Willy Peter" failed to set the forests aflame, it did set cane fields afire and destroyed a Japanese cave fortification. Our 20- and 40-mm guns also raked the woods, with doubtful effect.

Coming off line, we replenished ammunition from *Mount Rainier* (AE 5) and returned to Picket for another quiet evening. We would continue to provide TF 52 early-warning services for the next few days as plans to assault Tinian were finalized and then executed.

CONCEPT OF OPERATIONS

The plan was to keep the Army division in reserve and land the Marines in LSTs, LCIs, LCUs, and LCVPs staged from the southern tip of Saipan. There would be no transport ships involved. Because the selected beach, in the northwest quadrant of the island, offered only narrow egress to the interior of the island, the hope was that the defenders [knowing that] would concentrate their forces to repel a landing on the wider beaches along the southwestern side of the island, centered around Tinian Town. To support the direct cross-strait assault, the Army and the Marine Corps had emplaced their organic corps artillery on the southern rim of Saipan and registered [pre-aimed, by correcting trial rounds] the guns so they could provide the Marines a heavy volume of supporting fire from H-hour minus one (i.e., H−1) throughout the first two days of the Marines' push inland.

At dawn on July 24 the Japanese defenders witnessed a large amphibious force off Tinian Town—a feint intended to hold the main garrison in place.

THE ASSAULT

The landings at Tinian took place on schedule virtually to the minute, in spite of a spot of foul weather, the tail of a typhoon that was charging north, skirting the Marianas. We on *Bennion* had visited with the transport group off Charan Kanoa from the end of June until D-day working with the Marines and annotating our charts, as we were to be in the front line of the gunfire-support ships. We

17. Six-inch naval gun mounted in the hillside overlooking the southern end of the island of Tinian Official U.S. Marine Corps photo

would maintain our fighter/director function with our combat air patrol of trusty little Wildcats orbiting over Saipan; P-47s from the Army Air Forces would be available as a backup, flying off Aslito Airfield.

The fire support was described in the post-action reports as the most effective yet seen in any amphibious operation. The Japanese were essentially silenced by the time the Marines hit the beach in a very difficult assault. They could beach only two landing craft abreast at the same time, because of the cliffs that ringed Tinian and the offshore reefs, through which the UDT people had needed to blast a path. But if the naval gunfire was excellent, it was not without its cost. The destroyer *Norman Scott* (DD 690), firing at Japanese positions around Tinian Town, was hit by six successive rounds that made almost half the crew casualties, including the captain. The old

18. Aerial view of the first wave hitting the beach at Tinian, July 24, 1944
Official U.S. Marine Corps photo

battleship *Colorado* also was taken under fire and experienced heavy casualties among its topside personnel.[20]

The Japanese guns causing this damage were British Armstrong/Whitworth coastal-defense guns that had been captured at Singapore and were destined for the defense of Saipan but had not gotten beyond Tinian before the U.S. Navy struck. They were very cleverly emplaced at the base of cliffs east of Tinian Town and were never fired until the *Colorado* and *Norman Scott* showed up and closed to a thousand yards, to receive terrible beatings.

As a matter of historical and personal interest, *Norman Scott* was named for the father of a very close friend of mine at the Naval Academy a year behind me in the Class of 1944. Rear Admiral Scott had been on board the light cruiser *Atlanta* (CL 51) during the first night of the Naval Battle of Guadalcanal and had been killed in what may have been a friendly-fire incident.[21] The destroyer *Norman Scott* was given its name just before commissioning to honor Admiral Scott. His son Lt. Norman Scott Jr. served throughout the Pacific War and later in 1945 went through flight training with me in Iowa and Florida.[22]

On *Bennion* we monitored the progress of the invasion on the various radio circuits and remained vigilant at Picket Station 6 off the west coast of Tinian. Finally, early on the third day, we took station closer to Tinian's west coast and spent the day firing on targets identified by NGLOs. About two thousand yards offshore in, again, safe water with no visible reefs, *Bennion* and two other destroyers began a period of gunfire support that would last almost twenty-four hours. This was both "called fire" from the NGLOs on specific targets and "area fire" into general zones a hundred meters square where enemy troops were known to be dispersed in caves and foxholes. That evening we stayed on station to lob star shells over the island throughout the night. We fired a star shell round every so often to keep the battlefield illuminated, so that the Marines would be able to spot Japanese infiltrators. Even when things were quiet on the battlefield, the Marines asked for "harassing fire"—one 5-inch round every minute into a designated zone in which Japanese were known to be. The idea was to give the Japanese troops no opportunity for a night's rest to make them fit for tomorrow's battle.

On the morning of the 27th we returned to the transport area for assistance in repairing our gyrocompass, which had been failing us. With repairs completed, we returned to the west coast of Tinian on July 29 for an intense day of shore bombardment; we unleashed 313 rounds on targets identified by our ashore NGLO. The pace continued the next day; we spent the hours before dawn firing star shells at mixed intervals averaging one every ten minutes. We were then called to the southwestern side of the island—another 308 rounds.

Those rounds would be our last contribution to the operation. On August 1, as we rendezvoused with an oiler to refill our oil bunkers, we received news that organized resistance on Tinian had ceased—though there would be holdouts in the hills for weeks to come. Tinian had been taken quickly, on schedule, with what was considered a minimal loss of life—less than four hundred Marines killed. Saipan had been brutal for the 2nd and 4th Marine Divisions, which had lost more than three thousand Marines killed in action and ten times that many as casualties that had to be evacuated. On the other hand, nearly six thousand Japanese troops on Tinian and over 30,000 on Saipan had been killed. A few prisoners were finally taken, Japanese too incapacitated by their wounds or sickness either to fight back or commit hara-kiri (or seppuku, ritual suicide by disembowelment).

An Army unit was brought in to garrison Saipan and Tinian, and Army engineers immediately started work to build airfields on both islands. The island of Tinian with its ten-thousand-yard B-29 runway was to be essential in the Army Air Forces' heavy-bomber campaign against the Japanese home islands. The atomic bombs that would be dropped on Hiroshima and Nagasaki were flown to Tinian and loaded on Army Air Forces bombers for their trips to Japan. Before the Army arrived and the Marines backloaded to be reconstituted for their next amphibious landing, *Bennion* along with the other eight ships of DesRon 56 headed for Purvis Bay, at Florida Island in the Solomons, to undergo much-needed maintenance by a destroyer tender that had arrived in the forward area and to get ready for the next operation—we knew it was coming but neither when nor where.

CHAPTER 9

ENIWETOK AND CROSSING THE LINE

DEPARTING THE MARIANAS

IN ABOUT A WEEK after the Marines landed at Tinian, the invasion commander declared the island secure. The occupation troops (an Army regiment) were moved in and the Marines were relieved and brought on board amphibious shipping. There was no further need for shore bombardment, even though there were some Japanese remaining on Tinian. [They had to be routed out with satchel charges, grenades, and flamethrowers.]

So on August 2, 1944—in company with two other *Fletcher*-class destroyers (*Newcomb* [DD 586] and *Bryant* [DD 665]), two cruisers (*Montpelier* [CL 57] and *Denver* [CL 58]), and the escort carrier *White Plains* (CVE 66)—we left Saipan and headed for the atoll at Eniwetok, arriving three days later. We were assigned an anchorage in the atoll, put the hook down, and were given permission to shut down 50 percent of our engineering plant. We had been under way with the screws turning or ready to turn for sixty-eight consecutive days. *Bennion* had had no cosmetic upkeep, and as a result there were patches of red rust coming through our fading camouflage scheme.

At Eniwetok there were beaches set aside for bathing, and every day *Bennion* sent liberty parties of from twenty to thirty men over to these beaches with a couple of cases of iced beer, a chief petty officer to make sure it was equally distributed, and lots of suntan lotion. It was the first relaxation for the members of the crew since departing Hawaii. Also, the mail caught up with us, and the supply department was able to replenish toothpaste and candy bars and restock our ship's exchange (which was about the size of a pro football player's locker). Arguably, the most valuable part of the Eniwetok stay was the opportunity to accomplish some much-needed maintenance on the hull and equipment. Gyros and instruments were taken to a nearby destroyer tender, *Piedmont* (AD 17), for adjustment, repair, and in some cases replacement. We had become concerned in the last weeks off Saipan when our Mark 1 fire-control computer had been breaking down. We were able to get a civilian factory representative from the AD to come on board and change several components. That seemed to reinvigorate the "old box" (the Mark 37 computer [to which the Mark 1 sent data]); we had no more outages of that absolutely essential piece of equipment, upon which our lives depended for the rest of the time I was on *Bennion*. Electric motors were dismantled and their rotors taken to the tender for rewinding, and in the engineering spaces valves were replaced and gaskets were refitted. Though some of the crew thought it was most unfortunate, we were able to procure a number of gallons of dark grey paint. The rust spots were chipped down, painted with zinc chromate primer, and then repainted—not in our familiar haze grey but in the darker and grimmer shade of grey that had become the standard in the fleet.

Commander Cooper enjoyed getting away for a swim. He preferred the relative solitude at the "officers' beach." He would take the captain's gig, usually with a couple of the ship's officers, and we would swim, sit on the sand, drink a couple of beers, and eat a bologna sandwich that tasted much better on the sands of Eniwetok than at our battle stations.

It was during our stay at Eniwetok that we received a dispatch directing us to consider ourselves transferred from the Fifth Fleet to the Third Fleet under the command of Adm. William F. Halsey. We would be assigned to Task Force 32 that was the invasion force, in

Task Group 32.1, where we would be part of the shore bombardment group, under Rear Adm. Jesse B. Oldendorf, along with six older battleships and five prewar cruisers. As I have mentioned, the American people may have been under the impression that there were two fleets fighting the war in the Pacific—the Third Fleet and the Fifth Fleet—but actually there was just one set of warships and support ships. They changed their designation from *3* to *5* depending on whether Admiral Halsey or Admiral Spruance was commanding. It seemed at the time a good arrangement and certainly today it stands the scrutiny of the analysts.

Amphibious warfare is by far the most complex military operation in the wartime manuals, and in the Pacific it included

- Strike operations with fast carriers and newer battleships and cruisers

- Marines going ashore over the beaches in opposed landings

- The Army providing occupying forces at those places taken by the Marines

- Air support by an entirely different set of CVs

- CVEs, OBBs, less-modern cruisers plus every available destroyer protecting the landing force with naval gunfire support.

I cannot recall one single occasion in my experience during World War II when I found a reason to criticize the planning or the logistic support of an operation. It seemed almost unbelievable that *Bennion* could get a message to proceed in the middle of the night to a certain geographic location and find waiting there an ammunition ship with the proper ammunition for our specific guns and the particular mission on which we were about to embark. I don't ever recall a shortage of ammunition, of fuel, or of food. However, the quality of food often left much to be desired. The pseudo-butter "oleo" was white with the consistency of candle wax, the milk was reconstituted from a greyish powder, and neither looked, smelt, nor tasted like anything that ever came out of a cow. The potatoes were frozen and, perhaps due to their preparation, there were usually large lumps of totally uncooked spud in the middle of a creamy spoonful. The most available meat was an indescribably bad form of salami or bologna that was about four inches in diameter and at least a half inch thick.

The operations plans were prepared by the fleet, Third or Fifth, staff that would carry them into execution, and these two staffs were ultimate professionals—senior, experienced, and driven by true leaders in Spruance and Halsey.

On August 18, 1944, *Bennion* was under way again, this time with three cruisers, six destroyers, and an escort carrier, headed south to Purvis Bay. We were told as we left Eniwetok that we would be joining the assault group for the seizure of islands in the Palau group. The message sent half the ship's company scurrying to the chaplain's office, which doubled as the ship's library, to find the one *National Geographic Atlas* on board. None of us had ever heard of Peleliu or Babelthaup [now Babeldaob, on which is the capital of the modern Republic of Palau].

Two days from Eniwetok, *Bennion* crossed the equator. In recognition of this, the admiral commanding our task force declared a day free from exercises and inspections for all ships to conduct the traditional Navy "Crossing the Line" ceremonies. Only about 20 percent of *Bennion*'s crew were Shellbacks—people who had not only crossed the equator but also been initiated into the "mystic rites of King Neptune" in the process. If one crossed again later on a different ship, it was not enough for an individual simply to show that he was on a ship that crossed the equator: he had to produce a certificate that he had been through the ritual initiation. Many of the old-timers would never be caught without a copy of this certificate. Nobody wanted to go through the Shellback initiation more than once.

On *Bennion,* planning for the ceremony had been under way for several weeks, not quite secretly but privately by the Shellbacks, who had to put on a ceremony with costumes and props following word-of-mouth tradition. I for one wondered where the initiation committee was going to find from what was on board *Bennion* the stuff from which to manufacture the costumes and the props. It had to be a tremendously innovative effort, and as we were to find out, it was.

On the day of Crossing the Line, all the Pollywogs (the rest of us) were assembled on the fantail. We had already been given our summons to appear before King Neptune: simply an elaborate mimeographed invitation with our names typed in, with any special attire in which we should attend. The captain was a Pollywog, and he was instructed to wear his service dress blue, which was an indication that his ritual initiation would be largely pro forma. The exec was a Shellback, fortunately for all of us, and he made sure that the bounds of propriety were not breached—but also that enough fun was had at the expense of all Pollywogs regardless of rank. Commander Cooper was so respected that no one really wanted to subject him to anything demeaning.

I was of course a Pollywog, and my instructions were to wear not only service dress blue but a blue overcoat with gloves and my visored cap, carrying an automatic shotgun—unloaded—and a radar screen that I had to make myself out of scraps of wire. When all assembled on the fantail we were ordered up to the fo'c'sle [open deck at the bow] and stood by to welcome King Neptune and his court. Then the CPO playing the role of Neptune—a fine old gentleman, very dignified actually—climbed up the anchor chain through the hawsepipe. In flowing robes, a heavy white beard, a wig of long grey hair, and large spectacles, and carrying a trident, he also had, under his arm, a logbook that contained the sins that we Pollywogs had committed "while pretending to be seagoing sailors aboard *Bennion.*" The other members of his court appeared out of the fo'c'sle hatch to join him and they arranged themselves before us.

Among King Neptune's Court, I remember best the Royal Doctor, the Royal Baby, the Royal Barber, the Royal Jesters, and the Royal Torturer. There were a couple of other hangers-on in costume with shillelaghs made of sections of canvas firehose stuffed with material to harden them, enough to sting when applied to a Pollywog's backside (but no effects stayed with a Pollywog for more than a half hour).

King Neptune then called on the Royal Scribe to take the logbook and read the charges against the defendants. These were mainly trumped-up accusations levied against the ship's principal officers and chiefs, all in a spirit of fun. The commanding officer was criticized for his navigation, the gunnery officer (*me!*) for poor eyesight and bad shooting, the chief engineer for producing saltwater out of the freshwater evaporators, the doctor for passing out seasick pills that nauseated the crew, and of course the supply officer and the chief commissary steward for the terrible food. These are just some that I remember.

Then King Neptune, said "Let the trials begin." The Pollywogs retreated to the fantail, where we took off all our outerwear, down to our skivvies, except the commanding officer, who was excused to return to the bridge. Then we lined up in a column and walked forward up the starboard side on the weather deck walkway. The Pollywogs had to pass through a gauntlet of Shellbacks with canvas batten–filled shillelaghs with which they tried to get good shots at our backsides as we ran by. That is, we all tried to run, but like any warship *Bennion* had watertight doors and raised sills, the "shin knockers," to keep down the free-surface effect on the weather decks. So we had a choice between bruising our shins or walking, and most of us made a compromise, dog-trotting, but getting sort of jammed up at each watertight door, where some of the more sadistic Shellbacks knew to gather.

Meanwhile another group of Shellbacks played firehoses on us, and every third or fourth hose contained firefighting foam, which is not at all injurious [as was thought until recently] but does make kind of a mess. Actually, we were well hosed off with seawater by the time we got back to the fo'c'sle. There each of us went before the Royal Prosecutor, and things happened very fast. The first task was to ingratiate ourselves with King Neptune by kissing the Royal Baby. The Royal Baby was a chief watertender who was about five feet six and weighed about 280 pounds; he was of German extraction and so blond he was almost albino. He was attired in diapers, booties of some description, and a baby bonnet on his head and had some awful-tasting grease smeared across his tremendous belly. Each Pollywog had to kiss the Royal Baby, and that meant kissing his tummy. Most of us approached it fairly gingerly, but when we got close the Royal Baby rubbed our faces in the grease. I think it had something awful like castor oil in it, and it was very nauseating.

Then we went to the Royal Barber. Most of us got a shampoo with some vile mixture (very sticky and bad smelling). The alternative, which some of the younger sailors who were trying to let their hair grow got, was to have their locks shorn in so uneven a fashion that the next day or two they all had to get burr cuts to get rid of the awful coiffures. Or the Royal Barber might simply give a sailor a dye job, in which his hair was turned bright green or bright red. All of these dyes came out within a day or two with a lot of washing, but certainly for forty-eight hours everybody knew these were former Pollywogs.

From the Royal Barber we went to the Royal Doctor who took our temperature by sticking in our mouths some vile instrument that had again been coated with something very nasty. Once that had been swished around and we were about ready to throw up he said, "Here, here, rinse your mouth out with this," and most of us—being trusting—then rinsed our mouth out with something even worse than the vile crap that the Doctor had spread with his tongue depressor. So while still retching we were turned over to the Royal Torturers (or perhaps they were "dungeon keepers"). They had a large tunnel made out of canvas. It was about four feet in diameter and about ten feet long. It had been filled with garbage that had been saved. Urged on with blows from the shillelaghs, each of us crawled on our hands and knees through this filthy mess. Shellbacks on the outside could see our forms moving through, and the tube was just flexible enough so they would give us a good push and down we would go, rolling in the garbage of the last fourteen days from the general [crew's] mess. We came out covered with rotting old baked beans and whatever. When hit by the fire hose we were very grateful.

Once we Pollywogs completed our trip through the Tunnel of the Dungeon and had been beaten about by the Royal Undertakers in the plywood coffin, we were released: we had completed our initiation into the "mysteries of the deep" and were full-fledged Shellbacks. We stood around naked (except for our skivvies), soaking wet, some with odd-colored and odd-shaped hairdos, but most of us with great big smiles on our faces. We had gotten through this ordeal, and it had turned out to be not very painful at all but really a great deal of fun. I think that everyone in authority on a ship that goes through the Crossing the Line ceremony faces the event with a certain amount of trepidation and concern that things will get out of hand, that the Shellbacks might take things out on the Pollywogs with their shillelaghs to the extent somebody got hurt. But I must say to the credit of American sailors that the spirit of sportsmanship rather than vindictiveness or any other emotion takes charge. Everyone has a good time. If a Pollywog is clearly suffering the Shellbacks ease up on him. It's not a case of hurting people, it's a case of good-natured fun and that's exactly what mine turned out to be. The Pollywogs actually felt they had had a good initiation and they were proud of their stamina in standing up as victims of King Neptune's Court.[1]

PURVIS BAY, FLORIDA ISLAND

On August 22 *Bennion*, with other destroyers in Squadron 56 plus the cruisers *Denver, Honolulu* (CL 48), and *Cleveland* and the CVE

Kalanin Bay (CVE 68), arrived at Purvis Bay. Florida Island is an elongated piece of jungle-covered land about six miles long and two or three miles wide. It lies about twenty miles north of Guadalcanal, where history was made when the Marines landed and drove the Japanese into the sea in 1942—arguably the first real success of the allies in World War II. Just off Florida Island is a much smaller island named Tulagi.

Tulagi had been an important Japanese strongpoint. Because of its terrain and its location it could control the anchorage at Purvis Bay and seaborne traffic moving generally east and west between Guadalcanal and Florida Island, a passage that came to be known as "the Slot." In the invasion of Guadalcanal, picked Marine forces—the Marine Raiders—were assigned to assault and capture this critical piece of real estate. What resulted was a very bloody battle in which all the Japanese on Tulagi were killed and the Marines took heavy casualties. Therefore, "Tulagi" came to symbolize the brutal fighting that had and would occur in the Pacific between the Marines and the Japanese.

Purvis Bay was a reasonably good anchorage, sheltered from heavy weather with good depth and good holding ground [i.e., for anchors]. When *Bennion* arrived to moor, I had the deck and was amazed to see six CVEs anchored in a line, virtually in formation. The fact that six American carriers anchor in formation like a group of destroyers was a dramatic demonstration of how far the fleet in the Pacific had come since the battles of Coral Sea and Midway, when the total number of operational carriers in the Pacific Fleet could be counted on the fingers of one hand.

As was the custom, *Bennion* nested with three other destroyers of our division. This arrangement was useful in that it provided an opportunity to visit among ships, and especially in sending liberty parties ashore to swim on the beaches on Florida Island. The four destroyers could pool their whaleboats to shuttle the liberty parties to the beach.

I made one trip ashore and found the beach pristine with its white sand and a row of palm trees separating the sand from the jungle. I had never been in a tropical jungle before. I followed a trail for a hundred yards into the dense growth. Although the trail was well marked and had probably been in use for a hundred years, by the time I had gotten a hundred yards from the beach I felt totally isolated, with jungle noises, none of which was familiar to me, the only sounds to be heard. There was a dismal gloominess about the jungle, because the canopy of the tall trees really did shut out the sun. The trail passed between the larger trees; jungle undergrowth made any effort to get off the path virtually impossible. The soil underfoot was damp and almost greasy in consistency, probably never really drying out. The number of insects was unbelievable, and they represented many varieties of all sizes from "no-see-ums" to ferocious-looking dragonflies almost as big as small birds. All of them were attracted to my bare skin, and if they didn't bite or sting they caused a terrible itching. I turned around and headed back to the beach without any desire to spend any more time in a tropical jungle. On the path I passed several of the native Solomon Islanders, who were attired simply in a T-shirt and a pair of shorts, barelegged and barefooted. Obviously they were inured to this environment and the insects did not seem to bother them.

All I could think about were the Marines and the Army troops that had had to fight the Japanese in this environment. I had read *Guadalcanal Diary*, by Richard Tregaskis, shortly after it was published in 1943, one of the best as well as the earliest accounts of the war in the Pacific. Tregaskis had captured better than most writers the terrible conditions under which our troops had to live and fight and carry on. Having won a piece of the jungle, the Marines would have to move on to the next section of real estate. Now for the first time I really understood how this jungle environment could compete with the Japanese in making the Marines' life almost unbearable.

PARENTAL ADVICE

In Purvis Bay our ships received mail for the first time in almost a month, and among my letters was one from my father. He was catching me up on his activities, and I was pleased to read that he had orders to command *Iowa*, lead ship of the Navy's newest and most powerful class of battleships.

This letter was a very important document in my career. I had gone to the Naval Academy with the intention of being a Navy pilot, and at graduation in 1942 that had remained my goal. However, since graduation my career had been in destroyers—two of them—and I had taken considerable satisfaction out of my job as gunnery officer on *Bennion*. Commander Cooper had told me that he expected me to be detached within the next six months to be executive officer of another destroyer.

With the constant and hectic pace of our activity and my total preoccupation with my jobs as gunnery officer, a department head, and as officer of the deck, I had not given much thought to my plans to become a naval aviator. My father said in his letter that I should apply for flight training at the earliest opportunity, because he—a veteran destroyer and battleship officer—was convinced that the carrier had replaced the battleship as the principal combatant in the U.S. Navy and that naval aviation would continue to grow in importance as the role of the surface ship diminished in the balance. He based his comments on his prospect as the future commanding officer of the largest and most modern surface combatant in our Navy, in combat against the Japanese in both Task Forces 38 and 58. But he said in effect that battleships, cruisers, and destroyers were mainly escorts for the carriers. In fact, he thought that sometimes his battleship would be perhaps not as useful as a destroyer, because he would have no ASW capability.

He recognized that his new command would be virtually invulnerable to air or surface or even submarine attack and that in a showdown with the Japanese fleet *Iowa* would play a role. But at

Coral Sea, then Midway, and most recently in the battle of the Philippine Sea, the long range of the carriers' aircraft had meant that both we and the Japanese had taken their respective enemies sunder attack well beyond the range at which surface ships could engage. Further, it was clear from our own experience in Guadalcanal and the Japanese experience subsequently that surface warships could not survive air attacks without their own fighter protection. It is true that the battleships would be difficult to sink by air, but they could be put out of action when their radars, optical tracking devices, and gun crews topside were destroyed or devastated by bombs.

FLIGHT PHYSICAL EXAM

This letter from my father in mind, I called on Commander Cooper on our first quiet day at anchor in Purvis Bay. I reminded him of my previous conversation with him, when I said I wanted eventually to become a naval aviator, and now it was clear that if I did not apply the window of opportunity would elude me. An ALNAV had come out from BuPers announcing the officer "year groups" that were eligible for flight training. Already, Naval Academy classmates of mine were being detached and returning to the United States to undergo flight training.

The captain was, as I expected, most understanding. He said he had hoped I would stay in the surface Navy, because my service in *Bennion* had made it clear that I had an aptitude for destroyer life. However, he understood the pressures on young people to move into the newer mediums, and not only would he write a favorable endorsement to my application for flight training but he would help me in another way. One of the captain's good friends and classmates was the XO of one of the six CVEs anchored in Purvis Bay. Josh Cooper would ask him by flashing light to arrange a flight physical for me; the captain would take advantage of the opportunity to call on his friend.

Two days later Commander Cooper, with me in tow, in the *Bennion*'s gig went alongside one of the CVEs. After he was piped on board [they would have boarded in reverse order of rank] he retired to the exec's cabin to catch up on old times, and I was turned over to the flight surgeon of one of the embarked squadrons.

The exam itself seemed almost per forma except for the eye examination. To be a pilot in heavier-than-air aircraft I had to have vision of 20/20 or better. I had no trouble with my eye exam. The flight surgeon remarked that the best thing for sharpening one's eyesight was to stare into the sky looking for enemy aircraft, and we agreed that I had been well prepared for my eye exam.

MAIL AND MORALE

I had managed to get my letter application for flight training, endorsed favorably by Commander Cooper, in the outgoing mail before we got under way, so now it was just a case of waiting until orders from BuPers came through. I had absolutely no idea whether this would be a matter of weeks, months, or years. The United States and the Navy Department could have been on the other side of the moon as far as those of us in Task Force 32 were concerned. We lived in our own little world, and the only news that came through was national or international, most of it relating the state of the Allies' progress against the Germans in Europe. The only information we received on what was happening back in the United States of direct interest to us came in our letters from home. I was getting on average one letter every two or three days from my wife, and I would guess that was about the average for wardroom officers.

As gunnery officer, I was division officer for O Division [within his own department] and as such was called on for counseling. Periodically a sailor or petty officer would come to me saying that he had not heard from his wife for months or that his neighbors were writing that his wife was misbehaving with another man. In some cases wives were cruel enough to write their husbands, deployed in the far reaches of the Pacific with no chance of getting home until their ship was sunk or the war was over, that they were no longer in love and were living their own lives, which in her case included live-in boyfriends. You can imagine the blow to a sailor's or an officer's morale when letters like this hit. Yet it was not uncommon. Most of us had married young after joining the Navy, without extended periods of engagement. But these problems were not limited to the younger men. A first-class petty officer, our leading air controlman, with whom I spent two to six hours a day in the Mark 30 director during General Quarters, was so despondent over his wife's unfaithfulness that I thought he was suicidal.

All mail leaving the ship had to be censored. This was one of the chores of the junior officers. On *Bennion* it did not become a regular "collateral duty" for me because of my department head status. Occasionally, when the load became too great, the XO would ask all the officers to pitch in to be sure that no outgoing mail was held up by censoring. It often seemed to me that it was pretty ridiculous. Those of us on the ship did not know usually our destination until we were under way for it and no mail would be leaving the ship until after the next engagement had been initiated. Nevertheless, it was a general order in the Navy and the XO, Red Balch, was a very fine and correct officer who understood the necessity of carrying out general orders from above.

The process was for the mail to be sorted by divisions. Each division officer would sit at the wardroom table with a pair of scissors and a stack of unsealed outgoing letters in front of him. The scissors were to snip out offending paragraphs—if any were discovered. I don't remember ever reading in an outgoing letter any classified information requiring excision. All of us found it very embarrassing to have to read each other's mail—the officers' mail was censored along with the crew's. The arrangement was for officers to censor each other's letters. At one point there was a tacit agreement that reading the letters would be superfluous as we knew each other well enough to trust them. However, Red Balch saw this happening and laid down the law, and he was absolutely correct. We could not have two standards on one ship by which people in authority were getting around general orders.

I don't recall any problems with wardroom censorship. Occasionally we would run across an officer's letter that referred to the skipper, the exec, or a fellow officer in very uncomplimentary terms, but this was not objectionable; it was simply a product of a very long time spent with a small number of other people in a rather confined space. As it was, we came close to some very serious arguments in the wardroom over table manners before the Pacific cruise was over. With the pressures on us, we were simply getting on each other's nerves. As I pointed out, censoring mail was time consuming, and it was additional to other duties. It was done during the time that the censors could have been sleeping, reading, or otherwise relaxing from their administrative duties, their watches, or GQ.

Correspondence between deployed folks and our stateside correspondents was slow and tedious at best, although the Post Office did its best to speed delivery. We were given three printed sheets of very thin tissue paper known as "V-mail." We wrote our letter on one side, folded over the edges (which were preglued to form an envelope), addressed it (using our Fleet Post Office return address [which did not betray the ship's location]), and put our initials in the upper-right-hand corner: all our mail going off the ship was "free." The problem with V-mail was that although it moved quickly, there was not much space for anything more than a brief paragraph, and quite often in transit the flimsy tissue paper would be chewed up or obliterated by water or oil spills.

Mail call was a very important event, and we all looked forward to our letters. Somehow the Navy had worked out a system that was really very good. I don't ever recall coming into a port or an anchorage and there not being mail waiting for us there.

DECODING MESSAGES

Another responsibility assigned to the junior officers was augmenting the communications people in code breaking. Every message that came into the ship by radio was encoded. Some codes were much more sophisticated than others, depending on the classification of the material in the message. We had a coding machine that lessened the arduousness of the decoding, but only the communications people were permitted to use it.

Our ensigns and lieutenants (junior grade) were faced with a beastly process involving inserting cardboard strips bearing letters into a form and thus breaking the code into intelligible elements. I don't remember exactly how it worked, except that in the heat and humidity of the tropics the cardboard strips in a very short while became limp, and our task was sort of like trying to push a piece of wet spaghetti through a keyhole. We were motivated to get these encoded messages broken quickly, though, first because each officer had a quota to fulfill, and second, each of us thought the next message we broke might contain our orders to return to the United States. It is amazing how we grasped at every straw to find some glimmer of hope in our immediate future.

CHAPTER 10

THE PALAU CAMPAIGN

UNDER WAY

WHILE AT PURVIS BAY we were informed that DesRon 56 with *Bennion* would be part of Operation Stalemate, the invasion and seizure of Peleliu in the Palau Islands. Purvis Bay was the staging area for Stalemate, and a full rehearsal was conducted in that area. The rehearsal went off well. By then all of Destroyer Squadron 56 as well as the cruisers and the CVEs assigned to the operation were battle experienced and had been operating in the Pacific for three or four months. The ships' crews were experienced in Pacific island–type operations and had also become accustomed to their commanders up the chain. When we left Purvis Bay on September 1 to conduct a few days of exercises all hands were glad to get under way. The anchorage had been hot and sticky, and very few people had taken advantage of the liberty boats that plied between our nest of destroyers and the sandy beaches. Morale was high, we felt well trained with Saipan behind us and that we had in that operation given a good account of ourselves. Furthermore, the news was universally good. The Allies seemed to be making progress on all fronts. We all realized that the closer we got to Japan the tougher the Japanese forces would be, and we could expect higher losses in the months ahead. But that realization was largely offset by the fact that we were making progress and that we had demonstrated that the Japanese could be defeated. We could foresee the possibility of an end of the war in the Pacific in the future. None of us would hazard a guess as to when that might be, but up until now many of us had had the feeling that the war could go on forever, the distances were so great, and the Japanese enemy so tenacious.

On September 6, having conducted preparations for our next tasking, *Bennion*, the rest of Destroyer Squadron 56, and the OBBs (minus *California* (BB 44)) and cruisers of Rear Admiral Oldendorf's bombardment force departed Purvis Bay.[1] We were headed for Palau, which the Marines would invade as the next step in our island-hopping campaign across the Pacific. It was hard for even the more senior and experienced officers on *Bennion* to understand the significance of Palau, but we believed that it would be easier than either Yap or Truk, two Japanese strongholds that would be fearsome to invade.

It was quite a powerful force: five old battleships—most of which had come out of the mud at Pearl Harbor—seven cruisers, four CVEs, eighteen destroyers, eight destroyer minesweepers (DMSs), and five destroyer transports. These APDs carried underwater demolition teams.[2]

BEFORE D-DAY

Oldendorf's force arrived at Peleliu early on September 12, D-day minus three. *Bennion* was assigned fighter-direction duty (*Bennion* was specially equipped for this mission, with specialized communications gear and a fighter-direction team embarked). This was to be in conjunction with shore bombardment. All the battleships, cruisers, and destroyers were assigned to Oldendorf's fire-support force, which was to support the Marines by prelanding bombardment to neutralize the Japanese defenses and then call fire as requested by the naval gunfire liaison groups assigned to the Marine battalions.

Bennion's fighter-direction activity proved minimal, because there were very few Japanese aircraft in the area. Those few that had been operational when we arrived had been pretty well neutralized after our first week there. *Bennion* was controlling fighters from the force's CVEs, and they gained local air superiority immediately on

D–3. On the first day two of the fighters under *Bennion*'s control shot down two Japanese aircraft. That was the extent of the penetration by enemy aircraft into our area of responsibility. On the other hand, *Bennion*'s shore-bombardment burden was very heavy during the nine days in which *Bennion* was a firing ship. Our 5-inch guns sent 4,142 rounds into targets ashore. We fired AA common–fuzed projectiles that detonated on impact. We had quite a few 5-inch influence fuzes on board, but they were reserved for aircraft targets. As always, the task group commander made sure that all his ships, including the destroyers, retained an inventory of armor-piercing shells. These would be used only if we encountered Japanese surface forces.

During the three-day prelanding bombardment, on D-day minus two, *Bennion* was assigned to cover the operations of the UDTs. This was the first time we had seen these people in action close up, and it was absolutely astounding. *Bennion* was lying to just off the reefs to the west of Peleliu near what became designated "Orange Beach One." The APDs with the teams came in between us and the reef. While still under way the APDs put rubber boats over the side for the UDT people to pile into and then retired seaward of *Bennion*'s position. *Bennion* moved in as close as we dared to the reefs to be able to use both our 5-inch (203 rounds would be expended) and 40-mm (454 rounds) on the Japanese if they opened up on the UDT. We were quite cautious, because we did not have a great deal of confidence in the charts, some of which were marked as having been issued by the British Admiralty in the mid-nineteenth century!

The rubber boats were pulled up on the reefs and the team members got out and actually walked on the high points of the reef, realizing that they were under full observation of thousands of Japanese on the shore. They were not fired on, because the Japanese did not wish to disclose their positions and the location of their defensive lines by taking what they considered a less-than-valuable target under fire. The Japanese were saving their camouflaged positions as a surprise

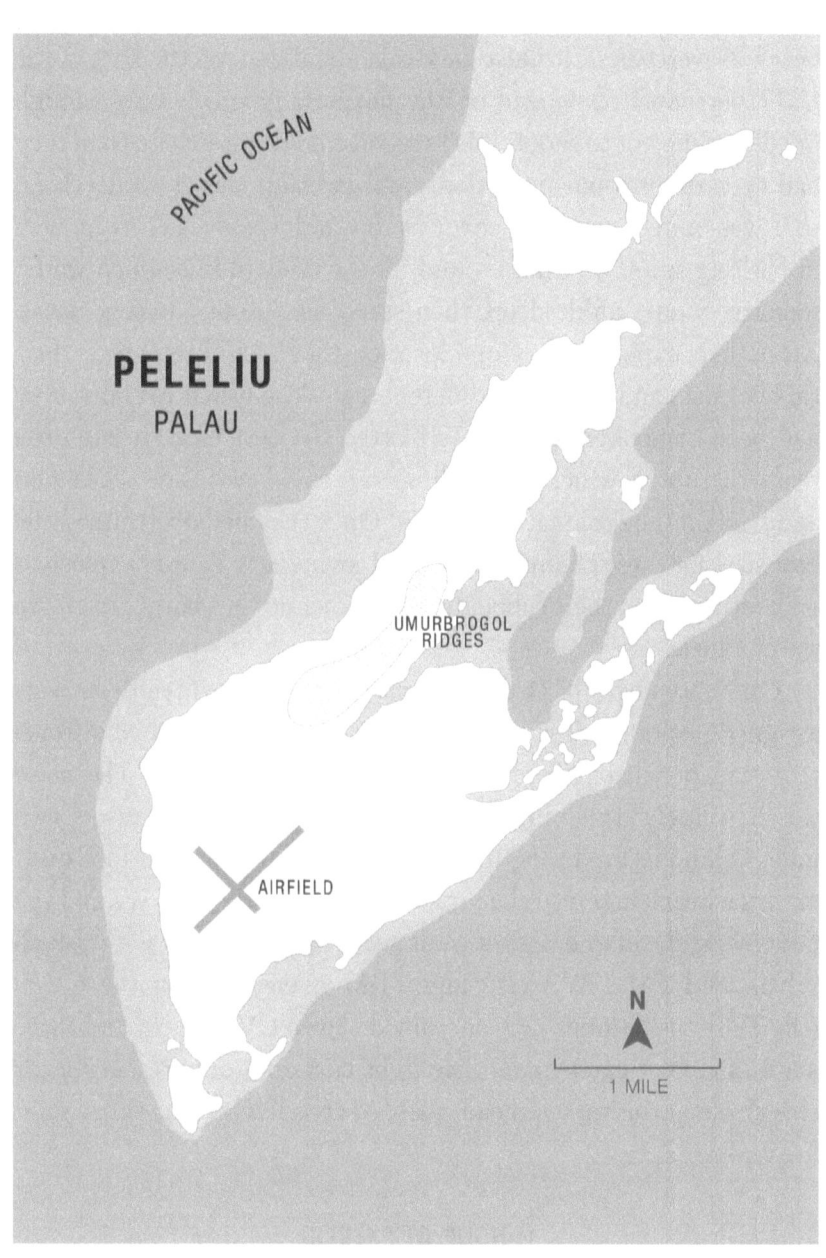

MAP 2. PELELIU

for the real threats that would be the Marines assaulting over the beach. Nevertheless, it must have taken real guts on the part of the UDT personnel to depend on the Japanese troops having enough fire discipline not to shoot. UDTs seemed bolder at Peleliu than they had been on previous operations, and *Bennion* was closer to them, so it was quite an experience for us to watch these UDT swimmers in bathing suits, walking around on the reefs in knee-deep water, sometimes only ankle deep, then standing still and taking notes. After their exploration of one location they would return to their rubber boats and move to a different one. When their initial survey had been completed, the UDTs plotted the best path through the reef structure by which the landing craft could get inside the lagoon and land on the designated beaches. Once they had determined the best sites for these channels, the UDT swimmers planted explosives and, returning to their rubber boats, detonated the charges to create the channels.

On September 15, D-day, *Bennion* was one of three destroyers assigned positions close to the landing beaches, and it had a front-row seat for what proved a classic amphibious landing. The noise was absolutely deafening as the battleships and the cruisers two miles behind us fired their 6-inch, 8-inch, 14-inch, and 16-inch guns onto the beach and into the jungle behind the tree line. We and the destroyers ahead and astern of us were banging away with 5-inch salvos, and FM-2 Wildcats and TBM Avengers from the CVEs (the Taffy task groups now contained eleven CVEs each, and three additional fleet carriers and five light carriers were present for air cover) were orbiting overhead ready to attack when the ships' gunfire ceased.

H-HOUR AT PELELIU

H-hour was spectacular. It had been preceded by the heaviest bombardment that we had seen, much denser than at Saipan or Tinian. Starting at 0530 the five battleships and cruisers just poured it in, as

19. Smoke and dust rise from Peleliu during the final stages of the preinvasion bombardment, September 15, 1944. Photographed from a modified LCI, the bow 40-mm gun of which is visible in the foreground. Official U.S. Navy photo, NARA

did the destroyers, which were able to get in quite close, just off the reef. At 0800 we began to fire salvos at predesignated targets. As we ceased fire about three minutes before the scheduled 0830 landing, Wildcats and the Avengers came in, the fighters leading and strafing the beaches and the Avengers dropping 500-pound bombs.

The smoke, debris, fire, and noise were overwhelming. On the first pass of aircraft longitudinally along the beach a TBM was hit, caught fire, and flew directly into the beach in a huge explosion of gasoline and TNT that stood out even in among the detonations of 16-inch shells. At H-hour minus three the ships' gunfire was lifted, and it was then that the aircraft bombing and strafing took place. At H-hour, as the Marine landing craft struck the beach, the aircraft moved their bombing and rocket attacks inland. Through our high-power optics, we could see the Marines running across the strip of beach, exposing themselves as little as possible before they reached the cover of the low-lying jungle canopy. We were surprised to see several landing craft hit by enemy fire before reaching the surf line, and it was not possible for us to tell how the Marines on the beach were faring. From what we could see most of the fire directed against them was from rifles and automatic weapons. We saw no sign of artillery or mortar explosions.

At H plus thirty minutes the naval gunfire liaison officers were crossing the beach and setting up their radios in the tree line. By H+40 the NGLOs were up on the net, calling for naval gunfire against specific targets. These calls were addressed to the naval gunfire coordinator on the command ship. He assigned the requests as firing missions to DDs in the best position to support those particular Marine units. These fire-support missions were a constant that morning for *Bennion*.

At 1300 we were pulled off the gun line, having expended a great deal of ammunition, and sent to rendezvous with the ammunition ship *Sangay* (AE 10) to take on fresh rounds. We were then directed to join *Richard P. Leary* (DD 664) and four LCIs (landing craft infantry) to form a barrier. We patrolled along the east coast of the Palau Islands to detect and intercept barges bringing Japanese reinforcements down from Babelthaup Island, mainly through Koror Harbor and then through the coastal lagoons inside the reef—where the Japanese craft were vulnerable to interception. It required special technique and a great deal of skill from the CIC and gunnery people. The destroyer would cruise outside the reef and sweep the lagoon on the shore side of the reef with its search radar to detect any barge or small-boat traffic. Detecting barge traffic was difficult because islands and dry reef coral heads in the lagoon gave radar returns similar to those of landing craft. The only way to identify a return as a boat rather than a coral head was to track all blips inside the lagoon and from those tracks determine which were moving. The moving targets obviously would be Japanese boat traffic.

Unfortunately, as a result of operator efficiency and atmospherics, a coral head could appear to have a course and speed. It took a skilled CIC evaluator to differentiate between these and Japanese boat traffic. When the evaluator had decided that contacts were indeed boats the captain would order the gunnery officer to take over, and one or two 5-inch guns would fire illuminating rounds—star shells. The star shells would illuminate the lagoon and normally make a landing craft discerned through the optics. In such a case the remaining 5-inch guns of the main battery would take the landing craft under attack, one or two of the 5-inch still providing illumination. The complication was that the illuminating guns were firing a different trajectory and loading different ammunition than the attacking mounts, and the director control had to keep these two functions separate and accurate. Nevertheless, that first night of picket duty was relatively quiet. That would change.

GUNFIRE SUPPORT

As the sun rose on September 16, we were assigned to a position on the west side of the island flanking the advancing Marines ashore. By now it had become clear that this was going to be a new kind of warfare for the destroyers, different from the gunfire support we had provided at Saipan and Tinian. Here on Peleliu we were dealing with an enemy who had dug an extensive network of caves and firing holes, and to inflict casualties it was necessary for us to put rounds right into the holes themselves. The destroyers were able to shoot very accurately, because we could get in close to the targets still staying just outside the reef, which ran about a mile offshore. Also the weather was generally favorable, which meant calm seas and a minimum degradation of our gun battery's accuracy by ship's motion. At Peleliu we used the 40-mm guns as well as the 5-inch battery for shore bombardment.

After the Saipan operation—when it became clear that none of the surface combatants would be using searchlights to illuminate targets in this kind of conflict—and working with the chief fire controlman, I had the 40-mm guns wired through the searchlight controller in the Mark 37 main-battery director. This provided level and cross-level control to the 40-mm guns and greatly improved their accuracy. It took away the difficulty for the pointers and trainers of compensating for the motion of the ship, particularly roll. We didn't have the 40-mm guns ballistic data in the searchlight controller, but with inputs for roll and pitch the 40-mm were very accurate under director control. It was possible after firing one or two rounds to spot a subsequent burst of 40-mm fire through the doorway of a house or the aperture of a pillbox. The 40-mm mount was primarily an antiaircraft weapon, and all its ammunition was fuzed to detonate at four thousand yards. So we had to be within two miles of a target to use those mounts. Even that was pretty far away, and we had to get into within about a mile of a target before we could get the sort of accuracy we were seeking. But the proximity of the Japanese fortifications to the waterline, the closeness of the reefs, and the availability of lagoons, enabled us to take destroyers in (sometimes) to two or three hundred yards of a target.

This system worked well. On one occasion a 5-inch salvo had blown away a great deal of jungle foliage in a particular target area, and we were able to see very clearly one of the cave entrances. Throughout the day to that point we had expended over six hundred 5-inch rounds. We had been conserving 5-inch ammunition because resupply had become so difficult, so we brought the 40-mm into action, by a technique of spot and adjust. We fired one round from a 40-mm then spotted that with the searchlight control directors. Then we fired successive single rounds, spotting after each one, until a projectile went right into the cave entrance. Then we commenced shooting in automatic rapid fire with a quadruple mount. We were very pleased to see that something important was in the cave when a great deal of smoke and debris came blasting out after our 40-mm rounds went in.

That evening after dark *Bennion* was again assigned a sector to the northeast of Peleliu. There we would fire a star shell every five minutes to illuminate the northern approaches of the island to assist LCIs that again had formed a picket line to deter reinforcements. At first light we were summoned back to provide fire support. En route, as we passed the southern tip of Peleliu we came upon three floating mines, which we dispatched using small-caliber weapons. We then proceeded to our assigned fire-support position to fire at Japanese positions in the central part of the island, expending over three hundred rounds of 5-inch AA common. For the remainder of the day and into that night we joined with *Newcomb* to screen the cruiser *Honolulu*, which had been designated as the standby fire-support unit. No fire missions were requested for that evening.

Instead, *Newcomb* and *Honolulu* spent a good portion of the next morning emptying their magazines in response to calls from ashore. *Bennion* met *Sangay* to replenish our magazines. Returning to Peleliu we responded to call-fire missions, expending some two hundred 5-inch rounds on what were believed to be enemy vehicle concentrations on the northern part of the island. We remained that night as fire-support ship. Our task was to fire star shells as directed when the Marines needed to observe movements of the Japanese, whose tactics were to hide in caves during the day and come out at night to infiltrate the Marine lines and counterattack. Also, the destroyers were called on for harassing fire in enemy-held areas during the night even when no specific engagements were in progress. This kind of fire involved sending several rounds every few minutes into a geographically designated area, moving the points of impact around, so as to disturb the enemy in that area, who might be assembling for an attack on the Marines or at least trying to get some rest.

Bennion also carried out combat air patrol responsibilities at the same time, always having between eight and sixteen Wildcats overhead during daylight hours. Except for a lone flier who played cat-and-mouse games with us on the third evening, drawing from us some eighty-five rounds of 5-inch before managing to slip away, there was no hostile air activity in our area of responsibility, allowing *Bennion* to concentrate on call-fire support.

By D-day plus four most of the really hard fighting ashore was concentrated along a ridge that ran northeastward on the northwest side of Peleliu. On the chart it was Umurbrogol Ridge, but we had nicknamed it "Bloody Nose Ridge." I doubt that name was original with us on the gunfire-support ships. We probably picked it up from the gunfire liaison people on the radio net. Bloody Nose Ridge is where the Marines were really having tough going. The Japanese had constructed a very complex system of tunnels, firing holes, and pillboxes throughout the tough, coarse terrain, and the Marines had to dig them out virtually man by man. That is where we poured in most of our 5-inch ammunition.

By D+4 our operations had settled down into a pattern. *Bennion*, along with all the other *Fletcher*-class destroyers, was assigned to gunfire support during the day. During hours of darkness the destroyers would be in gunfire support for two nights and the third night be detached for independent patrol of the coast. At nighttime the naval gunfire requirement might be for illumination over the battlefield to enable the Marines to detect enemy movements, either individual infiltrations or the assembly of a banzai charge. Or the destroyer might be called on for directed fire of 5-inch/38 AA common ammunition against formations that had been illuminated and spotted. During periods of no enemy activity, the destroyers would conduct harassing fire.

Bennion would lie to off Peleliu in an assigned gunfire-support sector in radio contact with the naval gunfire liaison people in the front lines with the troops, and under the oversight of the fleet gunfire coordinator on the flagship who monitored all our circuits. We would respond to requests for gunfire with great care to make our fall of shot precise, because we were firing at targets very close to our own front lines.

The way it worked was that the NGLO would call for a spotting round, and (based on our navigational position and the coordinates of the target, given to the closest yard) we would fire a single 5-inch round. Normally the NGLO would have in mind a point of impact such that a shot that missed the target was not going to fall on our own troops. From this first round he would then spot single rounds (maybe three or four) before he was satisfied that shots were impacting where he wanted them and with minimal chance of "shorts" or "overs" falling into friendly positions. Sometimes those preliminary single shots were enough to knock out a cave entrance or a pillbox. On other occasions the NGLO would call for several salvos of 5-inch rounds in rapid succession to saturate an area, in hopes that one of the, say, twenty-five projectiles would make a direct hit on the enemy position. In many cases it in fact required a direct hit from a 5-inch shell to blow up a cave, knock out a pillbox, or destroy a fortified crew-served weapon position. An indication of the intensity of our fire is the fact that we actually knocked feet of elevation off Bloody Nose Ridge.

Bennion's 5-inch magazine had a capacity of 2,500 rounds, a round consisting of a projectile and a brass cartridge case. Some of this ammunition could not be used for shore bombardment, as it was either AP or VT fuzed. The intensity of the gunfire support at Peleliu is also suggested by the fact that *Bennion* would regularly deplete its total inventory of AA common in two or three days. This meant making repeated trips to *Sangay*, which remained in the vicinity until after a few days she was empty, and after that leaving the gunfire-support group to replenish ammo elsewhere. Thus on the evening of September 23, following a day of heavy shelling of northern Peleliu and the adjacent Japanese-held island of Ngesebus, *Bennion* joined *Albert W. Grant* (DD 649) of our squadron to escort the cruiser *Minneapolis* (CA 36) north to rendezvous with the replenishment group at Kossol Roads, at the north end of the Palau Archipelago. Zigzagging northward at thirteen knots, it took most of the night to reach the rendezvous point.

Kossol Roads was protected from the weather by extensive reefs, and the depth of water was such that replenishment ships could anchor there with lots of room. The disadvantage of Kossol Roads was that the Japanese had mined it and, although U.S. Navy minesweepers had gone through there, we all knew that minesweeping was not infallible. Also, the Japanese had some big guns, probably 8-inch caliber, on Northern Babelthaup that could reach most of the anchorage. They didn't fire at the ships in the anchorage very often, probably because they didn't want to disclose their position and draw counterbattery fire. Since most of the replenishment ships were commercial-type vessels with up to four thousand tons of high-explosive ammunition on board, Kossol Passage was not as comfortable an anchorage as an advanced base site like Eniwetok might be, but fortunately there were no casualties here to our naval or commercial ships.

Arriving at Kossol in the early morning we went alongside a Victory ship—*Meridian Victory*. This one was manned by a merchant marine crew, an unusual situation because normally merchant marine ships would transfer their ammunition stores to a fleet replenishment vessel manned by sailors. This was helpful because U.S. Navy ammunition ships use techniques and procedures that we were quite familiar with. Not so with merchant mariner. They were not used to offloading to destroyers. Their experience was mainly pierside or alongside other ammunition ships at anchor. The 5-inch/38 ammunition came over to *Bennion* fifty rounds at a time in a skip box [a large, open-topped container]. This made for very slow going, because the skip boxes had to be lowered into the hold of the ammunition ship, manually filled with ammunition, then hauled up out of the hold, swung over the deck of the destroyer, and set down on the fantail. Then a line of sailors would walk by, each man picking up a 5-inch/38 projectile or a 5-inch/38 powder can, almost as heavy, and walk it to the main deck magazine hoist, which would strike the round below into the magazine or the upper handling rooms.

Bennion's first trip to Kossol Roads to refill her magazines was marked with some unique problems. Upon arrival we were assigned fighter-direction duties for the whole anchorage. At about this time our fighter-direction center picked up some Japanese air activity in the vicinity of Babelthaup. It was far enough away so that we would be able to cast off from the ammunition ship before any bogeys arrived in our vicinity, but it was an uncomfortable feeling to have 5-inch ammunition piled up on deck. The bottleneck was getting the rounds and the powder cans down the magazine hoists, a slow process. After only about a half hour of working with the Victory ship, it was apparent that we were not going to be able to take on board our required ammo and still make the evening's commitment on the fire-support schedule. Nothing seemed to be going right. This was a civilian-manned ammunition ship using rigs we were not used to working with—plus the fact the crew of the ammunition ship seemed to have no sense of urgency. I went over with a couple of gunner's mates and was shocked to see how few crewmen were working the holds moving the ammo into the skip boxes. Their boatswain told us that the problem was the civilian crews were much smaller than Navy crews and simply didn't have the manpower. Furthermore, the boatswain pointed out, they were going to have to stop loading for a midday break because of union rules. The first thought that came to my mind was, "My God, don't you know there's a war on?" However, the captain of the ammo ship was adamant that the midday break was set in stone. I asked if we could send some of our crew over to work in the holds and load the skip boxes; the answer was that was not legal.

The captain then called the boatswain over to him, said a few words, and disappeared into the superstructure. The boatswain came over to me and softly said, "The captain said he was going to lie down and rest a while, at least for an hour, and would not know what went on in the forward and after holds." This comment was followed by a wink and I immediately sent our chief gunner's mate back to *Bennion* to return with thirty men to load the skip boxes. By the time our sailors came over, which was in less than five minutes, a number of the supervisory personnel among the merchant crew had disappeared, and the merchant seamen remaining topside pitched in with our sailors to show them how the ammo was stowed in the holds and how to handle the dunnage [wood and padding used to hold the ammunition safely in place]. Also, we did not have winch operators who were skilled in the kingpost [vertical columns from which booms are guyed] system of cargo transfer, so the merchant marine winch operators remained at their posts. Our manpower, with the help of the merchant mariners, doubled the rate of transfer.

When our sailors went on board the ammunition ship they had blood in their eye: "We're going to bloody a few noses and get these guys squared away. Don't they know there's a war on?" But it turned out there was no fighting or hard feelings. The supervisors who were on board to ensure union rules were followed conveniently disappeared. The merchant sailors remaining topside pitched in to help our people. I am sure that many of our own sailors came from blue-collar families and understood union rules.

We finished reloading our 5-inch common ammunition, cast off, and after refueling from the oiler USS *Caliente* (AO 53) headed south in company with *Albert W. Grant* at twenty-five knots. Fortunately, there was a fairly flat sea, because we still had a great deal of ammunition stacked on the weather decks; we used the four hours of transit time back to Peleliu to get it below and properly stowed. We were somewhat limited personnel-wise, because we had to maintain a "condition watch" with one third of the armament manned, which substantially reduced the number of hands available to handle ammunition.

Upon our arrival Commander Task Group (CTG) 32.5 directed us to a position off the western side of the island to be on call for fire support. No calls were made, and our guns stood silent that night. The next evening, however, made up for it, as we were moved to a sector northeast of Peleliu facing Ngesebus. From 2100 to 0500 on the morning of the 26th we delivered harassing fire on the Japanese holdouts hunkered down on this small isle. The feedback we received from our naval gunfire liaison officer was that we had delivered just as ordered.

INTERDICTION

With the arrival of daylight on September 26, CTG 32.5 directed us north to assist LCIs that had been assigned to mop up after a failed Japanese attempt to reinforce Peleliu a few nights earlier. After midnight on September 23, *Heywood L. Edwards* (DD 663) had encountered a group of barges loaded with reinforcements. Illuminating them with a star shell, the destroyer opened with her main battery and was credited with sinking fourteen barges carrying enemy troops. While some Japanese soldiers who survived the fire managed to get to Peleliu, others were stranded on small reefs in the vicinity. With the LCIs spotting for us, we fired air bursts over the target area, raining down shrapnel on the suspected hiding places.

That evening we were assigned to fire star shells over the lagoon northwest of Peleliu to detect Japanese small boats and take them under fire. The fire-control radar was not effective, because of interference from the landmass and the coral heads. Star shells, to be effective, had to burst on a direct line from the director to the target but three thousand yards beyond the target, placing the objective in silhouette. It was not as if the star shells would illuminate overhead and change night into day. It still required considerable interpretation on the part of the director crew looking though the optics to sort out moving craft from stationary coral heads and karst [limestone] islands. Once the 5-inch guns opened fire, there was a problem of the smoke from the "flashless" powder—which we always used at night—temporarily obscuring the target from the director unless the wind was just right, and even when it was, the splashes of rounds in the vicinity of the targets would take several seconds to dissipate so that the target could be picked up again. On this particular night no enemy activity was observed except for some bogeys detected by our air-search radar between 2140 and 2300. We immediately ceased firing our star shells so not to give away our position. Having approached from the west, these bogeys turned northward and stayed well beyond range. With their departure we recommenced illumination.

With much of Peleliu in American hands after a week of bloody fighting, we were sent south to fire illumination over the small island of Angaur. Six miles southwest of Peleliu, the small island was defended by a regiment of 1,600 Japanese soldiers. Two U.S. Army regiments were landed on the morning of September 17. Within three days the island was declared secure but for a good many Japanese who remained dug in on a hill on the northwest corner of the island. So on the evening of September 27 and into the early hours of the next morning we fired about ten star shells per hour to illuminate any attempted Japanese movements against our forces. Incidentally, the resistance on Angaur would last another month. On Peleliu it would last well into 1945.

On September 28, we repositioned off the reef east of Ngesebus, off the northern tip of Peleliu, to provide fire support if needed as the Marines stormed ashore at 0900. By the evening it was securely in American hands.

The Peleliu campaign proved costly. For the 1st Marine Division ashore it was a bloody and slow process, and in retrospect I believe our planners [like others at the time and since] must have felt that the cost in lives and particularly in experienced field leaders—lieutenants and NCOs—was a high price to pay for an island that did not subsequently constitute a major strategic asset for the American campaign across the Pacific. But Peleliu with its airfield had to be eliminated or from it the Japanese could have always harassed the flanks and the main supply routes of the Allies as the advance across the Pacific proceeded. It is true the cost in lives was high and that the immediate rewards seem minimal, but it had to be done. Also, in the long run the Marines' aggressiveness and frontal assaults on the well-dug-in Japanese probably cost them fewer casualties than a more cautious, long-drawn-out battle would have.

For the U.S. naval warships in the Palau campaign, the contrast between our fairly benign environment and the savagery of the fighting ashore was evident to all of us. At sea we were not confronted by an air threat, there was no Japanese sea-based force to defend against, and—to my knowledge at the time—no warship was damaged by hostile fire. On the other hand, the amount of gunfire support we provided to the Marines ashore was as extensive in terms of both volume and preparation as any I witnessed going across the Pacific.

On D-day, *Bennion* had been assigned a target on Bloody Nose Ridge. I recall being informed by the plotting room that its instruments indicated a target height of 553 feet that coincided with its designation as Hill 553. It was the tallest point on the ridge and was being used as both an observation point and a strongpoint from which troops and guns were able to pour fire down on the Marines. A week later we were still being assigned fire missions at the same coordinates on Hill 553, but now as the Mark 37 director put its crosshairs on the target the operator saw not a green patch of tropical forest but a nasty reddish-brown scar in the jungle where all the growth had been destroyed and blown away. But what was remarkable is the fact that the plotting room called up that day and said, "With your crosshairs on the peak of Hill 553, we only register an elevation of 548 feet." In those four to five days we had literally blown five feet of earth off the crest of Bloody Nose Ridge, the knob that was the strongpoint for the Japanese defense of the island of Peleliu!

On D plus seven, a *Bennion* sailor in a fireroom sustained severe steam burns on his arms and shoulder in a noncombat accident. Our medical officer considered the injury well beyond his own capabilities and was life-threatening unless the patient was given proper medical attention quickly. Upon being made aware of the situation, our destroyer squadron commander (who was our task unit commander) detached *Bennion* from the gun line to deliver the casualty to one of the large transports equipped with medical facilities to handle Marine casualties evacuated from the fighting ashore. The transport was not in the transport area but was anchored fairly close to the beach, where shuttling landing craft could deliver casualties to this advanced care facility in a minimum of time.

Bennion came along the starboard side and made up to the transport as our casualty was hoisted on board in a Stokes stretcher [made of rigid framework]. In the fifteen minutes that we were alongside, I was manning the Mark 37 director in *Bennion*, which overlooked the weather decks of the transport. I could not help but observe the activity outside the triage area and operating room, which opened onto the main hatch covering of the transport. Every two or three minutes two stretcher bearers would come out of the operating room area with a body on a stretcher that they placed on the hatch cover. Then the stretcher bearers very carefully drew the blanket or sheet up over the face of what had been a living Marine. Although great care was taken to cover the features of the dead, quite often their feet were left sticking out from under their makeshift shrouds. It was somehow incongruous that bare feet were the only evidence that this lump under a blanket had once been a human being.

On September 29, *Bennion* plus six other destroyers and four cruisers were detached from Rear Admiral Oldendorf's group in the Palaus and ordered to proceed to Manus in the Admiralty Islands to stage for the next operation.

The seizure of the Palaus was a bloody victory for the ground forces especially the Marines, who bore the brunt of the fighting. It was somewhat stereotypical for the destroyers, cruisers, and battleships that supported the invasion. Nevertheless, the strategic results were important. I don't believe those of us on board *Bennion* appreciated this at the time. We simply moved out as soon as the island was secured and were not around to see the important airstrips constructed on both Angaur and Peleliu. A U.S. Navy seaplane base was set up in Kossol Roads, the site of *Bennion*'s incident with the merchant marine crew. Seaplanes operating from Kossol Roads were very important for the next four months of the war, as they provided long-range reconnaissance of Japanese fleet operations in reaction to the approaching U.S. naval task forces.

One point that we were aware of at the time, and were grateful about, was the fact that by seizing Palau the United States was able to bypass the island of Yap. It was a Japanese stronghold in the Pacific that was so well fortified as to have made an invasion a very costly operation in ships and men. Palau was about 150 miles southwest of Yap, and the more the U.S. forces extended their control toward Japan the more isolated Yap became. Within several months the combatant units based at Yap had been rendered ineffective by the attrition of their combat support, mainly in replacement aircraft, fuel, and ammunition.

CHAPTER 11

ON MANUS AND AT THE INVASION OF THE PHILIPPINES

MANUS, LARGEST OF THE ADMIRALTY ISLANDS

BENNION ARRIVED at Manus Island in the Admiralties in early October 1944. We anchored in Seeadler Harbor, which was filled with U.S. warships of every description, all in a fever of activity getting ready for the next operation, which, we knew, was an invasion of the Philippines. Manus lies almost directly on the equator, about a hundred miles north of New Guinea.[1] Although every effort had been made to equip the advance base on Manus with the basic amenities for crew liberty, the few visits by our people ashore were made more in desperation than for pleasure. Everyone was so anxious to get off the ship and have a drink of something besides ship's water. With the continuous steaming, *Bennion* had not extinguished fires "under her boilers" [in the traditional phrase] since leaving Hawaii. Breakdowns were beginning to occur, and in particular some of the water being produced by the ship's evaporators had more salt than was acceptable for potable water. The best and purest water from the "evaps" went to the boilers, and the crew got what was available for washing and drinking.[2] It had become customary to add a product similar to Kool-Aid to the drinking water to disguise the salty taste, and every time a pitcher of pink liquid appeared in the wardroom for our table beverage we knew that the engineers were having evaporator problems again.

Bennion's sailors were kept hard at work on board ship, because there was only about a week to top off fuel, food, ammunition, and any other "goodies" we could lay our hands on. In addition, we had to shut down one fireroom at a time, to go in [i.e., into the brick-lined firebox of each boiler, once minimally cooled] and plug [ruptured] steam tubes and clean firesides [outer surfaces of the tubes carrying feedwater being boiled], sweating in the engineering spaces. I do believe, however, that every sailor on *Bennion* had the opportunity to get ashore at least once during our week at Manus. The beer was plentiful, and cold, and any of us who wanted to build up enough of an edge to forget the war temporarily could do so. However, we all paid for it, because the "green" beer and our long period of abstention caused some violent headaches the next day. But nobody complained.

There was an officers' club on Manus. It was simply a large warehouse with a wooden plank set up at the height of a bar running down its longest side, with room enough behind the plank for "bartenders." The officers were six deep behind the bar in their khaki uniforms, most with their caps on because there was no place to hang a hat in the warehouse. The bartenders had devised a tool, something like a rake on the end of a hammer, with which they could puncture the tops of a case of beer cans. With three or four swings their special tool could very neatly put two holes in the top of every one, one swing taking care of four cans at a time. These cases were then simply laid on the plank, and the customers grabbed what they could.

Money was not a problem; most of the clientele simply put dollar bills on the plank and—since the beer was ten cents a can—that would cover one person for an evening. Nobody had the time to make change, and the customers didn't care about it. There was also hard liquor served, something called "Three Feathers," an unaged bourbon or rye whiskey. Then there was another liquor—a bourbon/rye type—with the very pretentious title of "Black Label," which sported a distinguished-looking shiny black label that told very little about the contents of the bottle. "Three Feathers" was known on Manus as "Three Prongs" and "Black Label" as "Black Death." Both were guaranteed to produce a hangover that would last for a minimum of eight hours into the following day.[3] The bartender would place about twenty glasses on an aluminum tray. These were very inexpensive six-ounce glasses. He would then—and this was before placing the tray on the bar—pour about three fingers of "Three Prongs" or "Black Death" into each glass (without benefit of a jigger). When all the glasses on the tray had three fingers of rotgut, the entire tray was placed on the bar and eager hands quickly grabbed them.

There were bottles of soda, ginger ale, and water on the bar for customers to add as mixers. I don't remember whether there was ice available or not. Probably so, because I seem to recall large washtubs filled with ice from which customers helped themselves. There were also tables on the side of the warehouse away from the bar. These were long mess tables, so there was not much opportunity for a small group from a ship (or a division on a large ship) to get together for a private celebration. It was pretty much a community affair, and there were occasional fights. Most, as I recall, occurred between the aviators and the destroyer and cruiser officers. It was never anything serious. Seldom were punches landed. It usually began with an argument arising out of a disdainful remark about the other's military affiliation, then perhaps a hat knocked off or a shirt front pulled. Cooler heads immediately jumped in and separated the quarrelers, who thirty seconds later had forgotten all about it.

When their respective clubs closed at about 2230, the officer and enlisted customers all departed and headed en masse for the fleet landing. There was no place else to go. Amphibious ships had furnished landing craft to shuttle between the fleet landing and the ships anchored in Seeadler Harbor. A more uncomfortable form of transportation cannot be imagined. There were no seats, just a steel deck and bulkheads. The craft were wet in any kind of chop, and when they were running downwind the diesel fumes tended to fill the wells, where the passengers stood. However, the inebriated cargo didn't seem to mind. All had accomplished what they went ashore for: to forget about the war and get off their cramped home away from home, if only for just a couple of hours. Many of the sailors, particularly younger ones who were probably unused to drinking so much in such a hurry, passed out. Every night a dozen or so inert forms were laid out like corpses on the floating steel pontoons that formed the fleet landing. It was very important that a buddy identified the unconscious sailor or that the sailor himself be able to mumble the ship to which he had to return. From then on his getting back safely on board ship was entirely a function of the coxswain of the landing craft. I suppose there were some young men who ended up on the wrong ships, but mostly everyone took care of each other.

Bennion with Destroyer Squadron 56 and the other battleships and cruisers of Rear Adm. Jesse B. Oldendorf's advance group deployed from Seeadler Harbor at Manus on October 12, 1944. En route to Leyte we were joined by additional units including a number of minesweepers.

TASK FORCE ORGANIZATION

The task organization for the invasion of Leyte, which was scheduled for October 18–25, 1944, is of interest. The Supreme Commander, Allied Forces Southwest Pacific Area, Gen. Douglas MacArthur, U.S. Army, was in overall command. Immediately under him was Vice Adm. Thomas C. Kinkaid, commander of the Seventh Fleet. As commander of the Central Philippines Attack Force, he was embarked in the command ship USS *Wasatch*. With him was Lt. Gen. Walter Krueger, commander of the expeditionary troops that would be landed in the Philippines as the Sixth Army.

The Seventh Fleet under Kincaid was further divided into two major task forces: the Northern Attack Force (Task Force 78) had

Rear Adm. Daniel E. Barbey in command, with the X Army Corps under Maj. Gen. Franklin C. Sibert embarked, and the Southern Attack Force (Task Force 79) under Vice Adm. Theodore S. Wilkinson, with the XXIV Army Corps under Maj. Gen. John R. Hodge embarked. The Southern Attack Force was composed of two task groups, TG 79.1 and TG 79.2, each made up of more than sixty Navy transports carrying the troops. *Bennion* was assigned to the Southern Attack Force as part of Fire Support Unit South, commanded by Rear Admiral Oldendorf. It included a battleship division comprising three old battleships—*Tennessee* (BB 43), *California*, and *Pennsylvania*—plus three cruiser divisions totaling six heavy and light cruisers. The battleships and cruisers were screened by Destroyer Squadron 56, composed of nine destroyers (including *Bennion*) under the command of Capt. Roland Smoot.[4]

BEFORE D-DAY

The advance force, which would arrive well in advance of D-day, was composed of Fire Support Unit South, which included not only DesRon 56 but also Task Group 77.3, the Close Covering Group, minesweepers and UDTs escorted by cruisers, and a destroyer squadron.

On October 17 the advance force was only sixty miles from Leyte when the advance force was hit by a typhoon. We had little warning of the oncoming storm; even if we had there was little we could have done to avoid it. We were committed to support the D-day landings on October 20. All we could do was maneuver independently on courses that would minimize the effect of the wind and the towering seas. Having been through some major storms in the North Atlantic, I found the typhoon not nearly as threatening or uncomfortable. The first factor was the temperature, which never got much below eighty degrees. Consequently, we were soaking wet but not cold. The spray was not freezing on the top hamper [masts and high parts of the superstructure, where the added weight of ice affected stability] as it did in the North Atlantic blows. *Bennion* was rolling between thirty and forty degrees, but we had plenty of fuel and were well ballasted, and so we were more in discomfort than in danger. However, the smaller ships were really tossed around; one of the minesweepers capsized and sank on the night of October 17.[5]

Fortunately, it was a fast moving, highly concentrated typhoon. By morning of the 18th the advance force found itself on a comparatively smooth sea, and we entered Leyte Gulf that afternoon despite the minefields that intelligence told us the Japanese had placed in the approaches.

On October 18 and 19, the main-battery guns of *Bennion* and the other combatants of the advance force supported the beach and landing preparations such as the UDTs' approach clearing and the minesweepers, which had to contend with an estimated 330 mines defending possible landing areas. *Bennion* and two other destroyers in the division were assigned the beaches in the vicinity of the town of Dulag [the landing beaches, on the northwest corner of the gulf, extended roughly from here north to Tacloban City, about twenty-two miles], mainly backing up the UDTs and firing on suspected shore batteries. At the same time, *Bennion*'s now very experienced CIC team took over fighter direction/air control of the CAPs being provided by the Taffy groups of CVEs outside the gulf east of the island of Samar. Prior to D-day, October 20, enemy air activity was at a minimum so most of our fighters were brought down in altitude to shoot at targets of opportunity, strafing the landing beaches and roads and small bridges approaching the areas that were to be assaulted by U.S. Army troops on D-day. One enemy air contact did occur during predawn hours of October 19, when we detected a bogey coming at us from land. At five thousand yards we opened up, expending twenty-three rounds of 5-inch AA common, which probably accounted for the plane's veering suddenly westward.[6]

On the night of October 19, USS *Ross* (DD 563), a *Fletcher*-class companion of *Bennion* in DesRon 56, was maneuvering not more than five hundred yards from us off Black Beach 2 when she struck a mine to port under the forward engine room. Twenty-two minutes later, maneuvering into safer waters, *Ross* ran into a second mine, which detonated in the vicinity of the after engine room. The advance force included fleet tugs and rescue vessels for the purpose of extracting battle-damaged combatants. By about two hours after the second mine strike, *Ross* had jettisoned all her torpedoes and depth charges, gotten her list under control, and transferred her medical officer and wounded to the fleet tug USS *Chickasaw* (AT 83), which then took her in tow. Four hours later *Ross* was anchored off Montoconan Island.[7]

Ross's casualties from the mine explosions were twenty-three men killed and nine injured, but *Ross* had to endure further assaults until she was out of the combat area. Shortly after noon on D-day the Japanese attacked the anchorage, and two more of *Ross*'s crew were injured. That afternoon the destroyer was towed to another anchorage that was expected to be safer, but at dawn the following day Japanese aircraft attacked it too. Nevertheless, salvage work on *Ross* had commenced immediately; air attacks caused frequent interruptions but did not stop the repairs.

U.S. ARMY TROOPS ASHORE

As noted earlier, D-day was October 20. *Bennion* was with the amphibious force that entered Leyte Gulf at first light and took the landing areas under fire with the battleships, cruisers, and destroyers of the advance force (also designated the Southern Support Force). In addition to the major combatants, converted landing craft equipped with rocket batteries approached the beach to fire rockets at point-blank range. Immediately behind these rocket-equipped LCIs followed smaller landing craft with troops.

Bennion was in the first row of fire-support ships off the beach. Again we had a front-row seat for the largest landing in the Pacific theater to date. The landing itself began at 1000 and was relatively easy for the infantry, and we were able to see most of the troops cross the beach standing up after the landing. The reason for this was probably because of the very large littoral area that was available for across-the-beach landings. The Japanese did not have enough troops to cover all possible landing sites, and because of the distances involved ashore and the poor highway network it took them time to move troops from one landing site to another. The Leyte landings were very different in this respect from Saipan and Peleliu, where the Japanese knew exactly where American troops were going to land—because there were no suitable alternatives.

JAPANESE COUNTERFIRE AND CREW CASUALTIES

At Dulag the Japanese had established a shore battery, and it was taking a toll on the amphibious ships, mainly the LSTs. When the troops hit the beach the Japanese shifted their fire to the fire-support vessels, singling out *Bennion* as a primary target. *Bennion* took a hit forward. The fragments pretty well covered the ship. Lt. (jg) A. L. Robertson, the assistant gunnery officer. who was standing next to me, suffered a grievous injury: his right arm was cut cleanly off, right at the shoulder. His severed arm, still in the buttoned shirt sleeve, was lying on the deck of the director platform.

Two fire controlmen standing next to me in the main-battery director hatches were wounded seriously enough to be evacuated. Interestingly enough, one of the shell fragments penetrated the warhead of a torpedo in the main torpedo tubes [exposed on the deckhouse amidships in two quintuple launchers]. That caused some concern, but we were able to get rid of that torpedo by firing it at a Japanese battleship five days later. Altogether, the Japanese shore battery wounded six men, but there was no slackening in our fire. Our medics immediately treated the casualties, our damage-control parties patched the small holes from the shrapnel, and we fired our shore-bombardment mission without missing a single salvo.[8]

THE AIR WAR OVER THE BEACHHEAD

For the next three days, *Bennion* and our sister ships in DesRon 56 carried out a wide variety of tasks:

- Shore bombardment under the direction of both Army and Navy liaison teams; control of both shore- and carrier-based fighter aircraft

- Support to UDTs clearing the beach approaches

- Cover for landing craft, rescue vessels, fast transports, and fleet tugs as they went about the very complex business of keeping the troops moving ashore and supplied

- Long-range artillery support for Army units as they advanced inland.

Over the first three days after the landing on October 20, Japanese air activity continued to pick up. The Japanese had established a number of landing fields in the central Philippines. Their army aviation branch used the fields to stage tactical aircraft into the area from major bases in the northern Philippines. At first, the only defense against these bogeys was the CAP from the CVEs off the east coast of Samar and controlled by fighter-direction teams such the one in *Bennion*. The ability of our fighters flying from CVEs to disrupt the almost continuous sorties of the Japanese was remarkable.

The CVEs operated well offshore, and their fighters were FM-2 Wildcats, the combat capabilities of which were well below those of the Marine F4U Corsairs (fairly well established on land airfields) and the F6F Hellcats that, operating from the CVs [fleet carriers], had taken such a toll during the Marianas "Turkey Shoot." (In retrospect, I am very impressed by what was accomplished with the rather primitive communications that existed in those days, compared to what is available in the fleet today.) *Bennion* was able to coordinate requests from both Army units ashore and naval units afloat to organize fighter cover and vector fighters against targets, using radar information of our own, from other ships in the force and—surprisingly enough—Army radar units ashore.

Japanese air attacks were characteristic in their traditional fanatical tenacity. They sent in large-scale raids, from fifty to sixty aircraft, of which handfuls reached their targets, the cargo ships and transports anchored at Tacloban. Our Navy fighters would intercept them twenty miles out and shoot them down in numbers we thought were unsustainable for the Japanese. As the surviving Japanese got closer to the force, we could see the smoking trails of burning Zeros falling the ten to twenty thousand feet from their operating altitudes to their eventual splashes in the waters of Leyte Gulf.

A sample log entry from *Bennion* on October 24, 1944, read [using a variant spelling of "bogeys"]:

0530: General Quarters. Bogies to NW.
0600: CAP, 36 VF fighters, F4F and F6F reported on station.
0752: Large raid coming in from NW.
0815: CAP shot down one twin engine bomber.
0840: 18–20 enemy planes at 15,000 feet.
____: CAP splashed two twin-engine bombers and three Tonys [Ki-61 fighters].
1120: CAP tallyhoed ten Zekes [i.e., Zeros, A6M fighters] at 17,000 feet.
____: Bogies split into three groups. All headed for transport area.
1140: CAP splashed one Zeke.
1220: CAP splashed five Zekes.
1224: CAP splashed two Zekes.
1718: CAP splashed two Vals [D3A dive-bombers], one Irving [J1N twin-engined bomber/scout].
1855: Bogies withdrew over land to NW.

As the groups of about fifty aircraft came in, our fighters would dive into the middle, shooting down five or six and scattering the remainder. The survivors would make individual attacks on the ships below, from which the destroyers, cruisers, and battleships were generally able to defend both themselves and the transports. We found that the most devastating type of attack and the hardest to handle was a coordinated attack of three or four planes. It was these that inflicted most of our losses in the destroyer force.

Destroyers had only one main-battery director, and their 5-inch guns were not very effective firing in the local-control mode. The 40-millimeters were controlled by three separate directors and were absolutely invaluable in shooting down "leakers" that had penetrated the fighter and the 5-inch shields and got within four thousand yards (two miles) of the ship—the maximum range of the 40-mm. It was my observation that the 40s were not really effective until range closed to about a thousand yards, or a half a mile. In the ensuing months the 20s were best at shooting down a kamikaze plane or killing its pilot in the last moments so that the plane would miss the ship, if only perhaps by a matter of feet. A kamikaze aircraft required a man's hand on the stick to get a hit. The plane was moving at over two hundred knots and the ship at thirty knots, and the pilot of the diving aircraft had to correct course continually to compensate for these two motions.

All that being said, our main battery could claim credit for one of the leakers on the evening of October 22. This fellow managed to overfly the transport area and land two bombs on the beachhead before we were able to get a fire-control solution and started to see bursts around the target. We followed the flight of this Japanese plane as it fell, exploding on impact into a hillside. That proved to be a highlight for *Bennion*, in that we had been pulled from the gun line having expended most of our ammunition over the preceding days. Having been relieved of our fire-support duties, we refueled from the battleship *Pennsylvania* at midday and spent the afternoon of the following day alongside USS *Mazama* (AE 9) to restock our magazines for the next day—which would prove timely, as we could see from reports of enemy fleet concentrations in the Sulu Sea.

CHAPTER 12

LEYTE GULF
The Battle of Surigao Strait

BATTLE PLANS

IT WAS APPARENT by October 23, 1944, that the Japanese navy was determined to attack the Allied forces in the Leyte Gulf area. Reports from our submarines and Navy patrol aircraft indicated that two separate Japanese task forces were headed in that direction. The hundreds of transports, supply ships, amphibious craft, and other vessels anchored off Tacloban supporting the Army ashore were certain to be prime targets for the Japanese fleet.

On the morning of October 24 we shifted down to the southern transport area to disembark two of our crew for further medical attention. One of the two, Lieutenant (junior grade) Robertson had lain wrapped in a blanket and strapped to the dining room table in the officers' wardroom, which at GQ served as the ship's main battle dressing station. The war was over for him. He was full of morphine. Easing the pain and stopping the bleeding were about all that we could do for him until we could get him to a hospital ship.

Following the transfer, the CO called me in and showed me a message indicating that the southern group of Japanese surface ships was moving in a direction suggesting a probable attack through Surigao Strait, the southern entrance of Leyte Gulf. The captain thought we would probably be involved in a night action that evening.

When I returned to the director, I called on the sound-powered telephone circuits to inventory our 5-inch ammunition and get it distributed among the magazines and the five upper handling rooms. As gunnery officer, it was my responsibility to ensure that we had the appropriate rounds for a night surface action available at each gun—star shell, AA common, and AP. It wasn't necessary to test firing circuits or night lighting in the mounts, because we had been firing guns at night on shore bombardment and against Japanese aircraft routinely for the past four months. Nevertheless, as a matter of routine the crew on their own went ahead to replace or repair any equipment that showed signs that it might fail in an extended firing engagement. We also made sure that the torpedoes, which had not been exercised since our shakedown training in the States, were "war shots" [i.e., not training dummies] and ready in all respects. I had the twelve-to-four watch as OOD. During that period, I was on the bridge and able to listen to and read the incoming voice-radio and flashing-light traffic that laid out the disposition of our own forces. Rear Admiral Oldendorf had six battleships, eight cruisers, and twenty-eight destroyers to take on the Japanese force that we expected to come through the Surigao Strait. It was our mission to prevent it from breaking through or outflanking us and reaching its objective: the transports and supply ships.[1]

Thirty-nine PT [patrol torpedo] boats were also assigned to the Leyte Gulf force. I was on the bridge wing at about 1400 on the 24th when their formation passed by on the way to set up an ambush in Surigao Strait. I had never heard such a racket. Their engines were unbelievably noisy. We could hear the PTs five miles away and see them even farther, because they were engulfed in clouds of their own exhaust. This was my first encounter with PT boats, and I was not impressed.

During the afternoon watch, Rear Admiral Oldendorf's detailed plan for the disposition of his forces came through by message, and we in his force spent the next several hours deploying to our assigned positions. Destroyer Squadron 56, organized in three three-ship divisions, would attack the column of Japanese battleships and cruisers after they emerged the strait. Oldendorf was specific that DesRon 56 destroyers would each expend only five of their ten torpedoes during this attack, holding the remaining five in reserve. [Torpedo reloads for destroyers were hard to come by in the Western Pacific, and a destroyer tender was normally required for the reload.] Commodore Smoot, the squadron commander, directed three separate but coordinated torpedo attacks by the three divisions: one against the eastern flank, the second head-on (led by Smoot's flagship), and the third (which included *Bennion*) against the western flank. Each division would approach in a column, and each destroyer in succession would launch a salvo of five torpedoes as its column made a "corpen" (column) turn and then retired. Because *Bennion* was the last in the third division, we would be the last to launch our fish. That meant the range from the enemy would be closing for us as our column executed the corpen maneuver. Smoot added that his destroyers should not fire their 5-inch guns during the attack, to avoid providing the Japanese gunners observable aim points.[2]

The ships of DesRon 56 joined up during the late daylight hours at the designated rendezvous point at the northern end of Surigao Strait to form our disposition for the anticipated night action. We remained at General Quarters; *Bennion* had been on picket station at the gulf's eastern entrance and, as the deck log entries quoted earlier illustrate, we had been under Japanese air attacks that continued when we left the station and steamed to the join-up point. These attacks fortunately were not well coordinated or effectively conducted. The cloud cover was about 60 percent cumulus, and enemy aircraft were popping in and out of the clouds searching for targets. By the end of the day we estimated that the CAP under *Bennion*'s control accounted for at least twenty-five enemy aircraft. Toward the end of the day *Bennion*'s 5-inch battery engaged a bogey, letting loose fifteen rounds when this hostile came within three miles. The bogey abruptly turned to the west, and we lost him on radar at a distance of ten miles.[3]

ENGAGING THE ENEMY

We were in our battle disposition by 2100. The crew had been fed in phases, a few men from each battle station going down to the mess line to pick up their battle rations, thick baloney sandwiches. With the number of pickets out on station, both PT boats and destroyers, we would not be taken by surprise. There would be plenty of warning before the enemy came within firing range. Indeed, before midnight we began receiving radio reports detailing a column of approaching Japanese warships.

CONTACT

Shortly after 0300 on October 25 we made our first visual contact with the Japanese heavies. I was standing up through the hatch in the Mark 37 director scanning the horizon with my 7×50 binoculars. The rumble of heavy gunfire had become continuous, and the lower southern sky was now aglow from the steady muzzle flashes. The PT boats in the strait had sprung their ambush on the Japanese column and had triggered a fierce firefight. The Japanese managed to escape the attacks by evasive maneuvers and effective gunnery, they would not fare as well against DesRon 54, under Commo. J. G. Coward, who had stationed two divisions of destroyers farther down the strait. These destroyers had launched some forty-seven torpedoes that would score hits on three destroyers, nearly blowing one out of the water, leaving a second in sinking condition, and blowing the bow off a third, which was retiring. Coward believed he also scored fatal blows against the battleship *Fuso* and a hit on another battlewagon. Having passed through the DesRon 54 gauntlet, the Japanese force came on yet another American destroyer squadron lying in wait.[4] Capt. K. M. McManes split DesRon 24 into two sections of three and approached an increasingly ragged Japanese formation to execute a torpedo attack. With fish away, one of the destroyer sections came under fire and countered with 5-inchers. Despite the blows the enemy pressed on, unaware of the firing squad that lay ahead, the American battleships and cruisers with turrets pointed at the mouth of the strait. However, before steaming into range of the Seventh Fleet's big guns, the Japanese would have to get past yet one more destroyer squadron.

There was a tug on my trouser leg, and the sailor at the pointer station next to me motioned to my eyepiece. Through the magnification of the director's optics the scene to the south was clearer. The lens crosshairs were fixed at the base of the massive pagoda superstructure of a Japanese battleship. The flashes from the continuous fire of her secondary battery on DesRon 24 were lighting up the entire ship. From her clearly visible bow wake she was making at least twenty-five knots.

The radar operator, sitting behind me, tersely reported that his radar had now picked that target out of the landmass return and was getting good ranges. I pushed down the bridge switch on the 21MC [speaker] intercom and reported to the captain that we were tracking a Japanese battleship and had locked on with the fire-control radar. The captain replied that the "Martinis" (collective call sign for the PT boats) had reported that two battleships, a cruiser, and at least three destroyers had passed through the narrows and that our commodore [squadron commander] had called on the TBS (Talk between Ships, voice radio) to assign the second battleship in the column as *Bennion*'s target. He added, "Let me know when you have a fire-control solution on the Big Boy. Have the gun battery ready, but don't shoot unless I specifically tell you to. We are to make a torpedo attack with five fish." His voice was calm and businesslike. Throughout the night in the background noise of the intercom I could hear on the TBS the excited chatter of the Martinis as they maneuvered to launch their torpedoes. Unfortunately, they were unable to score any hits. Then DesRons 54 and 24 engaged, to good effect. Going back to the optics, I could now see just two capital ships in close column—a battleship and a cruiser. I moved the crosshairs to the BB, got a confirmation from the radar operator that he was locked on, and called plot (the plotting room) to tell them to let me know when they had a firing solution on the new target.

Now that the battleship had emerged from the strait, its radar image was clear of ground clutter and our fire-control radar was ranging it consistently. In minutes plot reported "tracking in automatic." I passed this to the bridge, and the captain acknowledged, "Very well. Train out the batteries but don't shoot until I give the specific order to commence firing." I switched the 5-inch guns and both quintuple torpedo mounts to director control, and—standing up in the hatch—looked aft to see the forward torpedo mount train out on the port beam.

The ship was running in and out of rain squalls, and it was very dark. The gunfire was still well to our south. I could barely make out the other two destroyers in our division. We were keeping a three-hundred-foot interval in a loose column, loitering at five knots close to the coastline of Leyte Gulf, using land clutter to confuse the enemy radars. The only sounds were the popping of safeties [actually, roars—excess steam pressure suddenly vented up pipes affixed to the smokestacks] as the engineers kept a full head of steam for the run into the target. It was quiet in the director. Each member of the director crew was absorbed in his particular duties. Our small talk had been used up long ago. For the past seven months the five of us had been together eight hours a day in this hot, cramped, steel box, standing watches or at General Quarters, shooting at the Japanese. At Peleliu, *Bennion* had emptied her magazines three times in a single week. The crew considered themselves experienced veterans. We had fought together at Saipan, Tinian, Guam, and Palau. There was one new man in the director crew this night; the regular pointer had been wounded by shrapnel from that near miss forward days earlier and had also been evacuated off the ship that morning. Both that young fire controlman and the assistant gunnery officer, standing by my side, had been wounded.

I had been momentarily diverted while checking the readiness of the gun mounts and torpedo stations over the sound-powered battle phones, and I was startled to look through the director optics again and see how much larger the image of the Japanese battleship had grown. The remnants of the enemy column was headed in our direction at twenty-five knots, and the range was closing fast.

The soft purr of the idling fireroom forced-draft blowers suddenly rose to a high-pitched whine. The bridge had rung up full power. The director began to tremble and the deck plates to vibrate from the propellers' cavitation as the ship accelerated.

Almost together, the 1MC (the ship's general announcing system) and a sound-powered-phone talker announced, "Starting run-in for the attack."

Tactics had been preplanned to take advantage of the geography of the gulf. Our triad of three-ship divisions would operate individually but in coordination. Our division, then in its initial position lying in wait, would initiate an attack on the commodore's order, the column of three destroyers running at thirty knots for the ten-mile approach to the torpedo launch point. Meanwhile the Japanese column was continuing its own attack, rushing north at twenty-seven knots. It was the commodore's intention that we would meet the Japanese head-on before they got within their torpedo range of our cruisers and battleships.

TORPEDO ATTACK

With the signal to commence the run-in to the attack, our three destroyers turned in column to a southerly course to intercept the enemy, keeping a three-hundred-foot interval between ships. As we increased to thirty knots the engine rooms were ordered to make black smoke to screen our force. "Darken ship" had been set, and there was only the dim blue light from the battle lanterns of the ship ahead for illumination. Standing in the hatch of the director, I could watch the entire panorama of the two converging forces. Through the high-powered lenses of the Mark 37 director, the enemy ships could be seen in individual detail. When our destroyers broke out from the shadow of the shoreline we were immediately taken under fire by the Japanese battleship and cruiser.

It was strange to be rushing through the dark, closing with the enemy at a relative speed of more than fifty knots, not firing our own guns but seeing the steady gunfire of the Japanese ships and the explosions of their shots falling around us. The towering splashes of the 14-inch shells were close enough to wet our weather decks. Both sides were firing star shells, which added to the eerie character of the scene. As the Japanese came into range, Oldendorf's battleships and cruisers, deployed in an east–west line to "cross the *T*" at the top of the Japanese column, opened up with their main batteries. All along the northern horizon, enormous billows of flame from their 16- and 14-inch guns lighted up the battle line. Directly over our heads stretched a procession of tracers, our battleships' shells converging on the Japanese column. The apparent slowness of the projectiles was surprising. During the fifteen to twenty seconds they took to reach their targets, they seemed to hang in the sky. Through the director optics I could clearly see the shells bursting on the Japanese ships, sending up cascades of flame as they ripped away gun mounts and fiery sheets of molten steel as they tore into heavy armor plate.

When the first destroyer in our division reached the firing point, the enemy was only six thousand yards away. Each of the three destroyers in the column successively executed a hard turn to starboard, launching five torpedoes when the enemy was on the port beam. When it was *Bennion*'s turn, the bridge called on the 21MC and the sound-powered phones to "launch torpedoes!" The battleship *Yamashiro* with the force commander, completely filled the viewing glass of my optics. The crosshairs were stabilized on the waterline just below the pagoda foremast. Plot was repeating, "We have a good solution." Glowing dials showed the torpedo tubes were trained clear and the torpedo gyros set. I pushed the "fire torpedo"

20. Gun flashes of U.S. cruisers during the battle of Surigao Strait, October 24–25, 1944, photographed from USS *Pennsylvania* (BB 38) Official U.S. Navy photo, NARA

button on the console and stood up through the hatch to see our five fish shoot out of their tubes and hear them slap the water. All were running hot and straight.

Each destroyer, having turned and fired, began maneuvering independently to avoid the enemy gunfire. As *Bennion* retired to the north at thirty knots (still making black smoke) the scene astern was one of growing confusion. The Japanese formation had disintegrated, with ships circling out of control, dead in the water, on fire, shuddering from massive explosions, and unrecognizable with bows gone, sterns blown away, and topsides mangled. Our own destroyers were intermixed in this melee, and in *Bennion* we were trying to distinguish friend from foe. Commander Cooper on the wing of the bridge and the OOD in the pilothouse combined their efforts to identify visually the radar blips in the immediate vicinity. Most of these were the other destroyers of our squadron, maneuvering darkened at high speed, attempting to reestablish our column formation.

I had an almost unobstructed 360-degree view of the entire scene of action when, unexpectedly, I saw the loom of a large warship on our port bow. Using the slewing sight, I swung the director to point directly at this new target, instructing the range-finder operator to use his highest-power optics to track and identify the strange ship. If hostile, the fire-control radar would be locked on and the plotting-room computer would generate a target course and speed. I called down to Commander Cooper—no phone or intercom was needed, he was on the port wing of the bridge, one level below me— to report the strange contact. It was at this juncture that the unidentified warship commenced firing what appeared to be its secondary battery. Judging by the clearly visible tracers, the rounds were being directed at *Albert W. Grant*, which had already been hit and damaged by gunfire—some of it "friendly," from our cruisers—during the retirement from our torpedo attack. *Grant* had lost all way [movement] and was now adrift in the middle of the strait. Admiral Oldendorf, aware that an American warship had crossed into a kill zone, had put a cease-fire into effect up and down the battle line. The sudden respite enabled two capital ships, *Yamashiro* and the cruiser *Mogami*, as well as a destroyer to reverse course. In doing so, they continued to put up a fight and took their own shots at the damaged *Grant*.

By opening fire, the unknown large ship on our port bow immediately established itself as enemy by her ripple-fire salvos, characteristic of the Japanese navy, in contrast to the simultaneous salvoes of U.S. warships. Again bypassing the sound-powered-phone talker, I shouted to Commander Cooper that the unknown ship was now positively identified as Japanese. No sooner than the captain acknowledged this intelligence when the first-class fire controlman on the director range-finder reported that we were locked on with fire-control radar, tracking what he evaluated as a large, slow-moving target, and that the plotting room already had a good solution for launching torpedoes.

I shouted this information to the captain and recommended we fire our five remaining torpedoes at the Japanese ship, a cruiser or battleship, obviously too lucrative a target to ignore. Without hesitation Commander Cooper replied "Affirmative," even though he must have had in mind, just as I did, the instructions of Rear

THE SECRETARY OF THE NAVY
WASHINGTON

The President of the United States takes pleasure in presenting the BRONZE STAR MEDAL to

LIEUTENANT JAMES LEMUEL HOLLOWAY, III
UNITED STATES NAVY

for service as set forth in the following

CITATION:

"For meritorious service as Gunnery Officer of the U.S.S. BENNION in action against enemy Japanese forces during the Battle of Surigao Straits on October 25, 1944. Passing important fire-control radar and visual data to the Combat Information Center team, Lieutenant Holloway contributed materially to the assistance given by his ship in sinking a hostile battleship in a night torpedo attack and, by the skillful direction of the guns under his command, aided in the destruction of a disabled enemy destroyer. His courage and devotion to duty during this hazardous engagement were in keeping with the highest traditions of the United States Naval Service."

Lieutenant Holloway is authorized to wear the Combat "V"

For the President,

Secretary of the Navy

21. Lieutenant Holloway's Bronze Star citation Naval History and Heritage Command

Admiral Oldendorf to expend only five torpedoes in the squadron attack. Clearly now was not the time for equivocation, and the captain repeated his instructions on the 21MC and the sound-powered telephones to fire all five of our remaining fish at this close-in target.

I passed these instructions by sound-powered phone to Lt. (jg) Tom Bayliss, the torpedo officer. He was at the Mark 27 torpedo director, wearing the sound-powered phones himself and personally making the target data inputs and torpedo settings. I wanted to ensure that the torpedoes were set at "deep." This was the recommended depth setting for a battleship or cruiser target, to cause the torpedo to impact below the torpedo-defense side blisters. Bayliss had been monitoring my conversation with the captain on the sound-powered circuit and was aware that the target was a large man-of-war and he had already set the deep option. I looked aft and saw the quintuple Torpedo Mount 2 training out to port, the plotting room repeating on the 21MC, "We have a solution." I reached across to press the red torpedo-firing buttons on the interior bulkhead of the director to launch five torpedoes in a salvo. Again, standing up in the hatch, I could see the torpedoes come out of their tubes in quick succession with their motors already running, slap the water, submerge, and head for the Japanese heavy, now only three thousand yards away.

Bennion again heeled sharply as the captain ordered full left rudder and "all ahead flank," and we swung to a northerly course heading for the postattack rendezvous point. Commander Cooper did not wish to linger in no man's land, considering the fate of the hapless *Grant*.

THE CHASE

By 0430 DesRon 56 had reformed north of Surigao Strait. As first evidence of the morning twilight appeared, the destroyers were ordered to proceed south at high speed to engage and destroy the remnants of the Japanese force. In the pale predawn light the scene in the lower gulf was appalling. I counted six distinct fires, and the oily surfaces of the gulf were littered with debris. Groups of Japanese sailors were clinging to bits of floating wreckage but showed a strong disinclination to being rescued, at least by us, as we raced by. Needless to say, there was no time to pause to deal with survivors. In the smoke and the early morning gloom we sighted a Japanese destroyer, *Asagumo* as she proved to be, limping south, badly damaged and on

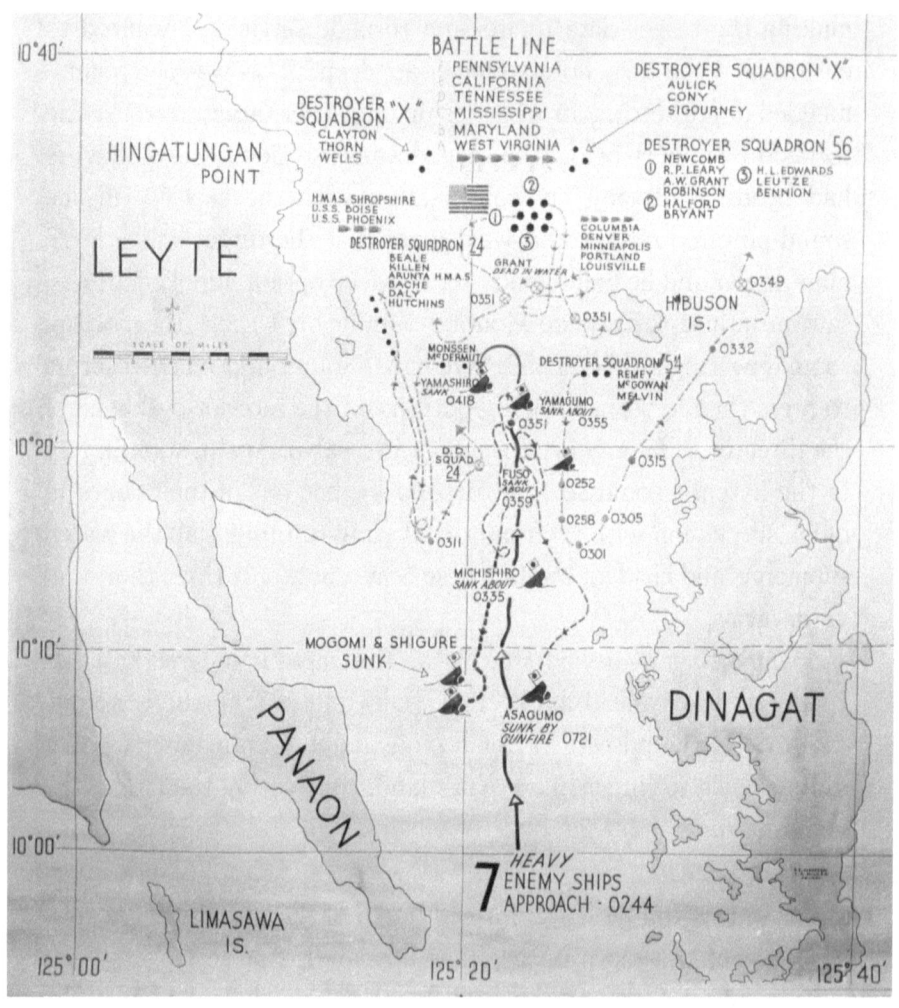

MAP 3. BATTLE OF SURIGAO STRAIT

fire. If *Asagumo* still had torpedoes on board she remained a deadly threat. As she was, she was valiantly fending off attacks from *Cony* (DD 508) and *Sigourney* (DD 643) with her aft battery; she soon came under heavier-caliber fire as the cruisers *Denver* and *Columbia* (CL 56) arrived. Changing course to close her, *Bennion* also opened fire with our forward 5-inch battery at ten thousand yards and began to hit on the third salvo. I shifted to rapid continuous fire at six thousand yards, and our rounds, in combination with others, penetrated *Asagumo*'s hull and exploded. Flames burst from her hatches. At about two thousand yards, the Japanese destroyer blew apart and slid beneath the grey, choppy waters as we passed close aboard. Listening to the chatter over the TBS and witnessing the survivors clinging to the floating remnants of what hours before had been Imperial Japanese Navy warships, we sensed that a great victory had been won. A major enemy force of battleships and cruisers had been virtually immolated at the cost of serious damage to only one of our ships, the destroyer *Albert W. Grant*. Samuel Eliot Morison was later to write that Leyte Gulf [of which the Surigao Strait action was a part] was the greatest naval battle in history.

ASSESSMENT

It was not until the day after the battle that we in *Bennion* had the time to analyze the engagement and submit our action report to Commander, Destroyer Squadron 56 for consolidation with the reports of the other eight destroyers, and to assess the performance of our own ship during the battle. Bayliss had timed the run of each torpedo salvo with a stopwatch to determine if an explosion occurred at the moment of expected impact. He reported seeing an explosion at the expected impact time of one of our torpedoes. He also said in his report that *Bennion*'s sonar had detected an underwater explosion at the time of his visual sighting. Bayliss unfortunately did not identify whether it was the first or second salvo that achieved the presumed hit.

Morison's account of the battle, the twelfth volume of his monumental 1958 *History of U.S. Navy Naval Operations in World War II*, is based on the official U.S. Navy after-action reports available at that time. It states that all of DesRon 56's torpedoes fired in the initial coordinated squadron attack missed, because the Japanese column reversed course at that very time. It does not mention *Bennion*'s second five-torpedo salvo against the unidentified Japanese heavy.[5] Morison does offer a caveat that tacitly reveals the ultimate authority for his own account of the battle: "Rear Admiral Richard W. Bates (Ret.) . . . and his staff have been working on an exhaustive and detailed study of the battle for Leyte Gulf which I have cited as the *War College Analysis: A Collection of Translated Japanese Action Reports and Memoirs*."[6]

The official analysis of the battle, conducted by the Naval War College and published like Morison's twelfth volume in 1958 but after the latter, has this to say:

> The *Yamashiro*, however turned to close the enemy as she advanced. Shortly after being taken under fire she started to burn. At 0356 she turned to the west and at 0405 she was hit by a torpedo fired by the *Bennion*. At 0359 *Bennion* had fired a second salvo of five intermediate speed torpedoes at what she thought was a second battleship . . . and made one hit on the *Yamashiro*. . . . At 0419, she [*Yamashiro*] suddenly sank.[7]

It should be noted that the War College analysis made extensive use of the interrogation of Japanese survivors of the battle, one of whom was a warrant officer from *Yamashiro*. Therefore, it can be firmly concluded that on the basis of a critical review of all official and authoritative information available on this subject, *Bennion* should be credited with a torpedo hit on the Japanese battleship *Yamashiro* in the battle of Surigao Strait at Leyte Gulf and so directly contributed to the subsequent sinking of the battleship only minutes later.

THE SURPRISE OFF SAMAR

As noted previously, at approximately 0700 on October 25, 1944, *Bennion* with cruisers and several other destroyers were racing south through the Surigao Strait in pursuit of the Japanese survivors of the previous night's violent battle. Our force had overtaken the badly damaged Japanese destroyer *Asagumo*, and *Bennion* assisted in rendering the coup de grâce.

Smoke from two additional Japanese ships, badly damaged but still able to travel under their own power, could be seen on the southern horizon, and the pursuing force continued the chase. Just as *Bennion* turned to rejoin the formation, a Zero broke out of the low clouds on our port beam heading directly toward us. Again using the slewing sight at the director officer's hatch, I swung the 5-inch battery onto the incoming plane and commenced firing, in a no-deflection, head-on shot. A 5-inch round scored a direct hit. The Zero was blown to pieces in a fiery explosion and the flaming debris fell into the sea around us.

It was now early morning of the 25th. The crew of *Bennion* was tired. We had been up since early reveille the day before. I was at my battle station in the Mark 37 director when the word was passed to secure from GQ and set Condition III, a condition of partial alert. At the same time Commander Cooper called from the bridge on the 17MC to tell me that the chase had been broken off, on orders from Rear Admiral Oldendorf. All Seventh Fleet cruisers and destroyers were to steam north, form up in their tactical units, and rendezvous with the battle line, which itself was forming up and steaming east across the entrance of Leyte Gulf to get to open waters east of Samar. I was replaced in the forward director by one of the assistant gunnery officers, a lieutenant (junior grade) who had the watch in the director from eight to noon. I was understandably tired but had to proceed directly down to the bridge, where I was scheduled for the 0800–1200 deck watch.

As I prepared to take over from the communications officer, the OOD during General Quarters, I found him in deep conversation with Commander Cooper, who beckoned me to join them. They were talking about message traffic from Commander Seventh Fleet to the effect that the Taffy [their collective call sign] groups, the task groups of CVEs, DEs, and DDs defending the landing beach, were being taken under attack by a large Japanese force of battleships, cruisers, and destroyers. There were three Taffy groups operating east of Samar and apparently two of them were under direct fire. Because of the distance and the landmass between our position and that of the Taffy groups, we could only hear parts of the radio exchanges between the CVEs and their escorting ships, but it was evident that at least one CVE had been hit by gunfire and was burning and that several of the DDs and DEs had been sunk. Rear Admiral Oldendorf was rallying his forces that had fought the Japanese at Surigao Straits and preparing to sortie from Leyte Gulf and save the Taffy groups.

This was a sobering moment. The exhilaration we had experienced from the realization of a great victory in Surigao Strait, the sight on the arrival of daylight of the sinking and burning Japanese ships, and the absence of major losses on our part was being replaced by the news that six Seventh Fleet CVEs and their surface escorts were facing annihilation. I quickly relieved as OOD, and the captain left the bridge to grab a bite to eat and to shave; he had been on his feet for the preceding twelve hours. At this point, ComSeventhFlt [Commander, Seventh Fleet or a staff member acting at his direction] came up on the TBS circuit directing the cruisers, destroyers, and battleships to report directly to him via voice radio the quantities of armor-piercing, major-caliber projectiles each had and for the destroyers the number of torpedoes on board. This was transmitted with urgent priority. I called up to the Condition III gunnery watch officer in the main director, using the 17MC, requesting that he query each of the 5-inch gun mount handling rooms for the number of AP projectiles available and then passed the word for Chief Gunner's Mate Omer Shriver to report to the bridge immediately.

Shriver almost immediately informed me through the sound-powered talker that he was in the forward magazines and would come to the bridge if desired but was taking a quick inventory of armor-piercing and AA common projectiles. Chief Shriver was doing so on his own initiative, and I felt fortunate to be serving with such professionals.[8]

As I listened to the ships' reports being made piecemeal of ammunition stocks on hand among the combatants, I understood ComSeventhFlt's apprehension. There was not much armor-piercing ammunition left. Most of the allowance had been expended in the night action at Surigao Straits. The available projectiles were mainly AA common, which would be relatively ineffective against modern Japanese battleships. Interspersed with these logistical reports were sporadic call-ups from destroyer division and squadron commanders attempting to round up their ships by broadcasting their positions, sometimes in latitude and longitude but more often with a bearing and distance to a geographical point. The voice circuit on the TBS was becoming overloaded to a dangerous extent. Normally this channel was available only for immediate tactical commands and warnings of enemy forces in the vicinity, particularly enemy air activity. Fortunately, various commanders realized the need for circuit discipline and imposed a self-restraint that quickly got the situation under control. This was a good example of the seasoning of competent leaders by months of demanding operations.

By 1030 we had joined up in a disposition prescribed by ComSeventhFlt and had increased speed to twenty knots standing toward the eastern entrance of Leyte Gulf. About this time a radioman gave Commander Cooper an intercept of a flash-precedence message from Taffy 3, Rear Adm. Clifton A. F. Sprague, that for unknown reasons the Japanese force attacking his units had broken off, reversed course, and seemed to be headed toward San Bernardino Strait. Shortly thereafter we received a confirming message from ComSeventhFlt that slowed the battle line and turned it 180 degrees toward a better position for defending the beachhead at Leyte Gulf. The immediate threat of the destruction of the Taffy groups by the Japanese fleet, and even worse the prospect of the Japanese battleships and cruisers turned loose inside Leyte Gulf against the thin-hulled troopships and cargo vessels off the beachhead, had dissipated. The fleet spent the rest of the day and the next assigning and moving the heavies to cruising stations and setting up submarine screens and air picket stations for the destroyers. *Bennion* took on an assignment to screen Oldendorf's OBBs through the evening of the 26th. In addition, we continued our fighter-direction duties on both days; an uptick in enemy air activity occurred on the 26th. Our air controllers took control of eight or ten Navy fighters, F6-F Hellcats from the fast carrier groups rather than FM-2 Wildcats flown by the Taffy groups. Our surmise was that the CVEs had lost most of their aircraft in the action off Samar or had been forced to withdraw by the Japanese force and had not returned. It made us all very, very nervous to have our fighter cover reduced, especially with the effectiveness of what we were now seeing as the new Japanese tactic.

CHAPTER 13

MY TIME IN DESTROYERS COMES TO A CLOSE

AT 2247, we received orders to steam back to the eastern entrance of Surigao Strait to take on picket duties. Two hours later, early on the 27th, we were back where the last duel between battleships had occurred a mere forty-five hours earlier.

The next day, October 27, *Bennion* was relieved at that picket station by the destroyer escort USS *Eversole* (DE 404). We returned to the beachhead area, where *Bennion* joined an ASW screen, patrolling with active sonar the area surrounding the beachhead anchorage, where the cargo ships and transports were anchored.

During the day there were Japanese planes overhead almost constantly but also enough Navy fighters to knock them down or force them to turn back before getting into the port area. Meanwhile, Commander Cooper became concerned about our fuel level and the fact that we had defanged ourselves with our expenditure of torpedoes and large quantities of ammunition. Though granted permission to refuel on the 28th, enemy air activity had us going to General Quarters throughout the day. Finally, on the morning of the 29th, we were directed to pull alongside USS *Caribou* (IX 114) [a commercial tanker taken up by the Navy] to replenish our fuel bunkers. That afternoon, to replenish our expended ammunition, we moored alongside the destroyer *Sigourney*, which was readying to depart for Seeadler Harbor to extract her ten torpedoes and load two hundred rounds of 5-inch AA common, smoke-generating canisters, and additional provisions. By then we had learned that *Eversole* had been torpedoed that morning by a Japanese submarine and sunk with heavy loss of life off Dinagat—the island fronting Leyte across the Surigao Strait.[1]

Sigourney would join with the majority of the Seventh Fleet's combatants to form up into a cruising disposition and depart, leaving behind the transports, supply ships, and a holding force. The main body of the Seventh Fleet was retiring for much-needed maintenance and resupply in preparation for the next major operation, which we expected to be an amphibious assault into the island of Luzon, to liberate Manila. The holding force was made up of three old battleships, three older heavy cruisers, and a dozen destroyers. We were left with the holding force because *Bennion* had on board a fighter-direction team—a small assigned detachment trained to guide the combat air patrol—and therefore would be crucial for the defense of the beachhead area, over which the Japanese had already challenged American air superiority.[2]

Of note, from this point on the paint scheme on the aircraft we took under our direction was no longer blue but green.

THE U.S. ARMY AIR FORCES

At least one Army Air Forces [or USAAF, as the U.S. Army Air Corps had been known since June 1941] fighter strip began operating in the vicinity of our beachhead near Tacloban. As Japanese high-altitude (ten thousand feet) raids entered the area, we could see the distinctive, twin-tailed P-38 Lightnings engage them. Those of us topside had a unique vantage point to watch some dogfighting. That showed us that not all of the experienced Japanese pilots had been lost.

Although the USAAF had now entered the battle to contest the Japanese control of the air over the Philippines, the poor condition of the landing fields ashore made substantial fighter augmentation from the Navy needed, and fortunately it was provided. Our fighter-direction team had some time ago installed a special communications link from their spaces to the Mark 37 director to keep me, as the condition watch gunnery officer, continuously informed of the air battle.

The Japanese mounted many assaults on the Leyte Gulf beachhead, probably because it was the only American force that could be targeted by their range-limited aircraft. By the third or fourth day after the landings they were sending two daylight raids per day—in the morning and afternoon—between fifty and seventy aircraft in each wave. The Japanese were staging their planes—multiengined bombers, single-seat dive-bombers, and Zeros for fighter cover—into fields in the Philippines within range of Tacloban. These Japanese aircraft were coming from the home islands as well as from Truk and Formosa. They usually approached at ten to fifteen thousand feet and were intercepted by the CAP twenty miles or so from the objective area off Tacloban, still filled with merchant ships supporting the 140,000 Army troops ashore. The CAP was remarkably effective, shooting down about half of the raiders in each wave and forcing the others to divert to emergency Japanese landing strips on northern Luzon. The Wildcats and Lightnings were working over the twin-engined bombers and the kamikazes; the Japanese fighters seemed unable to counter them. In the director I could hear through my earphones the Navy planes calling out "Tally Ho" as they sighted their targets and initiated their attack runs.

Some stragglers in each wave managed to evade our fighters and slip into the objective area, where they were taken under fire by the 5-inch guns of the destroyers, battleships, and cruisers.

The loss of *Eversole* was a grim reminder of the dangers that still lurked below the surface as well. A few days later, the light cruiser *Reno* (CL 96), operating with Task Group 38.3, would absorb a torpedo hit on her port quarter and struggle to make it back to Ulithi. Meanwhile, at Leyte Gulf we encountered yet another threat, in the form of a cyclone that bore through the area late on the 29th and into the 30th. There was a silver lining, however—a respite in enemy air activity thanks to the worsening weather. That respite would be short-lived.

AERIAL ASSAULTS

As the seas calmed, Commander Cooper received orders from DesRon 56 to relieve *Killen* (DD 593), which had ridden out the storm at a picket station guarding the eastern approaches to the gulf. The final two days of October for *Bennion* proved relatively peaceful at that easterly outpost. That too was about to change, and abruptly.

To our dismay, we heard on radio circuits Task Group 77.1 coming under heavy air attack and the Japanese scoring numerous direct hits. We heard that two sister *Fletcher*-class destroyers, *Claxton* (DD 571) and *Ammen* (DD 527), were hit—the former now suffering a major steering casualty and the latter structural damage around the stacks and bridge from a strike amidships by what were described as suicide planes. Then we received word that *Killen*, the destroyer we had relieved two days earlier, had been hit. I later learned she was attacked by seven enemy aircraft in a span of four minutes. The destroyer splashed four of the attackers before a bomb hit on the port side, killing fifteen.

Given the lethality on the ongoing air assault, *Bennion* and two other destroyers on picket stations were recalled to Leyte Gulf to beef up AA defenses.[3] *Bennion* proceeded first to a picket station about forty miles east of the beachhead near the entrance to Leyte Gulf, and relieved USS *Abner Read* (DD 526), another *Fletcher*-class destroyer, on station. As we approached *Abner Read*'s position we lost radar contact with her and at the same time observed a column of black smoke in the vicinity of where *Read* had been last seen. Then we received word through the fighter-direction circuits, which our fighter-direction team always monitored, that an enemy aircraft had dived directly into *Abner Read* and set her on fire. We later learned that a diving Val whose left wing *Abner Read* shot off had already released a bomb that would score a bullseye on the after stack and penetrate the deck, decimating the aft engine room and starting a fire that would soon detonate the forward magazine.[4] The word "kamikaze" was not used because this was really our first experience with this terrifyingly effective Japanese tactic. I believe for the first week there was a feeling that these planes were crashing into destroyers simply because the pilots were being killed during dive-bombing attacks, that the planes just continued its final course with dead hands on the stick.

Again *Bennion* was summoned to return to the beachhead area, this time to counter Japanese surface forces reported by intelligence in the Sulu Sea and Ormoc Bay. If the Japanese were to be nuts enough to force the Surigao Strait again, they would receive a similar reception.

As we maintained our position on the left flank guarding the egress from Surigao Strait that evening we reflected on the damage inflicted on our forces that day and perceived that there had been a shift in tactics. As our war diary notes, "self preservation" had been replaced by "daring and persistence." That the Japanese went after screening destroyers when there were much more lucrative targets in the vicinity also seemed puzzling. Perhaps we appeared as larger targets to pilots at altitude. Another theory was the Japanese, should they try again to force the strait, wanted to have eliminated the torpedo ships.[5]

Through the following morning we remained in a formation called Disposition 5, with the comfort of knowing that Adm. William F. Halsey had formed a new task group—TG 34.5—commanded by Halsey himself in *New Jersey* (BB 62) in company with *Iowa* (BB 61), three light cruisers, and six destroyers, now not far beyond the eastern horizon. By that time, Halsey's fast carriers, which had recently engaged and decimated much of the remaining Japanese fleet [especially its carriers], in what became known as the battle of

Cape Engaño had retired to Ulithi. With large numbers of Japanese aircraft shuttling down from airfields on Luzon to challenge control of the skies, those carriers would soon be under way with an objective of hitting the Luzon airfields, beginning on November 5.[6]

On the strength of a reassessment that the Japanese were not going to attempt another attack but instead land reinforcements at Ormoc Bay on the opposite side of Leyte, we reassumed a circular defensive disposition around the landing zone. Five or six other destroyers anchored in a protective arch around the northern part of the beachhead anchorage. The reason for ships being rotated through the picket stations and then anchored in a fixed antiair screen was to save fuel. Both fuel and ammunition were in somewhat short supply, but what was of greater concern was the difficulty of refueling and rearming alongside tankers or ammunition ships with the Japanese overhead.

I assumed the "dog watch" [the 1600–2000 was "dogged," divided in two, to allow the watch standers to eat] that afternoon. The defense of the beachhead was still entrusted to our force of old battleships, cruisers, and, now, crippled destroyers; when I looked around at the screen of destroyers the sight was absolutely bizarre. The ships were unrecognizable in many cases. One destroyer had had its forward stack knocked off and another's after stack was missing. Both were *Fletcher*-class ships but their silhouettes were now like that of the early *Mahan* class. One destroyer's fantail had been wiped clean of 20-mm guns where a kamikaze had crashed before going over the side. However, all of them could still steam at twenty-five knots and control at least two 5-inch guns in director fire.

That night was miserable for the holding force off Tacloban and was a harbinger of nights to come. The U.S. forces were unable to maintain local air superiority, and one reason was the failure of the U.S. Army Air Forces to get their land-based squadrons into the action. The plan had been for Army engineers to upgrade former

Japanese sod fields and to create new ones for P-38s and P-51 Mustangs. But the recent typhoon and ongoing monsoon season had left the ground too soft, and the deadline for additional fighter strips becoming operational had been passed days before. Much of this information came from the chatter picked up by our fighter-direction team.

The commander of the holding force was Rear Adm. George L. Weyler.[7] Because of the shortage of fuel, he had the battleships and cruisers anchor with the transports and supply ships and the dozen destroyers anchor in an arc around the offloading anchorage. We of course kept our boilers steaming, at low pressure to conserve fuel but enough to generate the power needed to operate the gun mounts and magazine systems.

That evening, November 2, shortly after dark, the force was approached by what we believed to be low-flying Bettys. The twin-engined naval bombers were not used for kamikaze attacks but delivered bombs or torpedoes from internal bomb bays. We tracked the Bettys as they arrived and saw them drop down and spread out in a wide arc from which they would initiate their runs on the transports, as if following spokes going into the hub of a wheel. They came in quite low, which made tracking them very difficult with the limited capabilities of our fire-control radars on the Mark 37 director. All at once one of the transports commenced firing. Each transport normally carried an old 5-inch gun with a Navy gun crew plus a half dozen 20-millimeters, also with sailors as gunners. There was little fire discipline on these ships, and apparently this transport's crew thought they saw a Japanese aircraft and commenced firing, and with that virtually every ship in the force opened up with all its weapons. It was bedlam: friendly 20-mm projectiles were passing between our stacks and exploding in the water around us. The commodore had ordered all destroyers to make smoke to obscure the ships in the anchorage, so *Bennion* and her compatriots were belching thick, black, nauseating smoke out of both stacks [produced by unbalancing the boilers' fuel/air supply]. We had two Bettys in our immediate vicinity flying at high speed through our disposition, but it was hard to tell whether they could be effective or not, as it was obvious they would have trouble selecting their targets and estimating the proper release point.

We suffered through two more raids that night. Two ships reported damage and casualties from friendly fire. In the subsequent attacks the fire discipline on the ships improved, but wild scenes still erupted when the Japanese planes passed over our formation at masthead height. With dawn and then daylight the attacks ceased, and once again we had our CAP overhead that was able to intercept, shoot down, or turn back Japanese raids, now coming in at between eight and fifteen thousand feet. These were kamikaze aircraft, which preferred to make their attacks from six thousand feet or higher, pitching over into a dive as if glide- or dive-bombing, hurtling down at a steep angle that made antiaircraft gunnery from the ships most difficult, and then crashing into a ship.

PICKET DUTY

Bennion was detached from the anchored screen and ordered to a picket station in the eastern entrance to Leyte Gulf, where we established an ASW patrol, cruising at about ten knots in a north/south pattern. Commodore Weyler was much concerned, as he should have been, about the threat of Japanese submarines entering the gulf and attacking the ships at anchor, sitting ducks. It was a worrisome situation. At the same time *Bennion* was controlling CAP, using our long-range radar to detect raids coming in from the east. The Japanese were sending planes from island bases that had been bypassed by the Leyte landings to airstrips on Mindanao and in the southern Philippines. Then during daylight they were flying to sea and approaching the Tacloban anchorage from the east in an effort to bypass the only USAAF strips that were expected to be operational at this time.

As darkness approached and our CAP bid *sayonara*, *Bennion* was recalled to the anchored screen of destroyers. A new wrinkle had been added to the defense of the anchorage. Craft such as LCVPs had been equipped with tanks filled with chemical smoke (FS) that they then laid in a screen outside the destroyers. Of course the FS smoke moved at the speed and in the direction of the prevailing breeze, and within a half an hour it was everywhere. It mixed with the noxious black smoke from the ships' fire rooms to make the local atmosphere very unpleasant for breathing and eye-watering in high concentrations.

We went to GQ at dusk as we picked up low fliers again forming up in the central gulf. It was another night of sleepless confusion, with more casualties—although somewhat fewer—among topside personnel from stray friendly rounds.

DETACHING

Despite the apparent confusion and chaos every night, the Navy's command and control in the anchorage and on the beachhead worked well. The organization of the Army advance to the north was remarkably effective, and the logistical operations were efficiently carried out in accordance with the operations plans. The one problem was continued delay in the operational readiness of the Army Air Forces. The generally lighter Japanese aircraft could operate from sod fields and wet expeditionary strips, whereas the heavier American fighters and light bombers demanded hardened landing, parking, and takeoff areas.

The flow of war material through the beachhead was continuous during the day. During the night the anchorage was dedicated to air defense, with its attendant hazards of bombs, crashing aircraft, and errant projectiles and shrapnel from our own forces. That was an opportunity to move the material away from the waterfront and into supply dumps farther inland along the main supply route. Each day, commercial ships that had discharged their cargos weighed anchor and headed east to pick up more cargo to sustain the Leyte beachhead or for the next landing of Army troops, which was expected on Luzon. Space on board these departing cargo ships was carefully regulated by the main logistical command. By October 29 there was still no regular air transport out of Leyte, so the first priority for the departing ships went to wounded who needed better care than could be provided by the mobile Army surgical hospitals ashore. Then came the retrograde [return to depots] of large equipment, military equipment, and vehicles needing repair. Lowest priority went to personnel being returned to "Zone of the Interior," the continental United States. Such was I, and there were very few of us.

On November 7, 1944, *Bennion* received a message that Lieutenant Holloway was to report on board the commercial cargo ship SS *Dorothy Lykes* prior to 1600 that day. *Dorothy Lykes* would be getting under way imminently, when the small convoy to which it would be attached was ready to move. Needless to say, my bags were packed. I had put my accumulated books, memorabilia, and souvenirs in a large "cruise box," constructed by the ship's carpenter, that *Bennion* would ship to me care of the Army when she next went alongside a cargo ship. I held back my toilet kit and khaki work uniforms in a full seabag—weighing about twenty pounds—that I could handle easily and that would not take up much room in the primitive conditions I expected. In fact, I had been told that though it was important to have orders, I basically would be hitchhiking back to California, grabbing a ride on anything moving in an easterly direction.

Early that afternoon the signalmen on *Bennion* did a great job of finding *Dorothy Lykes* in the anchorage, using a combination of flashing light and TBS radio. It was a large anchorage, the ships spread out all over the place, many of them moving to offloading areas closer to the beach, warships and cargo vessels intermixed, most of the cargo vessels with their names or identification numbers painted over and replaced in very small lettering. The whole anchorage seemed to be overhung by a pall of smoke left by gunfire, smoke from the ships' stacks, and the FS chemical smoke.

At about 1400 the skipper, still Cdr. Josh Cooper, called me to the bridge to say goodbye. He said he thought it was time I got going; neither of us showed it, but I know it was a sentimental parting for both of us. He thanked me for my contributions to *Bennion*'s war-fighting capabilities, and I thanked him for his consideration in overlooking the many mistakes that a young gunnery officer made over the past eleven months. My skipper, who was a splendid gentleman and a great destroyer captain, told me once again that he was sorry to see me leave the destroyer Navy. I thought for a moment before I replied: "Captain, we silenced four shore batteries, shot down three Zeros, sank a destroyer by gunfire, and made a torpedo attack that helped sink a Japanese battleship. I think I'd like to try something new."

He smiled and said, "It's still a long way to Tokyo, but by the time you get your wings this war will be over and I don't believe you'll ever see combat again in your naval career."

Josh Cooper turned out to be a better destroyer man than a seer. But he was expressing the universal conviction of war-weary Americans that our total victory in World War II could only result in a lasting peace.

He had been kind enough to make his gig available with his personal coxswain. It was a standard whaleboat with the canopy removed to minimize fire hazards and flying debris in the event the topsides were hit in battle, but the engine ran, and that was what counted. Just as I clambered down a Jacob's ladder into the gig I heard General Quarters sounded and looked up to see my comrades heading for their battle stations, no longer running but moving at a very steady, determined pace, knowing exactly what they had to do.

Before we had reached *Dorothy Lykes* [the gig having been dispatched notwithstanding] I could imagine the engineers on the Navy ships filled with glee as they were ordered to make lots of black smoke.[8] The coxswain of the whaleboat was a seaman first class—a "seaman 1st"—who would ordinarily have been the director/operator on the 40-mm director on the starboard side forward, right below the platform where I had watched him in action—standing on a pedestal at his handlebar-type director, totally exposed to the elements and the hail of fire and shrapnel but displaying no trepidation, only absolute concentration and focus on picking up and tracking the incoming kamikazes.

So I transferred in the captain's gig from *Bennion* to *Dorothy Lykes* to begin a long, slow hitchhike across the Pacific. I had orders to flight training. *Bennion* would go on to Lingayen Gulf, then to Okinawa, and to receive a Presidential Unit Citation without me, and I went on to a career as a carrier pilot.

As a footnote, I want to tell the "rest of the story" about the gig coxswain whose overall heroic performance I recounted above. Fifty-five years later we were to hook up again when he wrote me a letter to ask if I would help him get a Bronze Star Medal for which he had been recommended but that had been withdrawn because of a disciplinary infraction on his part. With the help of the staff at the Naval Historical Foundation in Washington, DC, where I was the president, I petitioned the Board of Decorations and Medals, which approved the medal after more than half a century. We all had great pleasure in seeing photographs of Adm. Vernon Clark, the Chief of Naval Operations and a career destroyer man himself, present the medal to Seaman First Class Harold Hartman at a Navy League dinner in Cincinnati in 2002.

EPILOGUE:
LATER YEARS,
FINAL HONORS

THE FATES OF *RINGGOLD* AND *BENNION*

BOTH DESTROYERS in which Admiral Holloway served would survive the war in the Pacific. Following his departure at Pearl Harbor in August 1943, *Ringgold* screened a fast carrier task force that conducted preliminary air strikes on Tarawa and Makin before heading on to Wake Island to soften up the Japanese garrison on that former American possession. Returning to Tarawa on November 20, *Ringgold* joined with *Dashiell* (DD 659) to steam into the lagoon ahead of the main body of the attack force and was hit by Japanese shore batteries twice. Fortunately, the shells were duds. There followed what proved to be a horrific day in Marine Corps history, but the close on-call gunfire provided by these two *Fletcher*-class destroyers prevented worse carnage. Specifically, it would be credited with disrupting a potential after-dark counterattack.

Following Tarawa, *Ringgold* participated in the capture of Kwajalein and Eniwetok Atolls in early 1944 and then headed to the Southwest Pacific to shell enemy installations at Kavieng, on New Ireland, in March. She then joined in the assault and capture of Hollandia, Dutch New Guinea, during late April. While in June and July *Bennion* was taking part in the Saipan and Tinian operations in the Marianas, Holloway's previous ship was the landing craft control vessel for the invasion of another island in the Marianas—Guam.

Subsequently, while *Bennion* was supporting the Marine Corps seizure of Peleliu, *Ringgold* performed similar duties five hundred miles to the southwest during the landing of American, Australian, and Dutch forces to capture the lightly defended island of Morotai in the northern Moluccas.

The invasion of the Philippines in October 1944 brought the two "Holloway ships" in the same vicinity as units of the Seventh Fleet. Given the scope of the invasion, it is unlikely that Holloway caught a glimpse of his former ship. *Bennion*, under Task Force 79, the Southern Attack Force and assigned to DesRon 56, was in the destroyer screen of Rear Admiral Oldendorf's battleships and cruisers. *Ringgold* was assigned to Task Force 78, the Northern Attack Force, and provided gunfire support for the landings on October 20 at Panaon Island, which flanked Leyte Gulf to the south. *Bennion* would be one of the combatants at Surigao Strait, but *Ringgold* missed out on the action, having departed the area three days prior for a scheduled overhaul at Mare Island, California.

The same day Holloway departed *Bennion* in November 1944, the Navy fighter-direction team also left, to be replaced by an Army air controller. *Bennion* continued to play a role in the air defense of the landing areas as units of the U.S. Sixth Army advanced across Leyte over the next week. Leaving Leyte Gulf on November 15, *Bennion* escorted convoys before spending Thanksgiving at Seeadler Harbor for repairs by the destroyer tender there. The destroyer then returned to Leyte Gulf, which was now a staging area for a mid-December amphibious thrust to seize Mindoro, a relatively lightly defended island in the Philippine archipelago south of Luzon. During the transit from the gulf to Mindoro by way of the Surigao Strait *Bennion* screened the CVEs, fending off several determined Japanese air attacks.

Another destroyer transiting Surigao Strait, escorting LCIs to Ormoc Bay, would not be as fortunate. On December 11, *Reid* (DD 369), commanded by former *Ringgold* XO Samuel A.

McCornock, in a span of less than sixty seconds shot down two approaching attackers and witnessed a third explode off her starboard beam, but a fourth aircraft and its bomb hit the ship at the waterline forward. A fifth plane strafed this ship and then crashed on the port bow, a sixth strafed the bridge before crashing off the starboard bow, and a seventh aircraft delivered the coup de grâce, crashing into the port quarter. Its bomb detonated in the aft magazine. *Reid* rolled over and sank with 103 of the crew; McCornock survived, with some 150 others. He would continue on active duty for another decade, retiring for health reasons as a captain. Promoted to rear admiral in retirement, McCornock settled in Iron Mountain, Michigan, where he died in early 1974.[1] McCornock's previous destroyer would "outlive" him.

On Christmas Eve 1944, back in Seeadler Harbor, Commander Cooper turned over command of *Bennion* to Cdr. R. H. Holmes and detached to remain in the theater on the staff of Amphibious Group 9. Cooper's subsequent tours would include command of the NROTC unit at Harvard and of *Iowa* during the Korean War; he would also head the naval sections of military aid groups in Greece and Norway. Cooper retired as a rear admiral in 1963, holder of the Navy Cross for *Bennion*'s actions at the Surigao Strait, and resided in Alexandria, Virginia, until his passing in 1998, having outlived his former destroyer by many years.[2]

Bennion, with her new commanding officer, left Seeadler Harbor in Task Group 77.6 en route back to the Philippines for the next amphibious operation, at Lingayen Gulf on northern Luzon. Along the way *Bennion*-directed CAP accounted for seven enemy aircraft, and passing northward across the entrance of Manila Bay the destroyer engaged in a running long-range duel with two Japanese destroyers that had emerged to contest the coming landing. Reassigned to support Task Group 77.2, the landing force, *Bennion* continued fighter direction and naval gunfire support during the successful landings of the middle two weeks of January 1945.

The U.S. Army would continue to liberate the Philippines all the way to the end of the war, but at the end of the month *Bennion* arrived at Ulithi Atoll, the staging area for the next major operation, against Iwo Jima. Over the eastern horizon *Ringgold* too returned, to be a screening ship for Vice Adm. Marc A. Mitscher's Task Force 58, which would fly air strikes to support the capture of Iwo Jima and then Okinawa. *Ringgold* steamed often beyond sight of land, but *Bennion* escorted *New York* (BB 34) close to the beaches of Iwo Jima.

Following another respite at Ulithi, *Bennion* operated off Okinawa for two and a half months beginning on March 21, 1945. There, owing to Japanese kamikaze tactics there were more American deaths at sea than ashore; *Bennion* played a crucial role as a fighter-director ship and came herself under frequent direct attacks. The destroyer's gun crews were credited with a dozen kills and four assists. She suffered slight damage during a near miss by a kamikaze.

Bennion then steamed to Saipan for a short break before spending much of July in the ASW screen of Task Group 30.8, the fast-carrier support group—escort carriers with spare planes for the frontline carriers, as well as oilers and other logistic ships. *Ringgold*, meanwhile, screened those frontline carriers and in addition operated directly against the Japanese homeland, conducting antishipping sweeps and taking targets ashore under fire. *Ringgold* would be off Japan when the atomic bombs were dropped and the Japanese announced their intent to surrender. In contrast, the war ended for *Bennion* during a Pacific odyssey that took her to Guam, east to Eniwetok, and north to Adak, then finally southwest to Honshu at the end of August to join the occupation forces. *Bennion* would be in Japan on September 2, but she would not be in the armada of ships at Tokyo Bay at the time of the surrender, and neither would *Ringgold*, which was undergoing upkeep at Guam. Holloway's first ship would then steam to Okinawa to embark eighty-three passengers for Pearl Harbor. From there *Ringgold* returned to the East Coast to be decommissioned on March 23, 1946. DD 500 subsequently was placed with other mothballed warships in the Atlantic Reserve Fleet near Charleston, South Carolina. She had earned ten battle stars for her World War II service.

Bennion returned to the West Coast, arriving at the Puget Sound Navy Yard on October 27, 1945. She would be decommissioned and placed in reserve at Long Beach on June 20, 1946. *Bennion* had received the Presidential Unit Citation for her actions off Okinawa (1 April–1 June 1945) and eight battle stars. Though *Ringgold* had been commissioned nearly a year earlier than *Bennion*, the overhaul she underwent at Mare Island in late 1944 likely left her in better shape when her crew filed off for the last time. Throughout *Bennion*'s war dairies are comments about cracks in boiler tubes, temporary repairs that failed to hold, and other engineering maladies. From her commissioning until her return from overseas she was ridden exceptionally hard. When the Navy pulled from the fleet reserve and then modernized follow-on *Allen M. Sumner–* and *Gearing*-class ships for service in Korea and Vietnam, *Bennion* would remain on the sidelines. Stricken from the Naval Vessel Register on April 15, 1971, she was sold on May 30, 1973, and broken up for scrap.

In contrast, after thirteen years resting at Charleston, *Ringgold* was transferred to the Federal Republic of Germany, along with five other sister ships to enable the Bundesmarine to form a *"Zerstörer"* (destroyer) squadron. Transferred July 14, 1959, the Germans designated her *Z-*2. In 1981 West Germany sold *Z-*2 to Greece, where she actively served in the Hellenic Navy as HS *Kimon* (D 42) for the next five years before being placed in reserve to be finally stricken and scrapped in 1993.[3]

JAMES L. HOLLOWAY JR.

As for a detailed overview of the future career of the young naval officer who served as a gunnery officer in these two destroyers, the already-published sequel to this narrative is well worth reading.

However, *Aircraft Carriers at War* has little to say on what became of Holloway's father, who has only two mentions in the memoir. But of these two mentions, the second is quite telling. On page 147, "Holloway III" wrote of his arrival for his first Pentagon tour as a commander in 1950 with his wife Dabney and three children, his father having just retired as a four-star admiral and living in Philadelphia. Holloway declared, "I make a point of this because there has been a tacit presumption that my father was in a position to advance my career as I gained seniority in the Navy." He argued such presumptions had little basis, as retired officers had little to no influence on the detailers who selected officers' future duty stations or on selection boards that recommended officers as worthy of promotion.[4]

Unfortunately, the reality was not so simple. Many who would be in positions to determine the future of the younger Holloway had served with or under his father, and from that arose the potential for bias. This point is illustrated by the younger Holloway himself, when his father's relief as head of the Training Command in Bermuda presumed that a slovenly officer with Holloway was in fact him. Still, given the senior Holloway's subsequent successful career, one could argue that favorable predispositions may have been left in his wake that could have benefited his son. On the other hand, recommendations made and actions taken by the father that were to shape the Navy through the present were not universally embraced at the time. In some cases the younger Holloway may have had to overcome preexisting unfavorable opinions on his own way to "stardom." Predispositions aside, the Navy's senior-officer selection process has long striven "to get it right," selecting on the merits of individual performance. All the evidence argues that James L. Holloway III's performance throughout his career was exceptional. As for the Navy's top job, Holloway's predecessor in it, Adm. Elmo R. Zumwalt, felt certain that "Mr. [(President) Richard] Nixon remembered Jimmy's father for his own period of naval service."

Since Nixon's service had been with naval aviation in the Pacific, it's hard to fathom how their paths might have crossed. However, Nixon when vice president would have been very familiar with the senior Holloway's role in the Lebanon crisis, which ended well for the Dwight D. Eisenhower administration.[5] Another Zumwalt assessment of his successor—"a father's achievements can place an unfair burden on the boy"—may have been more on target, suggesting that the junior Holloway "always thought he was being compared to his dad."[6]

Whether or not the senior Holloway's rise to full admiral had any influence on the success of his son's remains conjecture. However, it's worth a look at the final years of James L. Holloway Jr.'s career for the context readers might have looked for in *Aircraft Carriers at War.*

IOWA

As Lieutenant Holloway made his way back to the States from *Bennion* on board *Dorothy Lykes,* his father was beginning a rather short but active tenure in command of *Iowa,* vital in the air defense of the fast carriers as the Japanese turned to kamikazes ("Divine Wind"), inflicting serious damage. However, in December Admiral Halsey's fleet faced a true divine wind in the form of Typhoon Cobra, which cost the Third Fleet three destroyers lost, with nearly all hands, and serious damage to three additional destroyers, a cruiser, and five aircraft carriers. Some 146 aircraft were damaged or swept overboard, including one of *Iowa*'s floatplanes. Fortunately for Captain Holloway and *Iowa* no crew were injured. Damage to a propeller shaft on another occasion would take Holloway's battleship away from the tip of the spear. Hope that repairs could be made in a floating drydock in Manus proved unfounded; it was quickly determined that only a stateside Navy yard could do the work. *Iowa* was due for her first overhaul anyway, and Holloway received orders to take his battleship to Hunters Point Naval Shipyard in San Francisco, where he was greeted by Dabney's parents "Rim and Lucy Rawlings"—Capt. Norborne L. "Rim" Rawlings had command of that shipyard.[7]

With a repaired shaft and improved radars, *Iowa* returned to join what was now the Fifth Fleet under Admiral Spruance. She relieved *New Jersey* in mid-April 1945 off Okinawa and helped during May and June fend off kamikazes trying to stop the fast carriers from launching raids against airfields on the southern Japanese island of Kyushu. Then in July *Iowa*'s 16-inch rifles targeted steel mills on the northern island of Hokkaido and industrial facilities on Honshu. Her captain would not have the pleasure of witnessing on the scene the cessation of hostilities. All of a sudden one day a dispatch came in: "From CINCPAC [Commander in Chief Pacific] to Iowa direct." It concluded: "When relieved Captain J. L. Holloway Jr., USN promote to rear admiral and detach and proceed to Guam for further instructions."[8]

CHIEF OF NAVAL TRAINING AND HOLLOWAY BOARD

Holloway would learn he had been chosen to head Fleet Training Command, Pacific. He was not thrilled with the orders but rationalized that his selection was due to his previous experience in Bermuda preparing sailors to go to war and a subsequent tour in BuPers as the director of training. Had the war continued into 1946 as anticipated, Holloway's mission would have been essential. However, with the atomic bombing of Hiroshima two days prior to his assumption of command and Nagasaki the day following, Holloway "realized right away that the war was over and people were about as interested in training as they were in getting a hole in their head because everybody was going to be thinking about getting home."[9] As his new assignment became somewhat pointless, the new rear admiral became a bit depressed. To snap out of it Holloway checked out of his housing at the San Diego Naval Station and crossed the bay: "I just splurged and went over and lived in the Hotel del Coronado." From there he would walk down to the old ferry landing, where his barge (an admiral's "gig" but grander) would be waiting. "With just the change of locale and everything I lost about 20 pounds from what I'd been in the *Iowa*." However, before he could wear out the soles of his surface line officer's black shoes, "I got this frantic call from Washington to come back right away and I never returned to Coronado for duty because when I got back there I found they were in quite a swivet because [former Chief of Naval Personnel, Vice] Admiral [Randall] Jacobs and Jo[seph Warren] Barker, the Dean of Engineering at Columbia University had sent a proposal to Mr. [James V.] Forrestal that the Naval Academy be converted into a two-year school and accept people at the junior college year level."

The incumbent Chief of Naval Personnel, Vice Adm. Louis Denfeld, understood that this concept was meant to provide for the projected Navy and Marine Corps officer requirements in the postwar era, but he had his doubts. Thus, Holloway was to chair a board consisting of leading academics and senior naval officers to review how the Navy procured and educated its officers.[10] This study group, which became known as the Holloway Board, eventually recommended the expansion of the prewar Naval Reserve Officers Training Corps program to over fifty colleges and universities. The initial NROTC units had come into existence in 1926 at six universities. Enrollees received a small stipend, pay during summer training cruises, and on graduation a reserve commission and assignment to a naval reserve unit.[11] Under what became known as "The Holloway Plan," NROTC units would now cover tuition in addition to stipends, and graduating NROTC midshipmen would be commissioned into the fleet alongside Naval Academy graduates, initially incurring a three-year obligation.

For the board's ultimate decision not to pursue the Jacobs-Barker recommendation Holloway credited the Academy's Commandant of Midshipmen, Capt. Stuart H. "Slim" Ingersoll, who had argued that conversion of the Naval Academy into a quasi-postgraduate institution would wreck the esprit de corps of the midshipmen and the young officer product: "I think in retrospect it was absolutely right and he really swayed us into that premise almost at once."[12]

After securing the support of Secretary of the Navy Forrestal, the next step involved legislation, as tuition and other aspects of the program cost money. The House Naval Affairs Committee chair, Carl Vinson (reverently referred to as "First Lord" and since 1982 the eponym of a nuclear-powered aircraft carrier, CVN 70) liked the concept. When the legislation seemed stalled in the summer of 1946, Rear Admiral Holloway and Rear Adm. Felix Johnson flew down to Milledgeville, Georgia, to meet with Vinson. When they arrived Holloway recalled Vinson asking, "What's the matter? You boys in trouble again?" Holloway responded, "No, First Lord, we're down here for counsel and advice."[13]

With Vinson fully energized, the bill passed through both chambers and on to the White House for President Harry Truman's signature. Knowing that Truman would be encouraged by the War Department to veto it, as the Army had other ideas about officer procurement, Vice Admiral Denfeld reached out to Truman's legal counsel, Clarke Clifford. With a reputation before the war as a brilliant St. Louis attorney, Clifford had served a two-year stint in the Navy with a direct commission as a captain. Clifford secured an appointment for Forrestal and Denfeld to see the president. The visit was productive, and Truman signed the legislation into law.

The Army's objections to the plan will be delved into later; meanwhile, there was not insignificant opposition from midshipmen currently attending the Naval Academy and from some alumni. They argued that midshipmen attending NROTC units would not experience the rigors of plebe year nor imbibe the discipline instilled throughout the four years at Annapolis. One dismissive chant went, "Keep your car, keep your gal, keep your pay—be an officer the 'Holloway'!" Naval Academy graduates in the fleet would quip, "Did you get your commission the hard way or the Holloway?"[14] Holloway would get his opportunity to respond.

WORLD WAR II NAVY DEMOBILIZATION CHIEF

Though the development and then implementation of the Holloway Plan would have seemed a full-time tasking, Holloway's earlier observation that "everybody was going to be thinking about getting home" had been spot on. By mid-1946 Secretary Forrestal was growing concerned with reports from the West Coast that the local naval districts had backlogs of sailors awaiting discharge through the processing centers that had been set up. Holloway found himself designated as the new Assistant Chief of Naval Personnel for Demobilization. Inspecting demobilization centers on the West Coast, Holloway confirmed the reports but recognized it as simply a human-resources problem. He called on each of the district commandants and would say, "Admiral, the first priority of anything you have to do at this time is to provide the yeomen, the pay clerks, the typists and strip every activity in your district as may be needed to fully staff these demobilization centers and get these people through and moving." The added personnel solved part of the problem. Then there was the challenge of transportation home for discharged sailors. Working with the American Railroad Association, the Navy acquired rolling stock. It was from southern rail lines and was not winter-proofed. Some trains would have to get across the Rockies, but to Holloway it didn't matter that the bathrooms froze so long as these men could be on their way and home for Christmas. In the event, the Navy discharged over three million men from the service within a year following the formal Japanese surrender.[15]

If the implementation of the Holloway Plan was to ignite any semblance of a mutiny within the fraternity of Annapolis graduates, the Navy took quick action to quell it in advance. Throughout 1946, as Holloway deftly handled his two major taskings (and some others, such as having the Navy given the lead role in creation of the Armed Forces Staff College), he heard the rumors circulating that he was being considered for the superintendent's job at the Naval Academy. He knew he was liked by Secretary Forrestal and the

Chief of Naval Operations (CNO) Fleet Admiral Chester Nimitz, and the Chief of Naval Personnel, Vice Admiral Denfeld, had been his mentor. The pushback on his candidacy had to do with his young age (forty-eight) and a war-fighting resumé that included combat operations only during Operation Torch in North Africa and near the conclusion of the war in the Pacific.[16]

SUPERINTENDENT, U.S. NAVAL ACADEMY

On January 15, 1947, Rear Adm. James L. Holloway Jr. became the thirty-fifth superintendent of the Naval Academy. A thundering roar rattled the armory after Holloway's predecessor read his orders. "Then I read my orders and there was complete silence. I felt a sort of a silence that I was getting."[17] New NROTC units were getting established throughout the country, and the resentment was palpable. "One of the first things the Academy staff asked me to do was to make a speech to the whole Naval Academy, and explain the Holloway Plan to them which I did," Holloway recalled. "I don't think I was very successful in putting that over but I didn't worry too much about that because I thought time was a good doctor and things would work themselves out." Notwithstanding resentment of some for his having created a competing officer-commissioning program, Holloway's passion about the institution that nurtured him was undiminished, as illustrated by the space he devoted to his Annapolis years in his recorded memoirs. By the time he departed the Naval Academy he had earned the admiration of Brigade of Midshipmen who titled him as "Lord Jim." Reflecting a quarter century later, Holloway concluded, "I don't think I ever worked any harder at a job."

A good portion of his recorded reflections deal with his efforts to implement recommendations from some of the nation's top educators. When he had been a midshipman during the First World War and his son at the start of the second, academic study had emphasized rote recitation and continuous cramming. The recollection had left him open to outside, better ideas. Books that influenced his thinking were *General Education in a Free Society*, by James B. Conant, president of Harvard, and work by Sir Richard Livingstone as president of Corpus Christi College at Oxford.[18] So inspired, Holloway would aim to broaden the class offerings to allow for a more general education and less focus on specifically naval matters. "I wanted to hew to fundamentals and stay away from specialization."[19] However, he did draw more attention to one naval matter, and that was aviation. Perhaps influenced by the advice he had given his son, who was by this time working toward eventual qualification in F9F-2 Panthers, Holloway made sure midshipmen gained exposure to this emerging form of naval warfare.

Besides broadening the curriculum, Holloway slackened somewhat the rigor, especially for first class (senior) midshipmen, who were allowed to own cars and charged with greater responsibilities. Such adjustments made sense, given that the incoming plebes were much different from his son's class eight years prior. Many had prior enlisted service and recent combat experience. Then there was Midshipman Wesley Brown, who would become the Naval Academy's first Black graduate in 1949 during Holloway's watch.[20]

Aside from how he affected life within the Brigade of Midshipmen, much of Holloway's transcript deals with events outside the Academy's walls. During 1947 the Defense Unification Act created the Department of Defense and established a separate U.S. Air Force. Subsequent efforts to reduce the Navy's and Marine Corps' role within this new establishment would be not be taken lightly by naval leadership.

Troubling to Holloway was the series of events leading to the "Revolt of the Admirals." Senior naval officers summoned in October 1949 to testify before the Carl Vinson–chaired House Armed Services Committee on service unity and strategy challenged the contention of the Secretary of Defense and the Air Force that nuclear-armed B-36 bombers should be the centerpiece of national strategy. Among those who would lose their jobs for speaking views contrary to what was now the administration's position was Admiral Denfeld, now CNO. In the preface to *Aircraft Carriers at War*, the junior Holloway also writes about Denfeld's firing. A subsequent Chinese translation of the book took that to mean he had been shot. Fortunately, however, for the senior Holloway's former boss and mentor, Denfeld was allowed to retire as a four-star admiral and lived on for twenty-two years.

In 1949, Capt. Arleigh Burke solicited Holloway's support and the prestige of the Naval Academy in the complex events leading to the cancellation of the "supercarrier" *United States* and later the resignation of the Secretary of the Navy. Holloway refused: "The Naval Academy role is not one for these callow youths [midshipmen] to be drawn into this controversy." Holloway didn't think Burke ever entirely forgave him.[21]

If Holloway kept clear of the nuclear strategy debate, he was given a seat on the Stearns-Eisenhower Board to look at how prospective American military officers were educated. Early in his tenure in Annapolis, Holloway had fended off a proposal from the Army Chief of Staff, General of the Army Dwight D. Eisenhower, to align the curricula at the military and naval academies and have each send their junior classes to the other. Holloway would have none of it. Now Eisenhower in retirement was president of Columbia University and was paired with University of Colorado president Robert L. Stearns to look at a concept being pushed by Secretary of Defense Louis Johnson to have one large military academy that sent its graduates to the Army, Air Force, or Navy/Marine Corps. At the first informal meeting Holloway recalled "Ole Ike" saying, "Now what we want is to have a general common education and we'll have a Navy specialist, an Army specialist and an Air Force specialist." Holloway replied: "The Navy is a profoundly rooted and deep-seated historical profession and that doesn't make sense for us." Holloway supported those who had been calling for a third service academy, for the Air Force. By the final board meeting, at the Naval Academy, Eisenhower had agreed to the establishment of an Air Force academy; the former Supreme Allied Commander was the honored guest as the Brigade of Midshipmen passed in review.[22]

COMMANDER, BATTLESHIP-CRUISER FORCE ATLANTIC FLEET

Following his tour in Annapolis, Holloway served for thirty months as the commander of Battleship-Cruiser Force, Atlantic Fleet. Taking command in the wake of a most embarrassing incident—the grounding of *Missouri* (BB 63) off Fort Monroe in Hampton Roads—Holloway managed to steer clear of such mishaps. Several of his gun ships would deploy to the Pacific to support the United Nations in Korea, where his son distinguished himself as the executive and then the commanding officer of fighter squadron (VF) 52. The younger Holloway would earn a Distinguished Flying Cross and three Air Medals for his combat exploits, and in the aftermath of the war his squadron—at the Navy's behest—was involved in production of the Hollywood blockbuster *The Bridges at Toko-Ri*. The senior Holloway then hoisted his flag in the cruiser *Albany* (CA 123) for a Mediterranean cruise, calling in ports in France, Italy, and Greece. In Malta he met Britain's Prince Philip, who commanded a Royal Navy minesweeper. The prince introduced Holloway to his wife at a ball, and Holloway had the pleasure of several dances with the future Queen of England.

A year later Holloway, still embarked in *Albany*, led a flotilla on a Northern European cruise that often had him transferring his flag to the battleship *Missouri* to host grander receptions. However, a summer of port calls comparable to those offered by modern-day cruise ships was followed by a winter deployment toward Greenland with a light aircraft carrier to test the effectiveness of ASW aircraft in detecting a line of submarines formed as an exercise blocking force. When he received a report "Rolling 40 degrees and icing heavily" from one of his destroyer skippers, Holloway determined they had

had enough. "I about-faced the task force and we came on home rolling not quite so heavily and out with steam nozzles and axes and cutting the ice off the ships which was really serious because they hadn't been able to fuel [and were thus lighter and less stable under such "top weight"]."[23]

At this point the senior Holloway's time in the Navy could have ended, though many in senior naval leadership had assured him that he was likely to attain three stars. However, the flag retention board periodically reviewed the records of rear admirals to "screen out" those not competitive for further promotion. Years later, the chair of that board confided that three of its five members happened to be "Green Bowlers," members of a secret society that had existed at the Naval Academy from 1909 through the 1940s and apparently had issues with Holloway—presumably holding him responsible for the society's being investigated in 1947 on suspicion that it had conspired to seek advancement of its members unfairly. The report, prepared for Rear Adm. Frank Lowry of the Navy's General Board, showed no evidence of such activity. Fortunately for Holloway, the CNO, Adm. William Fechteler (who also happened to be a Green Bowler), shot back the flag retention board's initial recommendation, that of retiring Holloway: "I won't send it forward unless you retain Jimmy Holloway. I know he's won his spurs and he's had two and a half years of fine type command and he is my selection for CNP [Chief of Naval Personnel]."[24] The board relented.

CHIEF OF NAVAL PERSONNEL

Thanks to Fechteler, the senior Holloway pinned on his third star and took over as the CNP, responsible for the selection and assignment of all naval personnel. One of the immediate challenges was how to downsize fairly, hostilities on the Korean Peninsula having ended with a truce in July 1953. Coming into the job, Holloway discovered a bill on Capitol Hill proposed simply demoting about five thousand lieutenants back to the rank of "junior grade." "It would

22. Vice Adm. James L. Holloway Jr. as Chief of Naval Personnel and Deputy Chief of Naval Operations addresses graduates of the Naval Supply Corps School, Athens, Georgia, on October 11, 1956. Naval History and Heritage Command

have been a catastrophic blow," Holloway recalled. Instead, Holloway had his staff look at cutting individuals in the Naval Reserve who had been on extended active duty. Holloway convened a review board led by a Reserve rear admiral to work under the precept that "people with 17 years service be put in a bombproof shelter because they were so close to their 20 [years required] for retirement stipend at the age of 60 that we didn't want to fool with them." Holloway remembered the reaction when the cuts were made: "You would have been surprised at the pressure I received from various senior officers to keep their pets on when they got these letters." Fortunately, Holloway found he had the backing of his senior leadership.

Holloway was also addressing the challenge of the personnel needs of a new sector in the Navy, the nuclear power community—starting with its leader, Capt. Hyman G. Rickover. Of note, Holloway does not in his recollections mention Rickover or the role he played to keep the "Kindly Old Gentleman" (KOG)—an acidly ironic epithet—on active duty and promote him to admiral. No doubt he was attuned to the consternation the KOG had caused for his son, now the CNO, in advocating nuclear-powered carrier escorts. By the mid-1970s, Rickover, in his mid-seventies with strong allies on Capitol Hill and the first nuclear-trained CNO in office, saw an opportunity to determine how the Navy would be propelled into the twenty-first century. Thus when his protégé CNO issued an ALNAV in May 1976 directing that only submarines and aircraft carriers were to have nuclear propulsion, Rickover was not to be deterred. In *Aircraft Carriers at War*, the junior Holloway details the challenges he had to overcome on Capitol Hill in explaining that operational advantages nuclear-powered surface combatants offered did not justify the steep cost. In the end, Holloway's logic triumphed, and funding went forward to build what would become the conventionally powered *Ticonderoga*-class guided-missile cruisers. For his having to endure his own "Revolt of an Admiral" he had—largely—his father to thank.[25]

An engineering duty officer, Capt. Hyman B. Rickover had his "first look" for promotion in July 1951. He was "passed over"— not selected for promotion. The Naval Personnel Act of 1916 had dictated that if he "failed to select" during the next annual cycle he could stay on active duty as a captain for another year and then would have to retire. During the year leading up to the next selection board public interest in nuclear propulsion grew. Rickover had opportunities to brief Congress, and arranged for Truman to participate in the keel-laying ceremony for the first nuclear-powered submarine, *Nautilus* (SSN 571). However, when the next board reported out, Rickover's name was still not among those selected. To say "it got ugly" might be an understatement, especially as the end of the Truman administration meant that the promotion list would not be submitted to the Senate for approval until the following February. By then hearings were being held in both chambers to look at Rickover's nonselection; the Senate Armed Services Committee (SASC) placed a hold on the Navy's 1952 flag-officer promotion list. On March 5, 1953, the new Chief of Naval Personnel, Vice Admiral Holloway, testified at a hearing that no statutory reason existed why the nuclear propulsion program could not be headed by an admiral. The way out of the quagmire was simple—create a flag billet and then fill it with Rickover. The next day, the SASC received a letter from Secretary of the Navy Robert B. Anderson explaining how the system could be legally altered to ensure that Rickover could attain the gold shoulder boards of a flag officer.[26]

By the end of the month the Navy had convened a retention board to consider retaining retiring engineering duty officers for one year. Rickover was among the five selected, which enabled him to have a third look for flag in July 1953. This time a condition was written into the instructions to the selection board's chairman that one of the engineering duty officers selected had to have experience in nuclear propulsion.[27]

With *Nautilus* on the building ways, now–Rear Admiral Rickover and Vice Admiral Holloway worked out processes for officer selection and training in that community. One agreement they made that would continue until the present day was that the director of naval reactors would personally interview officer candidates for the program. One of those future candidates (who would write about that interview in *Aircraft Carriers at War*) was James L. Holloway III. The senior Holloway strove to support Rickover in other ways as well. It would be the Bureau of Naval Personnel, not Commander, Submarines Atlantic, that would take the lead in nuclear training. Writing in the early 1970s, Richard G. Hewlett and Francis Duncan observed that Holloway "had the breadth of vision to recognize what Rickover was accomplishing. . . . Both Rickover and the Navy were fortunate that Vice Admiral James L. Holloway Jr. was Chief of Naval Personnel."[28]

Sadly, many of the vice admiral's recollections during his tour at BuPers necessarily centered on his wife Jean, who was battling cancer:

23. Family holiday photograph, circa 1954. *Left to right, sitting on floor*: Jimmy Holloway (JLH IV), Lucy Holloway, Skid Heyworth (Lawrence III), Gordon Heyworth. *Left to right, back*: Dabney Holloway, JLH III, Jane Holloway, Jean Gordon Hagood Holloway, JLH Jr., Jean Holloway Heyworth, Lawrence Heyworth Jr. Courtesy of Jane Holloway

A great deal of this time your mother was in Bethesda so my routine was often to go out at noon in the official car which I didn't hesitate to do as it was from one naval point [which Bethesda then was] to another and then at night I would go home late—work until 6:00 or 6:30 and have dinner alone and then drive out in the little black Ford and spend the evening with her. So, really my work was my lifesaver and I put my heart and soul into taking care of her and doing my job as CNP.[29]

Toward the end of his planned tour at BuPers in 1956 it became apparent that Jean's days were numbered. "I said she shall not pass away in a hospital so I organized the household and Bob Brown [CO of Bethesda Hospital] signed up for the necessary equipment and we brought her home and she was reasonably comfortable for that last week or so. And all of you all were there when we lost her and I will pass on from that and not dwell on it but so it was."[30]

During this time the new CNO, Adm. Arleigh Burke, asked Holloway about his interest in a follow-on three-star job. Holloway countered by asking about a four-star billet. Burke agreed but cautioned that one would have to come open. In the interim, Holloway would stay as the Chief of Naval Personnel for another year. Besides buying time to make a promotion possible, the extension enabled the bureau chief to begin a courtship with the widow of a Navy captain who had once been assigned to BuPers—Josephine Kelly Cook.

COMMANDER IN CHIEF, U.S. NAVAL FORCES EUROPE

In November 1957, Holloway relieved Adm. Walter F. Boone as Commander in Chief, U.S. Naval Force, Eastern Atlantic and Mediterranean (CINCNELM). Landing at Blackbushe, a former Royal Air Force station near Reading, west of London, Holloway would be taken to country quarters ideally situated—if one was a golfer—near golf courses. Holloway was not, and he would regret accepting his new housing when the commute to London and his headquarters in Grosvenor Square proved to be the "biggest chore and nuisance I have ever gone through in my life."[31] CINCNELM was a four-star billet, and Holloway received his fourth on January 1, 1958. Fifteen days later, he married Josephine.

Shortly after, the Chairman of the Joint Chiefs of Staff tasked Holloway to establish and serve as Commander in Chief, Specified Command, Middle East (CINCSPECOMME). The concept was to establish a contingency command infrastructure that could react to a crisis in the Middle East. In his CINCSPECOMME "hat"— the acronym made him cringe—Holloway worked with British counterparts on Operation Bluebat, a plan that facilitated the quick insertion of British and American forces in the Middle East should something go further awry.

For context: The rise of Arab nationalism, exemplified by the seizure of power in Egypt by Gamal Abdel Nasser, which was seen as a threat to many of the pro-Western monarchs in the region and an opportunity for the Soviet Union. In Egypt Nasser nationalized the Suez Canal Company, of which France and Britain were primary shareholders. The failure—thanks in good part to nonsupport by the Eisenhower administration—of an effort by France and Britain, with the aid of Israel, to seize back the canal elevated Nasser's stock in the Arab world. In early 1958 Syria joined with Egypt to form a United Arab Republic. Then, on July 14, a violent military coup occurred in Iraq, eliminating the pro-Western royal family. Fearing similar violence, Lebanon and Jordan appealed to the United States and Great Britain.

LEBANON LANDINGS

The British deployed forces to Jordan, and President Eisenhower agreed to land Marines in Lebanon to thwart any communist move against the government of Camille Chamoun. On the morning of July 15, U.S. Marines landed unopposed on the beaches of Beirut. Steaming offshore was USS *Essex* (CV 9) carrying the new Skyhawk A4D aircraft of Attack Squadron (VA) 83, commanded by Cdr. James L. Holloway III. In *Aircraft Carriers at War* the senior Holloway gets his second mention, as this was the one instance where the son served under the father in the chain of command.[32]

Arriving on scene after the Marines had seized the airport, the senior Holloway found that Chamoun had had second thoughts. At a traffic circle near the airport Holloway met with Gen. Fuad Chehab of the Lebanese army, the American ambassador, and other officials to negotiate a peaceful American entry into the city. Holloway was able to coordinate an escort by Lebanese units of the American ground force to strategic locations throughout Beirut. Holloway and representatives of the State Department reassessed the situation, determining that no international communist threat loomed after all, that Chamoun was dealing with domestic opposition to his government. Nearly two decades later Holloway observed, "I was down there in Lebanon and to this day I think that the weakest elements in my experience in my entire time were our intelligence and their political evaluations which weren't worth the powder to blow them to hell."[33]

To the Americans' credit, they facilitated a general election at the end of the month as a result of which General Chehab replaced the unpopular Chamoun. Over the next three months of the transition to a new unity government, Holloway oversaw the gradual withdrawal of Marines as well as of U.S. Army troops that had been deployed to the eastern Mediterranean nation from Western Europe. The last Americans departed on October 25, 1958.[34]

RETIREMENT

Holloway, having returned to England, still had well over a year in his tour as CINCNELM, but he desired to retire early and called Admiral Burke to inform him. It was a decision he would regret, as expressed in the final recording made for his son: "I want to tell you right now that retirement is the, after being a CINC [commander in chief] and a flag officer and some forty years in the Navy, is the biggest vertical drop that any person can go through. Never retire until you have to. Stay on active duty even when you have disappointments, because the turn of the hand of fate may come along and somebody stubs their toe or somebody dies and everything opens up to you like the Golden Gate. So stay with it until statutory retirement if at all possible."[35]

Holloway returned to Washington for his retirement in April 1959. He would eschew opportunities that certainly awaited in what President Eisenhower would label as the "military-industrial complex." With no more suitable opportunities immediately available, he and Josephine did some traveling. Also, eventually, he packaged his personnel records for retention at Syracuse University in upstate New York. Included in that collection would be an oral history—"It's not a particularly good oral history"—conducted by John Mason of Columbia University.[36] Finally, that postretirement opportunity came along: the current Chief of Naval Personnel, Vice Adm. William R. Smedberg III, mentioned to him that Adm. Donald B. Duncan wanted to step down as the governor of the Naval Home in Philadelphia [now in Gulfport, Mississippi, as part of the Armed Forces Retirement Home]. Holloway replied, "I'm an applicant!" Thus from 1962 through 1966, James and Josephine resided at the historic central Philadelphia home where lived some three hundred elderly naval veterans. For the first two years Holloway approached his job with gusto, securing funds to install a sprinkler system and making numerous aesthetic changes to improve the appearance of the facility.[37]

Tragically in 1964 the admiral received news of the death of his grandson, James L. Holloway IV. The life of Jim and Dabney's only son, a sophomore at the University of Virginia, had been cut short in an automobile accident. The following year, as his son was taking command of the nuclear-powered aircraft carrier *Enterprise* (CVAN 65), the senior Holloway experienced serious health issues that landed him at the Bethesda Naval Hospital. Holloway would recall his return to the Naval Home after several surgeries as "most thrilling."

FINAL HONORS: FATHER AND SON

The admiral was now looking to step down from what he considered his final tour of duty, and the couple began considering options for their final home. His daughter Jean Heyworth and her three children had settled in Virginia Beach, Virginia, thanks to her husband's back-to-back assignments as CO of the oiler *Pawcatuck* (AO 108) and as the first skipper of the aircraft carrier *America* (CV

66). During a visit to the Heyworth homestead, the admiral took a stroll in the neighborhood and came on an attractive two-acre lot. He soon acquired it and sought the assistance of his brother-in-law, Rear Admiral Rawlings (Retired), now the general manager of the Newport News Shipbuilding Company. "Rim, would you find out who the best architect in the Norfolk–Virginia Beach area is?" With Rim's help, a reputable construction team was assembled, and the

24. Chief of Naval Operations at right with his father, Adm. James L. Holloway Jr., USN (Ret.), in 1974. They were the only U.S. Navy father and son to have both attained four-star rank while on active duty. Official U.S. Navy photo, donation of Adm. James L. Holloway III (Ret.) to Naval History and Heritage Command, 2006

Holloways in due time had a fine home near family and friends for their sunset years.[38]

From his perch in Virginia Beach, the senior Holloway had the pleasure not only of seeing his son advance to commander of the Seventh Fleet, then Vice Chief of Naval Operations (VCNO), and then CNO but also of seeing his son-in-law achieve flag rank and eventually accept an assignment that he had held two decades earlier—superintendent of the Naval Academy. When his health declined, he moved to Vinson Hall in McLean, Virginia, a nonprofit community that had opened its doors in 1969 for retirees from the sea services. He passed away on January 11, 1984. Following a memorial service at the Naval Academy Chapel, the senior of the two four-star father-son admirals was laid to rest at the Naval Academy Cemetery. He would be joined by his first wife Jean, who had rested at a previously reserved plot at Arlington Cemetery, and a decade later by his second wife Josephine.

At the time of the senior Holloway's passing, his son Jim and daughter-in-law Dabney had retired to a lovely residence two miles up the Severn River. The location kept him close to the institution that both he and his father so dearly loved—the Naval Academy—and allowed him to pursue one of his favorite hobbies, sailing. Holloway worked in retirement with the Defense Science Board, the Iran hostage rescue investigation, and the task force on counterterrorism, Also, he led the Naval Historical Foundation and the nonprofit Association for Naval Aviation. Another notable role was his leadership of the U.S. Naval Academy Alumni Association, where he headed a $250 million–plus capital campaign for major renovations of the Navy–Marine Corps Memorial Stadium. In soliciting donations from alumni who had only nominal interest in the Navy football team, Holloway would always stress that they would be supporting a memorial to their fellow graduates who had fought and made the ultimate sacrifice—a memorial that also functioned as a football stadium. The pitch worked!

Recognizing that age would eventually take its toll, James and Dabney resettled to Goodwin House, a retirement community in Alexandria, Virginia. There he devoted more time to the Association of Naval Aviation and the Naval Historical Foundation. With the latter he led a capital campaign to build a Cold War Gallery addition to the Navy Museum at the Washington Navy Yard. That exhibit space would include "Into the Lion's Den," an immersive experience of his "Battle of Haiphong Harbor" chapter in *Aircraft Carriers at War*, with recordings from the surface confrontation with North Vietnamese torpedo boats and his own re-creation of calling in two Navy A-7 attack aircraft to support his surface action group. Of course, while living at Goodwin House he had time to write the chapters that would be organized into *Aircraft Carriers at War* as well as those published herein that covered his nonaviation career. Unfortunately, with age came memory loss and other health issues, so publication of his pre-aviation material was not pursued. He would pass away on November 26, 2019, at the age of ninety-seven.

A few weeks after his death, the remains of James L. Holloway III lay beneath the dome of the Naval Academy Chapel and over the crypt of John Paul Jones. The Naval Academy superintendent, Vice Adm. Sean Buck, began the celebration of the twentieth CNO's life with a passage from the admiral's farewell speech in 1978 at the Naval Academy: "Each of us needs certain anchors in our lives; anchors that offer a reminder of our beginnings, and a haven which we can return during the all-too-swift passage of the years. As with so many of my fellow officers, the United States Naval Academy has been that haven in my life."[39]

That passage certainly was applicable as well to his father, who had been laid to rest thirty-five years earlier. Among those paying tribute to the second Admiral Holloway was the current CNO, Adm. Michael Gilday, close friend Adm. Bobby Inman, and finally, Dr. D. Stuart Dunnan, headmaster of Saint James School. Dunnan related how the admiral, as a trustee of the school, had interviewed him in

1992 for the position. He recalled Holloway pointing at the football field at the Hagerstown, Maryland, campus and observing, "I learned to run the Navy while playing football at Saint James School."⁴⁰ In addition to eulogizing the recently deceased admiral, all the speakers paid tribute to his widow Dabney, who quietly watched the proceedings with the rest of the Holloway-Heyworth family. She would join her husband on April 7, 2020. With the COVID-19 pandemic restricting large gatherings, she was laid to rest at the Naval Academy Cemetery adjacent to her husband and her son James L. Holloway IV. Jim and Dabney's marriage lasted seventy-seven years.⁴¹

One of the pleasurable prerogatives of the office of Secretary of the Navy is the naming of naval vessels. It should not be surprising that secretaries often use the prerogative to honor previous incumbents—perhaps with the thought that they too may someday be so honored.

Currently six *Arleigh Burke*–class destroyers and two *Virginia*-class submarines in the fleet or under construction honor secretaries of recent decades. *Chafee* (DDG 90) is named for the Secretary of the Navy in office when Adm. James L. Holloway III was VCNO. *John W. Warner* (SSN 785) and *J. William Middendorf II* (DDG 138) are named for the secretaries that Holloway served directly under as VCNO and CNO. Then there is *John F. Lehman* (DDG 137), named for the secretary who credited Holloway as one of his "sea daddies." Holloway's predecessor as CNO, Admiral Zumwalt, is remembered by lead ship (*Zumwalt* [DDG 1000]) of a three-ship class of guided-missile destroyers. Zumwalt, as naval historian Edward Marolda acknowledges, in fact took important steps to modernize the post-Vietnam Navy. But Marolda insists that it was Holloway who put the Navy back on an even keel. He wrote in *Admirals under Fire*, "One of Holloway's most significant accomplishments was to bring stability to a Navy reeling from the effects of the war and adjusting to Admiral Zumwalt's progressive social programs."[42]

Other ships have been recently named to honor father-son and other family combinations that have served the Navy and the nation, such as *John S. McCain* (DDG 56) and *Mustin* (DDG 89).

With these observations, I'd like to close with a call for a USS *James L. Holloway* to honor the only father-son combination in U.S. naval history to became and serve on active duty as full admirals. The recognition would be based not on the mere fact that each attained four stars—quite a number of men and now women have reached this rank (and may be lucky enough to have streets named for them)—but rather on the body of work that both men accomplished in lifetimes of service to the Navy and nation in war and peace. The Holloway legacy needs to be preserved and honored with a memorial that will endure for decades.

NOTES

PROLOGUE

1. A native of Barnwall, South Carolina, Hagood served at the coastal artillery battery on Sullivan's Island, near Charleston, during the Spanish American War. There he met and married Holloway's maternal grandmother.
2. Johnson Hagood (1829–98) successfully defended Fort Wagner in 1863 from assault by the 54th Massachusetts Regiment of African American soldiers led by Col. Robert Gould Shaw. After the war, as a post-Reconstruction governor, he reopened the Citadel. The Citadel named Johnson Hagood Stadium for him.
3. Named for Gen. George Henry Thomas, "The Rock of Chickamauga." USAT *Thomas* was built in 1894 in Belfast as SS *Persia* for the Hamburg America Line and acquired by the U.S. Army during the Spanish-American War to move soldiers to the Pacific.
4. Holloway's cruise east would be the last for *Argonne* as a transport. Built for the War Department with funds authorized during World War I, *Argonne* was loaned to the Navy in 1921 for its use in the Pacific. The Navy subsequently converted the ship to a submarine tender; during World War II *Argonne* served as a flagship and in logistical support for the fleet.
5. His sister later married Holloway's U.S. Naval Academy (USNA) classmate Lawrence Heyworth Jr. His eldest son Lawrence "Skid" Heyworth III was to retire as a surface warfare commander and serve for two decades as director of alumni services, then executive vice president of the Naval Academy Alumni Association. His younger brother Gordon was a 1972 graduate of the Naval Reserve Officers Training Corps (NROTC) at the University of Virginia and flew F-4 Phantom IIs. Lawrence "Lawrie" Heyworth IV (USNA Class of 2005) would follow in his father's shoes, becoming a surface warfare officer and as of January 2023 commanding officer of *Forrest Sherman* (DDG 98).
6. By a general order dated December 6, 1922, the Navy reorganized its afloat forces as the United States Fleet. It had two major components: a Pacific Ocean–based Battle Fleet, incorporating many of the Navy's newest battleships including *West Virginia*; and a smaller Atlantic Ocean–based

Scouting Fleet. *West Virginia* was the flagship of Commander Battleship Divisions, Battle Fleet.
7. During World War II it would be an Italian prisoner of war camp.
8. Isaac Campbell Kidd Jr. would graduate early with the Class of 1942 on December 19, 1941, twelve days after his father, Rear Adm. Isaac C. Kidd, Commander Battleship Division 1, was killed on the bridge of *Arizona* at Pearl Harbor. He would retire as an admiral. A classmate, John D. H. Kane Jr., would make flag rank and later serve as the director of naval history. Victor Delano of the Class of 1941 would be at Pearl Harbor embarked in *West Virginia* during the Japanese attack and witnessed Petty Officer Third Class Doris "Dorie" Miller's action that would earn him a Navy Cross. Delano was to retire as a captain. A classmate of Delano, Joseph K. Taussig Jr. too would retire as an O-6.
9. See "Dictionary of American Naval Fighting Ships," *Naval History and Heritage Command*, www.history.navy.mil [hereafter DANFS], s.v. "Nevada II (Battleship No. 25)." See also Steven M. Younger, *Silver State Dreadnought: The Remarkable Story of Battleship* Nevada (Annapolis, MD: Naval Institute Press, 2018), 108–109.
10. Joseph F. Bolger's father, of the Class of 1921, would lead a successful career, commanding the carriers *Intrepid* (CV 11) and *Midway* (CVB 41) and retiring as a vice admiral. Sadly the son's career in naval aviation was cut short by his death in a crash landing on *Oriskany* (CV 34) in 1963.
11. Paul Stillwell, *Battleship Commander: The Life of Vice Admiral Willis A. Lee Jr.* (Annapolis, MD: Naval Institute Press 2021), 61–64.
12. Johnson Hagood, *Caissons Go Rolling Along: A Memoir of America in Post–World War I Germany* (Columbia: University of South Carolina Press, 2013), 28.
13. Capt. Alexander Sharp Sr.'s tombstone at Arlington Cemetery has him born in 1855 and passing on in 1910 at the age of fifty-five.

CHAPTER 1. MY MIDSHIPMAN EXPERIENCE
1. His *Lucky Bag* entry did note that Wilfred James "Roger" McNeil was the "shortest man in his class." He would reach the rank of commander before becoming a fatality on May 27, 1959, in a landing on the carrier *Intrepid* (CVA 11).
2. Lt. (jg) Willis "Bill" Edward Maxson III would receive the Navy Cross, posthumously, for action as junior officer of the watch while in *Skate* (SS 305) on October 7, 1943.
3. Neither Richard B. Frank's *Guadalcanal: The Definitive Account of the Landmark Battle* (New York: Penguin Books, 1990), 444–45, nor James

D. Hornfischer's *Neptune's Inferno: The U.S. Navy at Guadalcanal* (New York: Bantam Books, 2011), 296–98, mention Shepard as being with Capt. Cassin Young during his dying moments. Shepard would become a naval aviator, as Holloway had, after World War II, to retire from the Navy in 1973 in the rank of rear admiral.

4. Since plebes could not compete in varsity sports, they were awarded numbers instead of letters.

5. Following his commissioning in 1940, Ens. Ulmont "Monty" Irving Whitehead Jr. would be assigned to *Arizona* (BB 39) and be lost on December 7, 1941.

6. The superintendent—the flag officer in command of the Naval Academy—was Rear Adm. Wilson Brown, a graduate of the Class of 1902. In the months following the attack on Pearl Harbor he would, promoted to vice admiral, command Task Force 11, centered on *Lexington* (CV 2).

7. Both men would have long careers in their respective services. Stella retired as a colonel in 1970. Allan Alfred Bergner would be embarked in *West Virginia* (BB 48) on December 7, 1941, survive her sinking, and go into the submarine force, retiring in 1973 as a rear admiral.

8. Navy won 10–0 in 1939, 14–0 in 1940, and 14–6 in 1941.

9. It is fascinating that Holloway takes the "not being identified as a Navy Junior" mindset into his later years: he fails to mention that his father is on the staff of Rear Admiral Ellis, embarked in *Texas*. Likewise, Holloway's father, who discusses this Caribbean cruise extensively in his memoir *Lord Jim*, does not mention that his son was on the same ship.

10. After the Germans established a foothold on Crete, Lord Mountbatten departed from Malta with his 5th Destroyer Flotilla to search for survivors from the sunken destroyers *Gloucester* and *Fiji* and then attack a German convoy off western Crete on the night of May 22, 1941. Mountbatten received instructions to forge on to Alexandria, Egypt. Rounding the western side of Crete, his destroyer was attacked and sunk by Ju 87 Stuka dive-bombers. Mountbatten survived.

11. Born in Norfolk, Virginia, on November 9, 1923, Dabney was the daughter of Norborne Lewis Rawlings of the USNA Class of 1917 and Lucy H. Rawlings.

12. "Obscure" to a midshipman, perhaps—it was Adm. Ernest J. King, now Commander in Chief United States Fleet and Chief of Naval Operations.

CHAPTER 2. HARVARD AND BOSTON

1. Under the V-7 program, established on June 26, 1940, candidates with at least two years of college education could be enlisted and sent to sea for

a month-long training cruise. Those deemed to have leadership potential were sent to one of several recently established midshipmen schools.
2. Speaking of Harvard, a notable direct-commissioned officer was historian Samuel Eliot Morison, who was commissioned as a lieutenant commander on May 5, 1942.
3. According to the *Harvard Crimson* of July 1, 1943, Macgowan, USNA Class of 1914, retired with the rank of commander in 1935 and returned to active duty for the war.
4. More commonly known as a "garrison cap" or "fore-and-aft cap," an overseas cap could be tucked under the belt when indoors.
5. Having earned his PhD in chemistry from Harvard, Conant became president of his alma mater in 1933. At the time Holloway had tea with him, Conant was chair of the National Defense Research Committee, the organization that would have oversight of the Manhattan Project.
6. Price's Neck Naval Anti-Aircraft Training Center was at the tip of a peninsula on the southern shore of Aquidneck Island (of which Newport occupies the southern half), facing the ocean.
7. At the beginning of 1942, Holloway's father became the commissioning commander of Destroyer Squadron (DesRon) 10 and "broke" his "broad command pennant" in the destroyer *Ellyson* (DD 454). Though his memoir does not mention the Bogert dinner, it does recall having Holloway, his sister, and his mother to dinner on *Ellyson* during a port visit. DesRon 10 would that November participate in the invasion of North Africa (Operation Torch). Beverley A. Bogert (1915–94), son of a banker, did indeed have the credentials, memberships, and society connections of his class and time.

CHAPTER 3. JOINING THE FLEET

1. Edward "Ned" Allen Hannegan, Class of 1928, would retire as a rear admiral.
2. DesRon 10 had been assigned to escort troopships to the Panama Canal.
3. Located on the west bank of the lower Hackensack River where it empties into Newark Bay in northern Jersey, the Federal Shipbuilding and Dry Dock Company had been constructed during World War I as a United States Steel subsidiary. Federal Shipbuilding earned praise for building ships quickly and efficiently. A month prior to Holloway's arrival, two light cruisers built at Federal a year earlier, *Atlanta* (CL 51) and *Juneau* (CL 52), would be lost in actions off Guadalcanal. The yard also built the lead ship of *Ringgold*'s class, *Fletcher* (DD 445).
4. Holloway's new command was named for Rear Adm. Cadwalader Ringgold, a commodore in the U.S. Navy during the Civil War.

5. Located on the Upper East Side of Manhattan, the street has been designated a historic district, many of the current residences having originated in the nineteenth century as carriage houses for New York City's wealthiest.
6. Both the U.S. and Royal Navies had evaluated the 1934 Oerlikon 20-mm gun and rejected it due to low muzzle velocity and unsatisfactory rate of fire. In 1939 the British reevaluated an upgraded design. Satisfied, they procured some guns from Switzerland, but with the fall of France they used plans they had obtained to put the guns in domestic production. The U.S. Navy's Bureau of Ordnance also saw the need for an improved antiaircraft (AA) weapon and opted for an adaptation of the Swiss Oerlikon Mark I on November 9, 1940.
7. He likely is referring to the battle off Savo Island on August 9, where the U.S. Navy lost three cruisers; the first night of the Naval Battle of Guadalcanal on November 12–13, in which the U.S. Navy lost a light cruiser and several destroyers but thwarted a Japanese bombardment mission; and the battle of Tassafaronga on November 30, in which the United States lost the cruiser *Northampton* and suffered heavy damage to three more cruisers.
8. Cdr. Thomas F. Conley Jr., USNA Class of 1926, was actually still in his mid-thirties. He would earn a Navy Cross during the battle of Surigao Strait and serve in the Korean War. He ultimately retired with the rank of rear admiral.
9. Samuel Aldo McCornock would also retire from the Navy as a rear admiral. Holloway would recall doing a Nuclear Power Program preinterview of the son, a Purdue NROTC midshipman named James Maxwell McCornock. Admiral Rickover accepted him for the program.
10. In his 1939 *Lucky Bag* entry Almgren was described as "A New England Brahman by birth but not by inclination, Neal is nevertheless keenly but unostentatiously intelligent." He would retire as a captain.
11. Hackman was in *Bullhead* (SS 332), which was reportedly sunk on August 6, 1945, in the western Pacific, depth-charged by a Japanese aircraft.

CHAPTER 4. TO SEA

1. *R-12* was commissioned in Boston on September 12, 1919.
2. The inspections and evaluation drills were conducted by ComDesRon 30.
3. Established in 1882 in York, Pennsylvania, the York Lock and Safe Company earned the contract to convert the Bofors gun drawings from metric to feet and inches and was then selected as the prime contractor for the guns and mounts.

4. Nicknamed "Doc's Shoebox," the device had been produced under a partnership whereby Sperry Gyroscope contracted with Charles Stark Draper's Instrumentation Laboratory at MIT to help develop the specialized instrument that enabled Navy antiaircraft gunners to track fast-flying aircraft. For Draper, see Thomas Wildenberg, *Hot Spot of Invention: Charles Stark Draper, MIT, and the Development of Inertial Guidance and Navigation* (Annapolis, MD: Naval Institute Press, 2019).
5. ComDesRon 19 in *Stevenson* (DD 645) was the Senior Officer Present Afloat (SOPA) for the escorting ships that (aside from *Ringgold*) included *Claxton* (DD 571), *Charles Ausburne* (DD 570), *Schroeder* (DD 501), *Stockton* (DD 646), *Foote* (DD 511), and *Spence* (DD 512). "TransLant," transit across the Atlantic, was one of the many abbreviations that became familiar from naval messages—where, in that Morse Code era, maximum brevity was critical—and entered the spoken language of people in and around the Navy.
6. *Ringgold* arrived on April 20, 1943. After three days in port, she proceeded back to the States, returning to New York on May 8.
7. *Belleau Wood*—built at New York Shipbuilding in Camden, New Jersey, on a hull designed for a *Cleveland*-class light cruiser—had been commissioned on March 31, 1943, as a light aircraft carrier. She actually, notwithstanding Mr. Elmore's hurried turnover brief, did have superstructure, a very small "island" on the starboard side for the pilothouse and signal bridge.
8. The ship's war diary (now in the collection of the National Archives and Records Administration in College Park, MD) confirms Holloway completed the watch of Lt. R. L. Elmore. An obituary published in 2009 for a Robert Elmore of White Stone, Virginia, states he had been born in 1918, attended the University of Richmond, and earned a commission in the U.S. Navy in 1941, serving in destroyers during World War II and leaving at the rank of lieutenant commander. The "top watch" usage below changed later and more recently meant the engineer officer of the watch.
9. The small flotilla arrived on Monday, May 24.

CHAPTER 5. SIDETRACKED

1. Trinidad, a British island possession off Venezuela, was separated from the South American mainland by the nearly enclosed Gulf of Paria. By 1942, Trinidad hosted a U.S. Naval Operating Base; net, supply and fuel depots; a hospital; a degaussing range (to neutralize ships' magnetic fields as a protection against mines); and ship-repair facilities. Aircraft based at Waller Army Airfield deterred German U-boats from operating in the vicinity.

2. In addition to *Princeton*, *Belleau Wood* and *Lexington* (CV 16) were in the Gulf of Paria conducting workups.
3. Macqueripe Bay's deep water made it ideal for a U.S. submarine station. The Macqueripe Beach Club complex consisted of a hotel and several cottages built by Sir George Fredrick Huggins in 1924.
4. On June 2, 1943, Ensign Kinnick flying from *Lexington* when his Grumman F4F Wildcat developed an oil leak that forced him to ditch the aircraft. The impact apparently killed him. When rescue boats arrived they found only an oil slick. His body was never recovered. In 1972, the University of Iowa renamed its football stadium in his honor.
5. Commissioned on February 25, 1943, *Princeton* would be one of the first carriers to embark F6F-3 Hellcats. On July 26 the vessels with their escorts reached the Panama Canal, where they rendezvoused with *Lexington*. The three carriers and their escorts passed through the canal and two days later westward toward Hawaiian waters.
6. During Holloway's time in the Western Pacific the Navy's tactical manual was *Current Tactical Orders and Doctrine, U.S. Pacific Fleet,* known as PAC 10. For that and standardization of operations see Trent Hone, "U.S. Navy Surface Battle Doctrine and Victory in the Pacific," *Naval War College Review* 62 no. 1 (Winter 2009), esp. 69, available at https://digital-commons.usnwc.edu/.
7. Lawrence Heyworth Jr. later in the war reported to *Finback* (SS 230), where he would be involved in the rescue of Lt. (jg) George H. W. Bush on September 2, 1944. After the war, Heyworth would earn his gold wings and become one of the few naval officers to wear both wings and dolphins.
8. Holloway is correct in that the submarine service suffered the highest casualty rate in the U.S. armed forces. During World War II the United States lost fifty-two submarines, resulting in the deaths of 375 officers and 3,131 enlisted.
9. *Long Island* (CVE 1) was laid down on July 7, 1939, as *Mormacmail*, under Maritime Commission contract, by the Sun Shipbuilding & Drydock Co., in Chester, Pennsylvania. A flight deck was installed, and she was commissioned on June 2, 1941, as *Long Island*.

CHAPTER 6. BACK TO SQUARE ONE

1. EDOs continue to serve today as "engineering duty officers," members of a community of the "restricted line." In an April 1931 edition of U.S. Naval Institute *Proceedings*, Cdr. Albert M. Penn traces the earliest "Engineering Duty Only" officers to congressional legislation in 1916.

2. Hunters Point traces its origins to a commercial shipyard established in 1870. Bethlehem Steel acquired the yard at the beginning of the twentieth century and sold it to the government in 1940.
3. The Top of the Mark continues as a popular bar and restaurant atop the Mark Hopkins Hotel, which opened in 1926. During World War II the northwest corner became known as "Weepers Corner"—a gathering spot for wives/girlfriends watching their husbands/boyfriends depart on ships through the Golden Gate.
4. Holloway's father would leave DesRon 10 on April 8, 1943, having received orders to set up a new destroyer escort shakedown command in Bermuda. He arrived there on April 13 and ran his school from the destroyer tender *Hamal* (AD 20).
5. The Cavalier continues as an exclusive Marriott-operated establishment. Its elevated site would have made it uniquely useful for a radar school; it is, however, no longer the only "high-rise resort" on the Virginia Beach waterfront.
6. "Jock" Cooper was a native of Georgia. His *Lucky Bag* entry boasted of his prowess as a baseball player and quipped, "The only hope the Navy has for keeping Jock for future use as an admiral seems to be keeping the big leagues from seeing him play baseball." Prior to *Bennion* (DD 662) Cooper held command of *Palmer* (DD 161).
7. Built in 1883, the stately rowhouse currently consists of three condos; the most recent sale price for a unit approached $3 million.
8. Of the four restaurants the Durgan-Park and Locke-Ober closed in 2019 and 2012, respectively. The Union Oyster House carries on, as the nation's oldest dining establishment, and the Grill at the Parker House continues to be known for its signature Boston cream pie.
9. The destroyer was named for Capt. Mervyn Sharp Bennion, commanding officer of the battleship *West Virginia* during the Japanese attack on December 7 on Pearl Harbor. He took a piece of shrapnel in the abdomen standing in an exposed position on the bridge.

CHAPTER 7. PACIFIC BOUND

1. Dashiell L. Madeira, a graduate of the Class of 1921, would serve for thirty-six years and retire as a rear admiral. He subsequently became a partner in Brown, Madeira & Company, a mutual fund specialist.
2. Holloway's reference acknowledges that a majority of the "baby flattops" constructed for the Navy during World War II were built at the Henry J. Kaiser shipyard at Vancouver, Washington. By this time they were being "laid down" as carriers with merchant-type hull designs, not converted from completed or under-construction merchant ships.

3. Work began on a variable-time (VT) proximity-fuzed shell in the United Kingdom prior to World War II. Progress on the project was shared with American scientists thanks to an agreement between Winston Churchill and Franklin D. Roosevelt in 1940 to share military-related scientific research.
4. An *Independence*-class light carrier built on a cruiser hull by New York Shipbuilding in Camden, New Jersey, *Bataan* was commissioned on November 17, 1943. Having returned from her shakedown cruise off Trinidad on February 14, the carrier readied for departure, which took place on March 2 with *Bennion* as an escort. The two ships reached the Panama Canal on March 8.
5. Y-guns were depth-charge "projectors" with two launchers arranged in a *Y* shape to fire to both sides. Depth charges were also arranged on sloping racks from which they could be rolled overboard directly astern. Holloway was about to employ both. Helm and engine orders are taken only from the officer who has announced out loud that he (in those years) is the "conning officer" or "has the conn" and been so acknowledged in the pilothouse; the captain or officer of the deck can take the conn unilaterally.

CHAPTER 8. THE MARIANAS CAMPAIGN

1. It's worth noting that the Navy's senior leadership during World War II mostly graduated from the Naval Academy during the first decade of the twentieth century—Kimmel '04, Nimitz '05, Spruance '07, Turner '08, Mitscher '10. In contrast, except for Douglas MacArthur, most of the Army's senior leaders graduated during the next decade.
2. For specifics on the command structure and composition of Task Force 58 see Evan Mawdsley, *Supremacy at Sea: Task Force 58 and the Central Pacific Victory* (New Haven, CT: Yale University Press, 2024).
3. Battleships included *Maryland, Pennsylvania, Tennessee, California, Colorado, New Mexico,* and *Idaho*. The first four listed had been returned to service after being damaged in the attack on Pearl Harbor. See Wikipedia, s.v. "Central Marianas Naval Order of Battle," accessed October 23, 2023. The "second-line battleship," OBB, designation mentioned below had been established by General Order 541 of July 17, 1920—when, of course, the ships now officially "old" were new and first-line; "Standard Nomenclature for Naval Vessels," *Naval History and Heritage Command*, history.navy.mil.
4. Gen. Yoshitsugu Saito, a graduate of the Japanese Army Academy in 1912, had come up through the ranks as a cavalry officer, seeing extensive service in China before taking command of the 43rd Division on Saipan.

5. The FM-2 was a General Motors–manufactured version of the Grumman-produced F4F Wildcat. Likewise, Grumman TBF Avenger bombers manufactured by General Motors were designated as TBMs.
6. TF 58 also conducted air strikes against airbases on Guam and nearby Tinian to suppress any reaction to the approaching amphibious forces. After the 13th, the other two task groups continued air attacks against Saipan, but at a reduced pace, as they were refueling and rearming. See Samuel Eliot Morison, *Two-Ocean War: A Short History of the United States Navy in World War II* (Boston: Little, Brown, 1963), 326–27.
7. Per Morison, *History of United States Naval Operations in World War II*, vol. 8, *New Guinea and the Marianas, March 1944–August 1944* (Boston: Little, Brown, 1953), 183, *Braine* suffered three killed and fifteen wounded. *California* was also hit, losing one killed and nine wounded.
8. Task Group 52.12 was commanded by Capt. Ruthven Elmer Libby, USNA Class of 1927, who also commanded Destroyer Squadron 56. He would retire as a vice admiral.
9. Kauffman was to achieve flag rank and serve as the forty-fourth superintendent of the U.S. Naval Academy. His career prior to Saipan is detailed in James D. Hornfischer, *The Fleet at Flood Tide: America at Total War in the Pacific, 1944–1945* (New York: Bantam Books, 2016), 41–44.
10. Morison reports (vol. 8, p. 192) that the first wave hit Red Beach at 0844.
11. The battle became known as "The Marianas Turkey Shoot": Admiral Spruance allowed the Japanese to get their airstrikes into the air to be decimated by TF 58's fighters and antiaircraft defenses. A late-day U.S. counterstrike on the 19th destroyed a Japanese light carrier and damaged three more. Submarine attacks accounted for two more carriers.
12. Morison recounts (in vol. 8, p. 329) that the torpedo bomber struck SS *Mercury* at 2318 on the 26th. Its torpedo dropped onto the cargo ship but failed to detonate.
13. The CO was Cdr. William Marchant Cole, USNA Class of 1924. He would earn a Navy Cross as the *Fletcher* survived the first night of the Naval Battle of Guadalcanal unscathed. He would leave *Fletcher* in December 1942 after six months in command to serve in a staff job for the next sixteen months before being given a destroyer squadron command.
14. Elements of the division started to land the day following the first Marine landings. During the seizure of Makin Island, elements of the division encountered stiff resistance.
15. For a more extended overview of this controversy see Hornfischer, *Flood Tide*, 233–42.
16. Magicienne Bay is more commonly known as Laolao Bay.

17. Making matters worse for members of the 105th Regimental Combat Team was that having established a defensive perimeter against the Japanese, they came under friendly artillery fire that drove them to the shoreline.
18. Holloway notes that William Renwick Smedberg III, USNA Class of 1926, had a career that ran somewhat parallel to, but later than, his father's, and the two had become good friends.
19. The Aldis lamp, invented by the Englishman Arthur Cyril Webb Aldis, sends signals in, generally, Morse Code, by the opening and closing of shutters, exposing or suppressing its light. The signaling method, later known simply as "flashing light," entered common use starting in the late nineteenth century.
20. Hornfischer, *Flood Tide*, 322–26. While firing on Tinian on July 24, the battleship *Colorado* came under fire from shore batteries. Attempting to draw fire away from the battleship, *Norman Scott* was hit six times within a few seconds. Cdr. Seymour Owens and twenty-two others were killed.
21. Rear Admiral Scott commanded the five-destroyer Task Group 62.4 in *Atlanta* (CL 51) on the first night of the Naval Battle of Guadalcanal, becoming effectively an observer when his group was directed to join the thirteen-ship TG 67.4, under the slightly senior Rear Adm. Daniel Callaghan, assigned to blunt the assault of a Japanese force centered on the battleships *Hiei* and *Kirishima*. Unfortunately, Scott became, apparently, the victim of friendly fire from Callaghan's flagship *San Francisco* (Callaghan too was killed that night, by Japanese fire).
22. Norman Scott Jr., USNA Class of 1944, would as a midshipman receive his late father's Medal of Honor from President Roosevelt. Scott was then on the battleship *Iowa* (BB 61). After the war he became a naval aviator, was discharged in 1947, and went into the merchant shipping business.

CHAPTER 9. ENIWETOK AND CROSSING THE LINE

1. On May 20, 1936, Adm. Joseph Mason Reeves took the United States Fleet into the Southern Hemisphere off the west coast of South America to initiate 29,751 Pollywogs. For details see David F. Winkler, *America's First Aircraft Carrier: USS Langley and the Dawn of U.S. Naval Aviation* (Annapolis: Naval Institute Press, 2024), 238–39.

CHAPTER 10. THE PALAU CAMPAIGN

1. On the morning of August 23, en route from Eniwetok, *Tennessee* suffered a steering casualty and collided with *California*, striking her port bow and killing seven *California* sailors in their berthing compartments.

Both battleships proceeded to Espiritu Santo in the New Hebrides, where repairs enabled *Tennessee* to steam on to Purvis Bay, arriving on September 4 in time for the Palau operation. *California* would steam on to Seeadler Harbor at Manus Island for additional repairs and would rejoin Oldendorf's OBBs for the Leyte Gulf invasion in late October. See *DANFS* for *Tennessee* and *California*.

2. *Bennion*'s war diary identifies the battleships as *Maryland, Pennsylvania, Tennessee, Idaho,* and *Mississippi* (BB 41), the first three Pearl Harbor veterans.

CHAPTER 11. ON MANUS AND AT THE INVASION OF THE PHILIPPINES

1. The capture of the islands (Operation Brewer) involved Gen. Douglas MacArthur's 1st Cavalry Division and began with a landing on Los Negros on February 29, 1944. Though the campaign to rid the islands of the Japanese would continue into May, Navy Seabees made substantial headway in April to convert Seeadler Harbor into a major logistics base.
2. As often thought by non-engineer officers like Admiral Holloway. The evaporator output was in fact all the same; the boilers got all they needed, and whatever was left went to any other uses or to tanks for freshwater storage. Thus the ship's fresh water was produced to feedwater standards (as free of minerals, or "soft," as possible) and had a rather unpleasant taste.
3. "Three Feathers," produced by Oldetime Distillers, began production in 1882 and was bottled in New York and Jersey City, New Jersey. As for "Black Label," Holloway was referring to a product of Schenley Industries that took its name from a whiskey-producing town in western Pennsylvania. The company, New York–based with a distillery in Indiana, produced a Canadian whiskey called "Schenley Black Label."
4. Kinkaid broke his flag on *Wasatch* (AGC 9) on October 14. Oldendorf broke his in the heavy cruiser *Louisville* (CA 28).
5. The loss of motor minesweeper *YMS 70* on this date could correlate with Holloway's observation.
6. *Bennion*'s war diary recorded 297 rounds of 5-inch AA common, 10 rounds of 5-inch white phosphorus, and 840 rounds of 40-mm fired on the afternoon of October 18, 1944.
7. Per the *Ross* entry in *DANFS*, the first mine detonated at 0133 on the port side under the forward engine room and fire room, and the destroyer began to list to port. At 0155 *Ross* struck a second mine in the vicinity of the after engine room. The list increased to fourteen degrees.
8. The *Bennion* war diary confirmed the loss of the arm along with five flesh wounds to sailors. On "A-day" (assault day) *Bennion* fired 476 rounds of

5-inch AA common and eight WP rounds, as well as sixty-two rounds of AA common "at Nip planes."

CHAPTER 12. LEYTE GULF

1. Samuel Eliot Morison, *History of U.S. Naval Operations in World War II*, vol. 12, *Leyte: June 1944–January 1945* (Boston: Little, Brown, 1958), 199.
2. Morison on page 202 points out that the destroyer force's magazines overall had been depleted to 20 percent of capacity, which may have been an additional factor in curtailing gunfire.
3. *Bennion* war diary for October 24, 1944.
4. Morison, *Leyte*, 218–20.
5. Morison, 221–23.
6. Morison, foreword.
7. U.S. Naval War College, *The Battle for Leyte Gulf, October 1944: Strategical and Tactical Analysis*, vol. 5, *Battle of Surigao Strait, October 24th.–25th.* (Newport, RI, 1958).
8. "Gunner" Shriver will be commissioned in 1945 as an ensign.

CHAPTER 13. MY TIME IN DESTROYERS COMES TO A CLOSE

1. Morison, *Leyte*, 306–307. *Eversole* (DE 404) was lost early on October 29, reportedly dispatched by two torpedoes from *I-45*, a Japanese submarine that surfaced to finish off the destroyer escort with gunfire. *I-45* would be sunk by American ASW forces soon afterward.
2. Battleships included *Mississippi*, *California*, and *Pennsylvania*. Cruisers included *Phoenix* (CL 46), *Nashville* (CL 43), and *Boise* (CL 47). HMAS *Shropshire* was also present.
3. Morison, *Leyte*, 344, according to which *Richard P. Leary*, *Bennion*, and HMAS *Arunta* were recalled from ASW duties to augment the antiair warfare screen around the Seventh Fleet battleships and cruisers.
4. The *DANFS* entry for *Abner Read* states that at approximately 1341, a Val burst into flames, dove toward *Abner Read*, and crashed into her. The ship lost firefighting-water pressure. At 1352, a tremendous internal explosion occurred, causing her to list about ten degrees to starboard and to settle by the stern. At 1415 *Abner Read* rolled over onto her starboard side and sank stern first. Destroyers and a fleet tug quickly came to the site and between them rescued all but twenty-two of the crew.
5. *Bennion* war diary, November 1, 1944.
6. Morison, *Leyte*, 345–46.
7. A graduate of the USNA Class of 1910, Weyler would earn a Navy Cross for his role in the Surigao Strait, retire as a vice admiral, and pass away in 1971.

8. Admiral Holloway is either being ironic or had been and remained unaware that overfiring boilers, deliberately or not, was a major contributor to soot buildup on firesides (see chapter 11). The engineers knew well that it would have to be scraped off—manually, by them—to prevent tube failure.

EPILOGUE

1. "Adm Samuel Aldo McCornock," *Find a Grave*, accessed December 5, 2023.
2. J .Y Smith, "Navy Admiral Joshua Cooper Dies at Age 91," *Washington Post*, February 25, 1998.
3. The *Ringgold* narrative was derived from a well-written *Dictionary of American Naval Fighting Ships* entry and *Zerstörer 1*–class destroyers page on the website *Naval Encyclopedia*, naval-encyclopedia.com, accessed December 7, 2023. *Bennion*'s sketchy entry in *DANFS* was augmented by material from her war diary and a ship's history drafted on September 27, 1945, in response to a Pacific Fleet directive ALPAC 202 of September 18, 1945.
4. James L. Holloway III, *Aircraft Carriers at War: A Personal Retrospective of Korea, Vietnam, and the Soviet Confrontation* (Annapolis, MD: Naval Institute Press, 2007), 147.
5. Elmo R. Zumwalt Jr., *On Watch* (New York: Quadrangle Books, 1976). 474–78. Of note, Holloway was not Zumwalt's personal preference—he favored Adm. Worth Bagley. However, Zumwalt had been asked to submit additional candidates after Secretary of the Navy John Warner had recommended Adm. Isaac "Ike" Kidd for the job. Zumwalt submitted Bagley, Holloway, and Maurice Wiesner. Zumwalt also polled the current four-star admirals to rank his three candidates. Holloway came in first. Zumwalt shared the results of this poll with Secretary of Defense James Schlesinger, over the objections of Warner. Schlesinger submitted Holloway's name as his recommendation in February 1974; no action was taken, because, Zumwalt alleges, there was an "Ike for CNO" campaign being lobbied by those who had taken issue with turns the Navy had made during Zumwalt's watch.
6. Edward J. Marolda, *Admirals under Fire: The U.S. Navy and the Vietnam War* (Lubbock: Texas Tech University Press, 2021), 114. Ironically, Holloway may have been more concerned about his comparison to Zumwalt. Once I surveyed the U.S. Naval Institute Oral History Program at Holloway's direction to discover whether there were more references to Zumwalt than to Holloway. Unfortunately, Holloway's reputation is often shaped by how one views Zumwalt.

7. James L. Holloway Jr., *Lord Jim* (self-pub., 2009), chap. 32; *DANFS, Iowa*, NHHC.
8. Holloway Jr., chap. 32.
9. Holloway Jr., chap. 33.
10. Board members included Cornell University provost Arthur S. Adams, Williams College president James P. Baxter, Illinois Institute of Technology president Henry T. Heald, Rear Adm. Felix L. Johnson, Rear Adm. Stuart H. Ingersoll, Capt. Charles D. Wheelock, Capt. John P. W. Vest, Cdr. Charles K. Duncan, and Cdr. Douglas M. Swift.
11. See David F. Winkler, *Ready Then, Ready Now, Ready Always: More than a Century of Service by Citizen Sailors* (Washington, DC: Naval Reserve Centennial Committee, 2014), 54.
12. Holloway Jr., *Lord Jim*, chap. 33.
13. Holloway Jr., chap. 33.
14. Michael T. Isenberg, *Shield of the Republic: The United States Navy in an Era of Cold War and Violent Peace* (New York: St. Martin's, 1993), 466–67.
15. Holloway Jr., *Lord Jim*, chap. 34.
16. Holloway Jr., chap. 34.
17. Holloway Jr., chap. 36.
18. James B. Conant, *General Education in a Free Society* (Cambridge, MA: Harvard University Press, 1945). Among the books written during Livingstone's tenure at Corpus Christi, Holloway may have been referring to either *The Future in Education* (1941) or *Education for a World Adrift* (1943).
19. Holloway Jr., *Lord Jim*, chap. 36.
20. For the Wesley Brown story see Robert J. Schneller, *Breaking the Color Barrier: The U.S. Naval Academy's First Black Midshipmen and the Struggle for Racial Equality* (New York: NYU Press, 2007).
21. Holloway Jr., *Lord Jim*, chap. 37. For a detailed overview see Jeffrey G. Barlow, *Revolt of the Admirals: The Fight for Naval Aviation, 1945–1950* (Washington, DC: Naval Historical Center, 2001).
22. Holloway Jr., *Lord Jim*, chap. 37.
23. Holloway Jr., chap. 38.
24. Holloway Jr., chap. 38; "Lowry Report Absolves 'Green Bowlers' of All Charges: 18 Admirals Listed," *Armed Force*, October 11, 1947. Rear Adm. Ernest Herrmann, the president of the Naval Postgraduate School, would not be retained. He committed suicide with a pistol.
25. Holloway III, *Aircraft Carriers at War*, 375–78.
26. Norman Polmar and Thomas Allen, *Rickover: Controversy and Genius* (New York: Simon & Schuster, 1982), 203–204.

27. Francis Duncan, *Rickover: The Struggle for Excellence* (Annapolis, MD: Naval Institute Press, 2001), 117–31.
28. Richard G. Hewlett and Francis Duncan, *Nuclear Navy: 1946–1962* (Chicago: University of Chicago Press, 1974), 349.
29. Holloway Jr., *Lord Jim*, chap. 39.
30. Holloway Jr., chap. 39.
31. Holloway Jr., chap. 40.
32. Holloway III, *Aircraft Carriers at War*, 140.
33. Holloway Jr., *Lord Jim*, chap. 40.
34. Holloway Jr., chap. 41.
35. Holloway Jr., chap. 42.
36. "James L. Holloway, Jr. Papers," *Syracuse University Libraries Special Collections Research Center*, https://library.syracuse.edu/digital/guides/h/holloway_jl.htm.
37. Holloway Jr., *Lord Jim*, chap. 42.
38. Holloway Jr., chap. 42.
39. Naval Historical Foundation, *Pull Together* (Winter 2020), 10.
40. Naval Historical Foundation, 11.
41. Dabney Rawlings Holloway obituary, *Washington Post*, May 10, 2020.
42. Marolda, *Admirals under Fire*, 371.

SELECTED BIBLIOGRAPHY

Barlow, Jeffrey G. *Revolt of the Admirals: The Fight for Naval Aviation, 1945–1950*. Washington, DC: Naval Historical Center, 2001.
Conant, James B. *General Education in a Free Society*. Cambridge, MA: Harvard University Press, 1945.
Duncan, Francis. *Rickover: The Struggle for Excellence*. Annapolis, MD: Naval Institute Press. 2001.
Frank, Richard B. *Guadalcanal: The Definitive Account of the Landmark Battle*. New York: Penguin Books, 1990.
Hagood, Johnson. *Caissons Go Rolling Along: A Memoir of America in Post–World War I Germany*. Edited by Larry A. Grant. Columbia: University of South Carolina Press. 2013.
Hewlett, Richard G., and Francis Duncan. *Nuclear Navy: 1946–1962*, Chicago: University of Chicago Press, 1974.
Holloway, James L., III. *Aircraft Carriers at War: A Personal Retrospective of Korea, Vietnam, and the Soviet Confrontation*. Annapolis, MD: Naval Institute Press, 2007.
Hornfischer, James D. *The Fleet at Flood Tide: America at Total War in the Pacific, 1944–1945*. New York: Bantam Books, 2016.
———. *Neptune's Inferno: The U.S. Navy at Guadalcanal*. New York: Bantam Books, 2011.
Isenberg, Michael T. *Shield of the Republic: The United States Navy in an Era of Cold War and Violent Peace*. New York: St. Martin's, 1993.
Marolda, Edward J. *Admirals under Fire: The U.S. Navy and the Vietnam War*. Lubbock: Texas Tech University Press, 2021.
Morison, Samuel Eliot. *History of United States Naval Operations in World War II*. Vol. 8, *New Guinea and the Marianas, March 1944–August 1944*. Boston: Little, Brown, 1953.
———. *History of U.S. Naval Operations in World War II*. Vol. 12, *Leyte: June 1944–January 1945*. Boston: Little, Brown, 1958.
———. *Two-Ocean War: A Short History of the United States Navy in World War II*. Boston: Little, Brown, 1963.
Polmar, Norman, and Thomas Allen. *Rickover: Controversy and Genius—A Biography*. New York: Simon & Schuster, 1982.

Schneller, Robert J. *Breaking the Color Barrier: The U.S. Naval Academy's First Black Midshipmen and the Struggle for Racial Equality.* New York: NYU Press, 2007.

Stillwell, Paul. *Battleship Commander: The Life of Vice Admiral Willis A. Lee Jr.* Annapolis, MD: Naval Institute Press, 2021.

U.S. Naval War College, *The Battle for Leyte Gulf, October 1944: Strategical and Tactical Analysis.* Vol. 5, *Battle of Surigao Strait, October 24th.–25th.* Newport, RI, 1958.

Winkler, David F. *Ready Then, Ready Now, Ready Always: More than a Century of Service by Citizen Sailors.* Washington, DC: Naval Reserve Centennial Committee, 2014.

Younger, Steven M. *Silver State Dreadnought: The Remarkable Story of Battleship* Nevada. Annapolis, MD: Naval Institute Press, 2018.

Zumwalt, Elmo R., Jr. *On Watch.* New York: Quadrangle Books, 1976.

INDEX

AA (antiaircraft) defenses: ammunition with proximity fuzes for, 92; *Bennion* and, 110, 132–3, 211, 265n3 (ch 13); Bureau of Ordnance on weapons for, 257n6; pre-Pearl Harbor, 13–14; Saipan assault and, 112; training aboard *Wyoming*, 32; training at Price's Neck, 27, 256n6
AA common projectiles: on *Bennion*, 113–4; *Bennion's* use at Leyte of, 185; *Bennion's* use at Peleliu of, 171; *Bennion's* war diary on use of, 264n6, 264–5n8; inventory of, 208–9
Abner Read, 214–5, 265n4 (ch 13)
Adams, Arthur S., 267n10
Admirals under Fire (Marolda), 250–1
Air Force, U.S., 235
Air Force Academy, 236–7
Aircraft Carriers at War (Holloway III): "Battle of Haiphong Harbor" chapter, 249; on Denfeld's firing, 236; Holloway Jr. mentioned in, 229, 244; Holloway Jr. mentions in, 228; reviews, xi–xii; on Rickover and nuclear propulsion, 240
aircraft recognition training, 77
Albany, 237
Albert W. Grant, 171–2, 174, 201, 205
Aldis lamp, 138, 263n19
Almgren, Neal, 38, 257n10
Altair, 87
American Railroad Association, 233
Ammen, 214
ammunition: replenishing at Kossol Roads, 172–4; ships with stores of, 166, 169, 171; Turner's concerns at Saipan on, 113, 133; types, 113–4; *See also* torpedoes

amphibious ships, 99, 106. *See also* LCUs; LCVPs
amphibious warfare components, 146
amtracs (amphibious tractors), 108, 110
Anderson, Robert B., 241
Angaur Island, 176, 178
Annapolis, MD: boarding houses, xxv, 3; *See also* Naval Academy
antiaircraft (AA) defenses: ammunition with proximity fuzes for, 92; *Bennion* and, 110, 132–3, 211, 265n3 (ch 13); Bureau of Ordnance on weapons for, 257n6; pre-Pearl Harbor, 13–14; Saipan assault and, 112; training aboard *Wyoming*, 32; training at Price's Neck, 27, 256n6
Argonne, xxi, 253n4
Arkansas, 11–14
Armed Forces Staff College, 233
armor piercing (AP) ammunition, 113–4, 171, 208–9
Army, Infantry Division, 27th: after Saipan assault, 136–7; banzai attack on Saipan against, 133–4, 263n17; Marianas campaign and, 99; Saipan assault and, 112, 130–2, 262n14; Saipan landing and, 101–2, 111; Tinian assault plan and, 139
Army, U.S., on NROTC, 232
Army Air Forces, U.S., 212–4, 216–7, 218, 219
Army Corps, X, 184, 185, 188
Army Corps, XXIV, 184, 185, 188
Arre, Frank, x
Arunta, 265n3 (ch 13)
Asagumo, 204–5, 207
Aslito Airfield, Saipan, 98 (map), 101, 112, 117
assault transports (APDs), 100, 161, 162

Association for Naval Aviation, 248, 249
ASW (antisubmarine warfare):
attack trainer simulations, 76–77;
Bennion at Saipan and, 122, 125;
Bennion in Leyte Gulf and, 211;
destroyers at Saipan on, 112–3; in
Leyte Gulf, 218; Task Group 30.8
and, 226; training, at New London,
Connecticut, 51; training at
Guantanamo Bay, 43, 257n1
Atlanta, 256n3
Atlantic Fleet Training Command
(TRALANT), 72–73
atomic bombs, 226, 230

B-29 heavy bombers, 143
B-36 bombers, nuclear-armed, 235–6
Babelthaup (now Babeldaob), Republic
of Palau, 147, 166–7, 172
Bagley, Worth, 266n5
Balch, Jon Bernard "Red," 78, 86,
135–6, 157, 158
Barbey, Daniel E., 184
Barker, Joseph W., 231
base fuzes, 114
Bassett, Frederick, Jr., xvi
Bataan, 93, 261n4 (ch 7)
Bates, Richard W., 206
battleships, old (OBBs), 100, 146, 210,
261n3 (ch 8)
Baxter, James P., 267n10
Bayliss, Tom, 203
Beacon Street townhouse, Boston, 79,
260n7
Beale, 42–43, 46–47
Beatty, Frank, xxxi
beer and liquor: at Eniwetok, 144;
on Manus Island, 181–2; Naval
Academy on, 9; in Trinidad, 56, 58
Belleau Wood: commissioning, 258n7;
deploying to the Pacific, 61, 62;
escorting to Delaware Bay, 59;
escorting to Norfolk, 52–53; Gulf of
Paria workups, 259n2; identifying,
51–52
Bennion: aerial assaults in Leyte Gulf,
214–8; ammunition types aboard,
113–4; Betty shot down by, 118–20;

bodies in the water and, 129; chasing
Japanese, 205; code breaking
aboard, 159; commissioning, 81;
"Crossing the Line" ceremonies,
147–51; departs Saipan, 144; dining
aboard, 115–6; fate of, 223, 225–6,
227, 266n3; in Fifth Fleet under
Spruance, 94; fighter-direction
duty at Peleliu, 161–2; fire-control
system aboard, 115; fog of war at
Saipan and Tinian and, 130–5;
gunfire support at Peleliu, 167–75;
Holloway III as gunnery officer on,
63–64; Japanese banzai attack on
Saipan and, 133–4; Leyte campaign
and, 184, 187, 188–91, 264–5n8;
mail at Purvis Bay, Florida Island
for, 154–8; maintenance on, 143,
145, 180–1; Naval Gunfire Liaison
Force at Saipan and, 132–3,
262n16; near-friendly fire incident
and, 127–8; noncombat accident
aboard, 178; Operation Stalemate
and, 160–1; paint schemes for,
36, 145, 212; Peleliu invasion and
seizure and, 164–7; on picket
station in Leyte Gulf, 218–9; on
picket station in Marianas, 111–30,
138–9; precommissioning detail of,
70, 72–73, 78–81; radar coverage
gaps, 123–5; radars on, 72; refueling
and arming of, 211–2; replenishing
ammunition at Kossol Roads,
172–4; in "Retirement Group" at
Saipan, 112–3; Saipan assault and,
102, 106–7, 110; shakedown cruise,
86–92; Suriago Strait campaign
and, 193–4; Surigao Strait campaign
and, 195–8, 205, 206; Tinian assault
and, 135, 139–40, 142–3; torpedo
attack on Japanese, 198–203;
transferred to Third Fleet, 145–6;
twenty-four hour alerts aboard, 116;
wardroom table manners on, 158;
under way for the Pacific, 92–93;
weapons of, 74
Bennion, Mervyn Sharp, 260n9
Benson/Gleaves-class destroyers, 84

Bergman, Ingrid, 50
Bergner, Al, 10, 255n7
Bermuda, DE-DD Shakedown Group at, 83–84
Bettys (land-based Japanese aircraft): attacking TF 52 at Saipan, 117–8, 121; *Bennion* shoots down, 118–20; flying over *Bennion*, 126–7; flying right at *Bennion*, 124–5; homing in on *Bennion*, 122–3; LCU guns against, 113; raiding Leyte Gulf ships, 217–8; at Saipan, 112
Black Label (liquor), 182–3, 264n3
Blady, William H. P., 111
Bloody Nose Ridge, Peleliu, 170, 171, 177–8
Bluebat, Operation, 244, 245
Bofors guns, 73–74
Bogart, Humphrey, 50
Bogert, Beverley A., 27, 256n7
Boise, 265n2 (ch 13)
Bolger, Joseph F., xxxii–xxxiii, 254n10
Boston, 26, 78–81
Boston Navy Yard, 82
Braine, 103, 262n7
Brewer, Operation, 264n1 (ch 11)
Bridges at Toko-Ri, The (film), 237
Brigade of Midshipman, Naval Academy, 234, 235, 237
Brooklyn Navy Yard, 36–37, 60–61
Brown, Bob, 243
Brown, Wesley, 235
Brown, Wilson, 255n6
Bryant, 125, 128, 144
Buck, Sean, 249
Bureau of Naval Personnel (BuPers), 25–26, 78, 238–43
Burke, Arleigh, 236, 243, 245
Bush, George H. W., 259n7
Byrnes, James F., xxxviii

Caine Mutiny, The (Wouk), 89
California, 184, 261n3 (ch 8), 262n7, 263–4n1 (ch 10), 265n2 (ch 13)
Callaghan, Daniel, 263n21
CAP (combat air patrol): *Bennion* at Leyte and, 185, 218; *Bennion* at Peleliu and, 169–70; *Bennion* at

Saipan and, 107, 115; *Bennion* at Surigao Strait and, 194; *Bennion*-directed, 225; *Bennion*'s fighter-direction team and, 212; Japanese over Tacloban beachhead and, 213; Leyte campaign and, 188; Marianas campaign and, 102
Cape Engaño, battle of, 215–6
Caribou, 211
carriers, World War II production of, 260n2 (ch 7)
Carrington, Paul D., xxxviii–xxxix
Casablanca (movie), 50
Casablanca, North Africa, 48–49, 258n6
Casco Bay, Maine, 42–43
casualties, TF 52 in Marianas and, 100–101
Cavalier Hotel, Virginia Beach, 71, 260n5
censorship, World War II, 18, 157–8
Chafee, 250
Chamoun, Camille, 244–5
Chapin, Harry, ix–x
Charan Kanoa, Saipan, 111, 135–6
Charles Ausburne, 258n5
Chehab, Fuad, 244–5
Chicago, xxx–xxxi
Chickasaw, 186
chief petty officers (CPOs), 82
Churchill, Winston, 261n3 (ch 7)
CIC (combat information center): Army fighter and Betty from Rota and, 118; on *Bennion*, 102, 123, 127–8, 185; *Ringgold* training and, 32
Citadel, xv, 253n2
Clark, Vernon, 222
Claxton, 214, 258n5
Cleveland, 125
Clifford, Clarke, 232
Close Covering Group, Leyte campaign and, 184
code breaking, 159
Cole, William Marchant, 262n13
Colorado, 100, 141, 261n3 (ch 8), 263n20
Columbia, 205

combat air patrol (CAP): *Bennion* at Leyte and, 185, 218; *Bennion* at Peleliu and, 169–70; *Bennion* at Saipan and, 107, 115; *Bennion* at Surigao Strait and, 194; *Bennion*-directed, 225; *Bennion*'s fighter-direction team and, 212; Japanese over Tacloban beachhead and, 213; Leyte campaign and, 188; Marianas campaign and, 102
combat information center (CIC): Army fighter and Betty from Rota and, 118; on *Bennion*, 102, 123, 127–8, 185; *Ringgold* training and, 32
ComDesRon 19, 258n5
ComDesRon 30, 257n2
Commander, TF 52 (CTF 52): *See* Turner, Richmond Kelly
Commander Task Group (CTG) 32.5, 175
Conant, James B., 27, 235, 256n5
Conley, Thomas F., Jr., 63, 257n8
Cony, 205
Cooper, Joshua "Josh" or "Jock": baseball and, 260n6; as *Bennion* commanding officer, 78; "Crossing the Line" ceremonies and, 148; enemy aircraft crash debris and, 120; Eniwetok R&R and, 145; farewell to Holloway III by, 221; on fuel and ammunition expenditures, 211; on Holloway III as gunnery officer, 154; Japanese banzai attack on Saipan and, 134; Maderia and, 89; on nonsubmarine near Panama Canal, 93–94; recommending Holloway III for flight training, 155; subsequent tours of, 225; Surigao Strait campaign and, 200–202, 207; on Thanksgiving leave in Boston, 80; Tinian assault planning and, 135, 136
counterterrorism, task force on, 248
Coward, J. G., 195
Creekman, Todd, x
Current Tactical Orders and Doctrine, U.S. Pacific Fleet (PAC 10), 259n6
CVEs (escort carriers): amphibious warfare and, 146; Japanese east of Samar threatening, 208–10; Leyte campaign and, 188; Marianas campaign and, 97, 102; Peleliu invasion and seizure and, 161, 164; Purvis Bay, Florida Island and, 152
CVLs (light carriers), 97
CVs (fleet carriers), amphibious warfare and, 146

Dam Neck, Virginia Beach training, 31, 73–76
damage-control parties, training, 76
Dartmouth, 19, 26
Dashiell, 223–5
Defense, Department of, 235
Defense Science Board, 248
Defense Unification Act (1947), 235
Delano, Victor, xxviii–xxix, 254n8
Denfeld, Louis, 231, 232, 234, 236
Denver, 144, 205
destroyer escorts: DE-DD Shakedown Group, 83–85; manning issues, 82–83; weapons of, 73–74
destroyer minesweepers (DMSs), 161. *See also* minesweepers
Destroyer Squadron (DesRon) 10, 256n2, 256n7, 260n4
Destroyer Squadron (DesRon) 24, 196
Destroyer Squadron (DesRon) 54, 195, 196
Destroyer Squadron (DesRon) 56: on *Bennion* relieving *Killen*, 214; deploying from Manus to Leyte, 183; Holloway Jr. and, 106–7; Leyte campaign and, 184, 188–91; maintenance in the Solomons for, 143; Peleliu invasion and seizure and, 160; Surigao Strait campaign and, 193–4, 203–4
destroyer transports, Peleliu invasion and seizure and, 161
destroyers: battered, in Leyte Gulf, 216; DE-DD Shakedown Group, 83–85; defending against multiple enemy aircraft, 190; honoring specific naval officers, 250–1; Peleliu invasion and seizure and, 161; preparing for Pacific War, 55–56; TF 52 in

INDEX 275

Marianas and, 99; TF 58 defense and, 97; weapons of, 73–74
direct-procurement system, 21–22
DMSs (destroyer minesweepers), 161. *See also* minesweepers
Dorothy Lykes, 220–1
Draper, Charles Stark, 45–46, 258n4
Dulag, Leyte Province, Philippines, 185, 187, 188–91
Duncan, Charles K., 267n10
Duncan, Donald B., 246
Duncan, Francis, 241
Dunnan, D. Stuart, 249–50
Durgan-Park (Boston restaurant), 79–80, 260n8

Egypt, Suez Canal Company and, 244
Eisenhower, Dwight D., 229, 236, 237, 244
Elizabeth, Princess of England, 237
Ellis, Hayne, xlii
Ellyson, 256n7
Elmore, Robert L., 51–52, 258nn7–8
engineering duty only officers (EDOs), 69, 259n1
Eniwetok, 144–5, 223–4
Ensey, Lyttleton Brockenbrough, 55
Enterprise, xi, 246
Enterprise-class carriers, 97
equator crossing ceremonies, 147–51, 263n1 (ch 9)
escort carriers (CVEs): amphibious warfare and, 146; Japanese east of Samar threatening, 208–10; Leyte campaign and, 188; Marianas campaign and, 97, 102; Peleliu invasion and seizure and, 161, 164; Purvis Bay, Florida Island and, 152
Essex, 244
Essex-class carriers, 55–56, 97
ETO (European Theater of Operations), 49–50
Eversole, 211, 212, 213, 265n1 (ch 13)
exhaustion, training for, 91
expanding-square searches, 86–87

F4F Wildcat fighters, 262n5
F4U Corsairs, 188

F6F Hellcats, 96, 102, 188, 210
F6F-3 Hellcat, 259n5
F9F-2 Panthers, 235
Fechteler, William, 238
Federal Shipbuilding and Dry Dock Company, 35, 36, 256n3
Fifth Fleet, 94–95, 230
fighter squadron (VF) 52, Holloway III as commander of, 237
Finback, 64, 259n7
Fire Support Unit South, 184
firefighting foam, 76
firefighting training at Dam Neck, Virginia Beach, 75–76
fire-support group, 100
fleet carriers (CVs), amphibious warfare and, 146
Fleet Training Command, Norfolk, 27–28, 73
Fleet Training Command, Pacific, 230
Fletcher, 127, 256n3, 262n13
Fletcher-class ships, 100
FM-2 Wildcat fighters: *Bennion* at Saipan and, 107; Leyte campaign and, 188; Leyte Gulf operations and, 210; Marianas campaign and, 102; Peleliu invasion and seizure and, 164, 165; production of, 262n5
Foote, 42–43, 258n5
fore-and-aft cap, 256n4
Forrestal, James V., 84, 231, 232, 233–4
French navy, in Casablanca Harbor, 48
friendly fire, 127–8
fuel: for *Bennion*, 211–2; *Ringgold* consumption of, 54–55; shortages, Leyte Gulf and, 217
Fuso (Japanese battleship), 195

garrison cap, 256n4
Gemsbork (tanker), 128
General Education in a Free Society (Conant), 235
Gilday, Michael, 249
Goldsborough, 111
Goodwin House, Alexandria, Virginia, 249
Green Bowlers, 238
Gressard, C. Fred, Jr., 17–18

276 INDEX

Gressard, Fred, 127
Grill at the Parker House, Boston, 79–80, 260n8
Guadalcanal, 37, 152, 257n7, 263n21
Guadalcanal Diary (Tregaskis), 153
Guam, 95, 223–4
Guantanamo Bay, Cuba, 43–44
Gulf of Paria, Trinidad, 46–47, 55–60
gunnery/fire control: on *Ringgold*, 39–41; training, Navy Department Atlantic Coast sites, 73

Hackman, Earl Drissel, 38–39, 257n11
Hagood, Johnson (1829–1898), xv, 253n2
Hagood, Johnson (1873–1948): at Fort Omaha, xxvi–xxviii, xxx; at Fort Sam Houston, xxxiv; Holloway's grandfather, xv; in the Philippines, xviii; Saint James School and, xxxv; Senate Armed Services committee and, xxxvii–xxxviii; Spanish American War and, 253n1
Halsey, William F., 97, 145, 147, 215–6
Hamal, 260n4
Hannegan, Ned, 33, 256n1
Harrell, John P., 7
Hartman, Harold, 222
Harvard University and Harvard Business School, 19, 21–27
hazing, Naval Academy, 6, 8–9
Heald, Henry T., 267n10
heavy cruisers, 100
Henson, Stan, 7, 8
Hepburn, Arthur J., xxii
Herrmann, Ernest, 267n24
Hewlett, Richard G., 241
Heywood L. Edwards, 175
Heyworth, Gordon, 253n5
Heyworth, Jean Gordon Holloway, 246, 253n5. *See also* Holloway, Jean Gordon
Heyworth, Lawrence, Jr., 246–7, 253n5, 259n7
Heyworth, Lawrence, III "Skid," 253n5
Heyworth, Lawrence, IV "Lawrie," 63–64, 253n5

History of U.S. Navy Naval Operations in World War II (Morison), 206
Hodge, John R., 184
Holloway, Dabney Rawlings: birthplace and parents of, 255n11; buried at Naval Academy, 250; dating Holloway, 17–18; Holloway's 1950 Pentagon tour and, 230; missed connection with husband in Brooklyn, 60–61; in New York, 34–35; Pentagon tour and, 228; retirement home, 248–9; in San Francisco, then Virginia Beach, 70–71; Thanksgiving in Boston (1943), 80–81; transcribing recorded recollections, ix; wedding, 33
Holloway, Francis Tiller, xv
Holloway, George, xv
Holloway, James L. (1860–1961), xv–xvi, xxxvi
Holloway, James L., Jr.: after World War II, 227–9; in Annapolis 1924–1926, xxi–xxii; as Battleship-Cruiser Force, Atlantic Fleet commander, 237–8; *Chicago* rammed by *Silverpalm* and, xxx–xxxi; as Chief of Naval Personnel, 238–43; as Chief of Naval Training, 230–1; as Commander in Chief, Specified Command, Middle East, 243–4; as Commander in Chief, U.S. Naval Force, Eastern Atlantic and Mediterranean, 243; as DE-DD Shakedown Group commander, 84–85, 87; DesRon 10 and, 260n4; Holloway Board on Naval Academy and, 231–2; as *Hopkins*' commanding officer, xxxi–xxxii; *Idaho* and, xxxvi, xxxvii, xxxix–xl; as *Iowa* commander, 53, 154–5, 229–30; Lebanon landings and, 244–5; marriage and early career, xvi–xvii; Naval War College and, xxviii, xxix; Newport liberty with his son (1942), 27; on nuclear propulsion, 241; Pacific Fleet battleships and, xxii–xxv; Panama Canal and, xl; in the Philippines and

China (1922), xvii–xxi; retirement, 245–6; Scouting Fleet under Laning and, xxv–xxvi; on son applying for flight training, 154; tape recorder gift from his son, ix; Virginia Beach home of, 247–8; as World War II Navy demobilization chief, 233–4
Holloway, James L., III: counseling and morale issues and, 156–8; dead GI on Saipan and, 136–7; deploying to the Pacific, 61–62; detaches from *Bennion*, 219–22; early life, xvi–xix; early recollections, xi–xiii; fleet training schools, 31–32; flight physical exam, 155–6; flight training reminder, 154; at Fort Omaha as child, xxvi–xxviii; high school in Washington, DC, xxxiv–xxxv; Lebanon landings and, 244–5; model airplanes and, xxxii–xxxiii; Naval Academy appointment, xxxvii–xxxix, xlii; Navy's nuclear program and, 241; on nuclear-powered surface combatants, 240; Pacific Fleet battleships and, xxii–xxv; qualifies as officer of the deck, 52; Radar School at Virginia Beach, 70–72; recording memoirs, ix–xi; retirement, 248–9; as *Ringgold* assistant gunnery officer, 39–41; as *Ringgold* officer of the deck, 59; Saint James School and, xxxv–xxxvi, xxxix, xlii; Sea Scouts and, xxviii–xxix; Surigao Strait battle preparations by, 192–3; Thanksgiving in Boston (1943), 80–81; Tinian assault planning and, 135–6; transferred from *Ringgold*, 62–64, 66; wartime officer schools and, 22–27; wedding, 32–33; See also *Bennion*; Naval Academy; *Ringgold*
Holloway, James L., IV, 246, 250
Holloway, Jean Gordon, xxi–xxii, xlii. See also Heyworth, Jean Gordon Holloway
Holloway, Jean Gordon Hagood: buried at Naval Academy, 248; in Charleston with her parents, xv; at Fort Omaha with children, xxvi–xxviii, xxx; health issues, 241–3; marriage, xvi; in the Philippines and China (1922), xvii–xxi; Scouting Fleet deployment and, xxv–xxvi; two young children and, xxii–xxv
Holloway, Josephine Kelly Cook, 243, 244, 246, 248
Holloway, Keith Leaming, xv–xvi
Holloway, Mary Leaming, xv–xvi
Holloway Plan, 231, 233, 234
Holmes, R. H., 225
Honolulu, 169
Hopkins, xxxi–xxxii
hose teams, for firefighting, 75–76
Hotel del Coronado, 230–1
Hudson, 60–61
Hunters Point Naval Shipyard, San Francisco, 69, 229–30, 260n2 (ch 6)

I-45 (Japanese submarine), 265n1 (ch 13)
Idaho, xxxvi, xxxvii, xxxix–xli, 264n2 (ch 10)
Independence-class carriers, 55–56
Ingersoll, Stuart H. "Slim," 231–2, 267n10
Inman, Bobby, 249
Iowa: escorting to Casco Bay, 60–61; Holloway Jr. as commander of, 53, 154–5, 229–30; returns to New York, 258n9; *Ringgold* and screening of, 53; TG 34.5 in Leyte Gulf and, 215–6
Iowa-class capital ships, 97
Iran hostage rescue investigation, 248
Iraq, coup in (1958), 244
Iwo Jima, 226

J. William Middendorf II, 250
Jacobs, Randall, 231
Japanese: air attacks at Leyte by, 189–90; aircraft, Saipan campaign and, 121–2; aircraft at Peleliu, 162; banzai attack on Saipan, 133–4, 263n17; captured on Tinian, 143; D-2 of Peleliu invasion and, 162, 164; dead, on Saipan, 136; evacuating Saipan, 112; low-flying

night bombing by, 115; Marianas defense by, 101; mass suicide at Marpi Point, Saipan and, 129–30; Pearl Harbor attack by, 15–17, 260n9; staging their planes at Leyte Gulf beachhead, 213; Surigao Strait campaign and, 195–8; surrender, 226; Taffy groups operating east of Samar and, 208–10; Tinian defense by, 141; *See also* Bettys
Jean Bart, 48
John F. Lehman, 250
John S. McCain, 251
John W. Warner, 250
Johnson, Felix L., 232, 267n10
Johnson, Louis, 236
Juneau, 256n3
jungle environment challenges, 153

kamikazes: American deaths at sea and, 226; *Bennion's* first experience with, 214–5; defending against, 190; exhaustion and, 91; over Tacloban beachhead, 213, 218
Kane, John D. H., Jr. "Jack," xxviii–xxix, 254n8
Kauffman, Draper, 106, 262n9
Kennedy, John F., 5
Kidd, Isaac Campbell, Jr. "Ike," xxviii–xxix, 8, 254n8, 266n5
Killen, 214
Kimmel, Husband, 97, 261n1
"Kindly Old Gentleman" (KOG), 239–40
King, Ernest J., xl, 255n12
Kinkaid, Thomas C., 183, 264n4
Kinnick, Nile, 58, 259n4
Kissinger, Henry, xi–xii
Korean War, 237, 238–9
Kossol Roads, 171–2, 179
Krueger, Walter, 183
Kwajalein Atoll, Marshall Island, 95, 223–4

Langley, xxxiii
Laning, Harris, xxv, xxviii, xxix, xxx
LCIs (landing craft infantry), 109, 166, 169, 175

LCUs (landing craft utility), 108, 109, 113, 134
LCVPs (landing craft vehicle, personnel), 107–8, 134, 219
LDOs (limited duty officers), 79, 82
Lebanon crisis, 229, 244–5
Lee, Willis "Ching," xxxiv
Lexington, xxxiii, 62, 259n2, 259n5
Leyte (island): air war over western beachhead, 188–91; before D-day at, 184–6; exhaustion concerns during assault on, 91; task organization for invasion of, 183–4; U.S. Army troops ashore, 186–7
Leyte Gulf: aerial assaults in, 214–8; *Bennion* returns to, 224; cyclone, 213–4; surprise off Samar Island, 207–10; *See also* Surigao Strait, battle of
Libby, Ruthven Elmer, 262n8
light carriers (CVLs), 97
light cruisers, 100
limited duty officers (LDOs), 79, 82
Lindbergh, Charles, xxiv
Livingstone, Richard, 235, 267n18
Locke-Ober (Boston restaurant), 79–80, 260n8
LOD (line of departure), 108
Long Island, 66, 259n9
Lord Jim: *See* Holloway, James L., Jr.
Lord Jim (Holloway III), x–xi
Lowry, Frank, 238
LSDs (landing ship docks), 108
LSTs (landing ship tanks), 82, 99, 100, 108, 187
LVTs (launching amphibious tractors), 108

MacArthur, Douglas, 183, 264n1 (ch 11)
Macgowan, C. A., 21–24, 256n3
Macqueripe Beach Hotel, Trinidad, 56–57, 58, 259n3
Madeira, Dashiell L. "Dash," 87–90, 92, 260n1
Mahan, Alfred Thayer, xxxv
mail, Pacific War and, 154–8
Manus, in Admiralty Islands, 178, 180
maps: Battle of Surigao Strait, 204;

Peleliu, 163; Saipan and Tinian, 98
Marianas: amphibious warfare and, 146; as *Bennion* objective, 95; *Bennion* on picket line at, 111–30, 138–9; invasion oversight and planning for, 96–97; Saipan and Tinian in, 98 (map); Turkey Shoot, 188, 262n11; *See also* Saipan; Tinian
Marine Corps: Department of Defense creation and, 235; Guadalcanal landing, 37; Lebanon landings and, 244–5; losses during Pacific War, 65–66; Peleliu invasion and seizure and, 165–6, 177, 179; Saipan assault and, 107–8, 109–10, 112, 143; Tinian assault and, 139, 140–1, 143; Umurbrogol Ridge, Peleliu and, 170
Marine Division, 1st, 176–7
Marine Division, 2nd, 101–2, 134–5
Marine Division, 4th, 101–2, 134–5
Mark 1 computer: *Bennion*'s, 74, 126; maintenance, 145
Mark 4 fire-control radar, 115
Mark 12 radar, 115
Mark 14 gun sight, 44, 45–46, 258n4
Mark 27 torpedo director, 203
Mark 37 director: air battle communications and, 213; on *Bennion*, 74, 115; as fire-control radar, *Bennion*'s problems with, 123–4; Holloway III on Saipan assault from, 109–10; maintenance and, 145; Saipan assault and, 107; watching advancing enemy ships from, 198–9; wiring 40mm guns through searchlight and, 168
Mark 51 director, 44, 46
Mark Hopkins Hotel, San Francisco, 70, 260n3
Marolda, Edward, 250
Maryland, 100, 261n3 (ch 8), 264n2 (ch 10)
Mason, John, 246
Maxson, Bill, 4–5, 254n2
Mazama (ammunition ship), 128, 190
McCornock, Samuel A., 38, 63, 224–5, 257n9
McManes, K. M., 195

McNeil, Roger, 4, 254n1
medical corps, 100–101
Mercury, 262n12
Meridian Victory, 172–4
midshipmen schools, 82. *See also* Naval Academy
military academies' curricula, 236–7
minesweepers, 185, 264n5. *See also* destroyer minesweepers
Minneapolis, 171–2
Mississippi, 264n2 (ch 10), 265n2 (ch 13)
Missouri, 237–8
Mitscher, Marc A. "Pete," 96, 97, 226, 261n1
Mogami, 201
Montpelier, 144
Morison, Samuel Eliot, 205, 206, 256n2, 262n10, 265n2 (ch 12)
Morotai Island, invasion of, 224
Mount Rainier, 139
Mountbatten, Louis, 15, 255n10
Mustin, 251

names, naval vessel, 250–1
Nashville, 265n2 (ch 13)
Nasser, Gamal Abdel, 244
Nautilus, 240, 241
Naval Academy: admission process, 3–5; Army-Navy game (1939), 10–11; battleship cruise, 11–14; Dabney Holloway buried at, 250; graduation, 18–20; Holloway Jr. and wife buried at, 248; Holloway Jr. as superintendent of, 233–7; Holloway III memorial service, 249; Holloway III's appointment to, xxxvii–xxxix, xlii; Holloway III's childhood at, xxi–xxii; junior college proposed for, 231–2; plebe year, 6–10, 255n4; senior leadership during World War II and, 261n1; September leave, 14; at war, 16–17; World War II adjustments at, 14–15
naval aviation: hazards, 58; Holloway Jr. at Naval Academy and, 235; Holloway III on career in, xxiii–xxiv, 14; Holloway III seeking training in, 154–5

Naval Historical Foundation, 248, 249
Naval Home, Philadelphia, 246
Naval Housing Office, Boston, 79
Naval Personnel Act (1916), 240
naval reactors, director of, 241
Naval Reserve, 239
Naval Reserve Officers Training Corps (NROTC), 231, 234. *See also* Holloway Plan
Naval Sea Frontier, 24
Naval Training School, Harvard, 25
Naval War College, 206
navigation: *Bennion* shakedown cruise and, 86–87; landing craft at Saipan, 109
Navy, U.S.: Charan Kanoa, Saipan landing beaches and, 137; command and control in Leyte Gulf, 219; DE-DD Shakedown Group, 83–85; officers for World War II under, 21–22; paint schemes for donated yachts, 24; Peleliu campaign casualties, 178; Revolt of the Admirals (1949) and, 235–6; Rickover promotion, 239–41; warships in Palau campaign, 177; World War II senior leadership, 261n1
Navy juniors, at the Naval Academy, 8
Navy Museum, Washington, D.C., Cold War Gallery, 249
Navy Signal Book, 62, 259n6
Navy–Marine Corps Memorial Stadium, 248
Nevada, xxix–xxx
Neversink, 83
New Jersey, 215–6, 230
New London, Connecticut, ASW practice at, 51
New Mexico, 261n3 (ch 8)
New York, 11–14, 226
New York City: East 73rd Street, 33–34, 257n5; as *Ringgold* homeport, 34–36; *Ringgold* topside armament changed at, 44–45; *Ringgold*'s return to, 50–51
Newcomb, 144, 169
Ngesebus (Japanese-held island), 171, 175, 176
NGLF (Naval Gunfire Liaison Force), 132–3, 262n16
NGLOs (naval gunfire liaison officers): Peleliu invasion and seizure and, 166, 171; planning for Tinian and, 137; targets for *Bennion* and, 132, 142, 166
Nimitz, Chester W., 96–97, 234, 261n1
Ninety-Day Wonders, V-7 program and, 21, 82
Nixon, Richard, 228–9
Norfolk: *See* Fleet Training Command, Norfolk
Norfolk Navy Yard dry docks, 60
Norman Scott, 140, 141–2, 263n20
North Africa, Holloway Jr. and Operation Torch in, 84
Northern Attack Force (Task Force 78), 224
nose fuzes, 114
nuclear power, debates on use of, 235–6, 239–40

Oceana Naval Air Station, Virginia Beach, 71
Oerlikon Company, 31, 36–37, 73–74, 257n6
officer manning, 82, 89–90
Okinawa, 226
Oldendorf, Jesse B.: arrives at Peleliu, 161–2; deploying from Manus to Leyte, 183; ends chase in Surigao Strait, 207; Leyte campaign and, 184; *Louisville* and, 264n4; Operation Stalemate and, 161; TG 32.1 and, 146; on torpedo use in Surigao Strait, 193–4, 202–3
Onderdonk, Adrian, xxxv
OS2U spotting aircraft, 103–4
overseas cap, 24, 256n4
Owens, Seymour, 263n20

P-38 Lightnings, 212, 213, 217
P-47 Thunderbolts, Army, 112, 140
P-51 Mustangs, 217
P-61 night fighters, Army, 117, 120, 122, 127

INDEX

Pacific Fleet organization, 96–97
Palau, 125, 147, 160–1
Panama Canal, xxxix–xli, 61–62, 93
Panaon Island campaign, 224
patronage, Saipan assault and promotions by, 131
PB4Y Liberators, 102
Pearl Harbor: attack, 15–17, 260n9; *Bennion* and Fifth Fleet in, 94–95; Naval Air Base in, 62–64; Submarine Force Pacific Fleet in, 64–65
Peleliu: with airfield and Umurbrogol Ridges, 163 (map); airfield on, 177, 178; *Bennion* crew locating, 147; *Bennion* emptying magazines at, 197; before D-day at, 161–2; gunfire support at, 167–75; H-hour at, 164–7; interdiction, 175–9; rehearsal for campaign against, 160–1
Pennsylvania, 184, 190, 261n3 (ch 8), 264n2 (ch 10), 265n2 (ch 13)
Pershing, John, xxvii
Philadelphia Navy Yard, 92
Philip, Prince of England, 237
Philippine Sea, battle of, 111, 262n11
Philippines: capture of, 264n1 (ch 11); control of air over, 212–4; Japanese landing fields in, 188; *Ringgold* and *Bennion* and invasion of, 224; U.S. Army and liberation of, 226; *See also* Leyte Gulf
Phoenix, 265n2 (ch 13)
Piedmont, 145
Price's Neck Naval Anti-Aircraft Training Center, Rhode Island, 27, 256n6
Princeton, 54, 61, 62, 259n2, 259n5
PT (patrol torpedo) boats, 193, 195, 196
pumps, "Handy Billy," 76
Purvis Bay, Florida Island: *Bennion* arrives for liberty at, 151–3; Holloway III's flight physical exam at, 155–6; Holloway Jr. letter to his son at, 154–5; mail and morale at, 156–8

Radar School, Virginia Beach, 70–72, 77
Ranger, xxxiii
Rawlings, Dabney: *See* Holloway, Dabney Rawlings
Rawlings, Lucy H., 230, 255n11
Rawlings, Norborne L. "Rim," 18, 69, 230, 247, 255n11
Reeves, Joseph Mason, 263n1 (ch 9)
Reid, 224–5
Reilly, John C., xi
Remey, 78
Reno, 213
Renshaw, 132
Revolt of the Admirals, 235–6, 240
Richard P. Leary, 166, 265n3 (ch 13)
Rickover, Hyman G., xxviii, 239–41
Ringgold: carrier shake downs in Gulf of Paria and, 59; to Casablanca, 48–49; commissioning, 33, 35; departs New York, 42; in dry dock at Portsmouth, Virginia, 59–60; escorting *Iowa* to Casco Bay, 60–61; fate of, 223–4, 226–7, 266n3; fuel consumption, 54–55; Holloway III assigned to, 28; living conditions, 37; New York City as homeport for, 33–36; to North Africa, 47–48; officers, 38–41; predeployment overhaul, 36–37; returns to New York, 258n9; topside armament changed, 44–45; training at Guantanamo Bay, 43–44; to Trinidad, 46–47
Ringgold, Cadwalader, 256n4
Robertson, A. L., 187, 192
Rocky Mount, 120
Roosevelt, Franklin D., xl, 9–10, 261n3 (ch 7)
Roper, John W., xlii
Ross, 185–6, 264n7
Rota Island, 95, 117–8
Royal Hawaiian Hotel, Pearl Harbor, 64–65
rum, at Naval Air Base Trinidad, 55–56, 58

Saint James School, xxxv–xxxvi, xxxix, xlii, 249–50

Saipan: assault, 107–10; assault overview, 102–4; intelligence on Japanese troops on, 101; invasion, 104–34; invasion challenges, 101–2; invasion components, 104–7; Japanese control of, 95; in Marianas, 98 (map); Marianas campaign and, 99; mass suicide at Marpi Point, 129–30
Samar Island, Philippines, 207–10
San Francisco Naval Shipyard, 69
Sangay (ammunition ship), 166, 169, 171
Saratoga, xxxiii
Savo Island, 36, 37, 91, 257n7
Schlesinger, James, 266n5
Schroeder, 46–47, 258n5
Schultz, Lieutenant, 87
Scott, Norman, 141–2, 263n21
Scott, Norman, Jr., 142, 263n22
Sea Scouts, xxviii–xxix
Seeadler Harbor, Manus Island, 180, 182–3, 224, 225, 264n1 (ch 11)
segregation, in Washington, DC (1930s), xxxiv
Senate Armed Services Committee (SASC), 240–1
Seventh Fleet, 183–4, 196, 207, 212, 224
Sharp, Alexander, xxxvi, xl, 254n13
Shaw, Robert Gould, 253n2
Shepard, Tazewell T., Jr., 5, 255n3
ship production, at peak (1943), 82
ship recognition training, 77
ship riders, *Bennion* shakedown cruise and, 87, 90
shore bombardment: Leyte campaign and, 185, 187, 188–9; Peleliu invasion and seizure and, 162; Saipan assault and, 103–4, *105*, 107
Shriver, Omer, 208–9, 265n8
Shropshire, 265n2 (ch 13)
Sibert, Franklin C., 184
Sigourney, 205, 211–2
Sirius, xli–xlii
Sixth Army, U.S., 224
skip bombing, by Japanese at Saipan, 115

Skyhawk A4D aircraft, 244
Smedberg, William R., III, 136, 246, 263n18
Smith, 79
Smith, H. M. "Howlin' Mad," 99, 131, 135
Smith, Ralph, 131–2
smoke: chemical, screening destroyers with, 219; darkening a ship with, 198, 199; harbor overhung with, 221; obscuring landing areas using, 122, 217–8; obscuring targets, 176; overfiring boilers and, 266n8; Saipan beaches and, 107
Smoot, Roland, 184, 194
SOC pontoon spotting aircraft, 103–4
South Dakota, 36
South Dakota-class carriers, 97
Southern Attack Force (Task Force 79), 184, 224
Spence, 258n5
Sprague, Clifton A. F., 209–10
Spruance, Raymond A., 94, 147, 230, 261n1, 262n11
Stalemate, Operation, 160
star shells: on *Bennion*, 113; Peleliu invasion and seizure and, 167, 169, 175–6; Surigao Strait campaign and, 199; Tinian assault and, 142
Statue of Liberty, 42, 44, 47, 49, 61
Stearns, Robert L., 236
Stearns-Eisenhower Board, 236
Stella, Harry, 10, 255n7
Stevens, 60–61
Stevenson, 52–53, 258n5, 258n9
Stockton, 52–53, 258n5, 258n9
submarines: honoring former CNOs, 250; Japanese, off Saipan's Cape Obian, 111; Marianas campaign and, 97; nuclear-powered, 240; Pacific Fleet, 63–65, 259n8; training, shakedown cruises and, 87
Suez Canal Company, 244
Sumners, Hatton W., xxxviii, xxxix
Sun Shipbuilding & Drydock Co., 259n9
supply ships, 99, 121

Surigao Strait, battle of, 204 (map); chasing Japanese, 203–5; contact with the enemy, 195–8; plans for, 192–4; torpedo attack on Japanese, 198–203
Surigao Strait, *Bennion* guarding, 215–6
Swartz, Ray, xlii
Swift, Douglas M., 267n10

Tacloban City, Philippines, 185, 188–91, 192, 213
Taffy groups, 102, 104, 107, 208–10
Task Force 32 (TF 32), 145–6
Task Force 52 (TF 52), 96, 97, 99–100. *See also* Turner, Richmond Kelly
Task Force 58 (TF 58): Marianas campaign and, 96, 97; Marianas Turkey Shoot and, 262n11; *Ringgold* and, 226; Saipan assault and, 102–3, 262n6
Task Force 78 (TF 78), 224
Task Force 79 (TF 79), 224
Task Group 30.8 (TG 30.8), 226
Task Group 32.1 (TG 32.1), 146
Task Group 34.5 (TG 34.5), 215–6
Task Group 51.1 (TG 51.1), 110–1
Task Group 52.12 (TG 52.12), 262n8
Task Group 52.15 (TG 52.15), 104
Task Group 77.1 (TG 77.1), 214
Task Group 77.2 (TG 77.2), 225
Task Group 77.3 (TG 77.3), 184
Task Group 79.1 (TG 79.1), 184
Task Group 79.2 (TG 79.2), 184
Taussig, Joseph, Jr., xvi, xxviii–xxix, 8, 254n8
TBM Avenger squadrons: Marianas campaign and, 97; Peleliu invasion and seizure and, 164, 165; Saipan assault and, 102, 107; as spotting aircraft, 104
TBS (Talk between Ships, voice radio), 196
Teeter, Phil, 78–79
temporary additional duty (TAD), 27
Tennessee, 184, 261n3 (ch 8), 263–4n1 (ch 10), 264n2 (ch 10)
Terry, 59

Texas, xlii, 11–14, 255n9
Third Fleet, 229
Thomas, xvii, 253n3
Three Feathers (liquor), 181, 182, 264n3
Ticonderoga-class guided-missile cruisers, 240
Tinian: Army runway built on, 143; assault, 139–43; concept of operations, 139; Japanese control of, 95; in Marianas, 98 (map); Marianas campaign and, 99; occupation, 144; planning operation at, 135–9
Top of the Mark, San Francisco, 70, 260n3
Torch, Operation, 84, 234
torpedoes: DesRon 56 destroyers at Surigao Strait and, 194; against the Japanese, 195–6; Japanese, at Saipan, 115; Surigao Strait campaign and, 199–200, 202–3
tow planes, for gunnery practice, 74–75
trains, World War II demobilization and, 233
TransLant (transit across the Atlantic), 258n5
transport ships, 121. *See also* assault transports
Tregaskis, Richard, 153
Trinidad, 46–47, 55–56, 258n1
Truman, Harry, 232, 240
Truxtun, xvii–xviii, xx
Tulagi, Naval Battle of Guadalcanal and, 152
Turner, Richmond Kelly: ammunition concerns at Saipan of, 113, 133; as Naval Academy graduate, 261n1; reserves at Saipan and, 130–1; as Task Force 52 commander, 96, 97, 99; Tinian operation plans and, 135
typhoons, 184–5, 229

Ulithi Atoll, 226
Umurbrogol Ridge, Peleliu, 170, 177–8
underwater demolition teams (UDTs): *Bennion* covering operations at Peleliu of, 162; Leyte campaign

and, 185, 188; Peleliu invasion preparations by, 164; Saipan assault and, 106, 109; TF 52 in Marianas and, 100; Tinian assault and, 140 underway replenishment, 55–56, 85–86, 91
uniforms, Naval Academy, 6
Union Oyster House, Boston, 79–80, 260n8
unions, merchant marine on *Meridian Victory* and, 173–4
United Arab Republic, 244
United States supercarrier, cancellation of, 236
USO (United Service Organizations), 34

V-7 program, Ninety-Day Wonders and, 21, 82, 255–6n1
Vest, John P. W., 267n10
Vinson, Carl, 232, 235–6
Vinson Hall, McLean, Virginia, 248
V-mail, 158
Volcano Islands, 102–3
voting, career military officers and, xxxvii
VT (variable-timed) fuzed ammunition, 92, 113, 171, 261n3 (ch 7)

Waller Army Airfield, Trinidad, 258n1
War College Analysis: A Collection of Translated Japanese Action Reports and Memoirs (Bates), 206
Warner, John, 266n5
wartime officer schools: candidates qualifications, 255–6n1; at Harvard, 22–23; organizing, 23–24
water, potable, on *Bennion*, 180, 264n2 (ch 11)
Waters, 111
West Virginia, xxii–xxv, 260n9

Weyler, George L., 217, 218, 265n7 (ch 13)
Wheelock, Charles D., 267n10
white phosphorus (WP) incendiary shells, 138–9, 264–5n8
White Plains, 144
Whitehead, Monty, 9, 255n5
Whitney, Dick, xxxii–xxxiii
Wiesner, Maurice, 266n5
Wildcat fighters: Japanese over Tacloban beachhead and, 213; manufacturers, 262n5; Marianas campaign and, 97, 102; as spotting aircraft, 104; Tinian assault and, 140; *See also* F4F Wildcat fighters; FM-2 Wildcat fighters
Wilkinson, Theodore S., 184
World War II: censorship during, 18; demobilization, Holloway Jr. as chief of, 233–4; Naval Academy and, 14–16; naval officers to support, 21–22; planning and logistic support during, 146–7
Wouk, Herman, 89
wrestling, at Naval Academy, 6–8
Wyoming, 32

yachts, Navy use in World War II of, 24
Yamashiro, 199, 201, 206
Yap Island, 125, 179
Y-guns, 93, 261n5
York Lock and Safe Company, 45–46, 257n3
Yoshitsugu Saito, 261n4 (ch 8)
Young, Cassin, 255n3

Zero, Japanese, 96, 207
Zumwalt, Elmo R.: destroyer named after, 250; on Holloway father and son, 228, 229, 266nn5–6; social programs of, 251

BIOGRAPHIES

AUTHOR

JAMES L. HOLLOWAY III graduated from the U. S. Naval Academy in 1942 and served in destroyers during World War II, shooting down three Zeros at the battle of Leyte Gulf as gunnery officer of USS *Bennion*. He became a naval aviator in 1945 and flew combat missions in Korea, where he was promoted to the command of a jet fighter squadron. After nuclear-reactor training under Vice Adm. Hyman Rickover, Holloway became captain of the first nuclear carrier, *Enterprise*, for two combat deployments to Vietnam. In 1968 he returned to the Pentagon and established the nuclear-powered carrier program. Four years later he took command of the Seventh Fleet in Southeast Asia. In 1974 he was selected as Chief of Naval Operations and member of the Joint Chiefs of Staff. Among Admiral Holloway's more than forty medals and decorations are the French Legion of Honor, Japanese Order of the Rising Sun, Grand Cross of Germany, Knight of the Italian Order of Merit, U.S. Distinguished Service Medal, and the Distinguished Flying Cross. He received the Admiral of the Navy George Dewey Award from the Naval Order of the United States in 2011. Holloway passed away on November 26, 2019, in Alexandria, Virginia.

EDITOR

DAVID F. WINKLER, PhD, an adjunct professor with the Naval War College, retired as a commander after serving twenty-eight years on active and Navy Reserve duty as a surface warfare officer. He earned his PhD in history from American University. Winkler was the staff historian with the Naval Historical Foundation and the Charles Lindbergh Chair of Aerospace History at the Smithsonian Air and Space Museum. He is the author of several books, including *America's First Aircraft Carrier: USS* Langley *and the Dawn of U.S. Naval Aviation* (2024). He resides in Northern Virginia.

THE NAVAL INSTITUTE PRESS is the book-publishing arm of the U.S. Naval Institute, a private, nonprofit, membership society for sea service professionals and others who share an interest in naval and maritime affairs. Established in 1873 at the U.S. Naval Academy in Annapolis, Maryland, where its offices remain today, the Naval Institute has members worldwide.

Members of the Naval Institute support the education programs of the society and receive the influential monthly magazine *Proceedings* or the colorful bimonthly magazine *Naval History* and discounts on fine nautical prints and on ship and aircraft photos. They also have access to the transcripts of the Institute's Oral History Program and get discounted admission to any of the Institute-sponsored seminars offered around the country.

The Naval Institute's book-publishing program, begun in 1898 with basic guides to naval practices, has broadened its scope to include books of more general interest. Now the Naval Institute Press publishes about seventy titles each year, ranging from how-to books on boating and navigation to battle histories, biographies, ship and aircraft guides, and novels. Institute members receive significant discounts on the Press' more than eight hundred books in print.

Full-time students are eligible for special half-price membership rates. Life memberships are also available.

For more information about Naval Institute Press books that are currently available, visit www.usni.org/press/books. To learn about joining the U.S. Naval Institute, please write to:

Member Services
U.S. NAVAL INSTITUTE
291 Wood Road
Annapolis, MD 21402-5034
Telephone: (800) 233-8764
Fax: (410) 571-1703
Web address: www.usni.org